CW00662219

YOU ARE STILL ALIVE, NOW ACT LIKE IT

EMPOWER, ELEVATE, AND ENLIGHTEN YOUR CONSCIOUSNESS

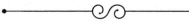

RAY CATANIA

www.LimitlessPublications.com

You Are Still Alive, Now Act Like It

Empower, Elevate, and Enlighten Your Consciousness

ISBN: 978-1-7370095-6-6 (eBook)

ISBN: 978-1-7370095-5-9 (Paperback)

ISBN: 978-1-7370095-4-2 (Hardback)

Content Warning:

This book deals with adult subject matter and adult language that may not be suitable for all readers. Possible triggers may include assault, abuse, sex, sexual assault, suicide, violence, profanity, post-traumatic stress disorder (PTSD), near-death experiences, and death.

Acknowledgments

Honored and grateful to all I have met. Each experience brings us one step closer together. Each interaction, one step brighter. Each exchange, one step wiser.

DEDICATION

To my love, for my love, with my love—and to my sons . . . you have given me more than you'll ever know.

CONTENTS

PREFACE

One of the exercises given to me by one of my medium mentors was to "let myself die." This was obviously not meant literally but metaphorically. I was hesitant to come out of the closet, so to speak, as an intuitive/medium because of the controversy that surrounds the topic. She said, "You need to let yourself 'die.' Let your old life cease to exist so that the new life and new person you'll become can flourish and thrive." I was trying to go as long as I possibly could, keeping this whole thing a secret, but that was proving more and more difficult. Eventually I was going to have to take her advice and let myself "die" in order to be reborn.

One day, in the summer of 2020, I received an email from a blog I follow about creative writing. I am rather new to writing, so I try to learn as much as I can from more experienced authors. I have subscribed to the blogs of many such authors, and each time there is a new article posted to their respective blogs it is automatically emailed to me.

I received one such article about how to motivate yourself when you feel down, feel like quitting, or feel like never writing again. It suggested that you reflect on the set of circumstances surrounding your situation, and then write a letter to remind yourself of why you should be writing your book, blog, paper, or article. I decided to give this a try. Before I began, I had no preconceived notion of what I was going to write. Below is the letter I wrote myself on July 29, 2020, about five months prior to the publication of my first book in this series.

Dear Ray,

It is nearing the end of summer 2020, and it is time for some personal reflection. Time to look back at the past, observe the present, and move into your future. It is obvious that significant changes are headed your way, and I need you to be focused wholeheartedly on this transformational process. It won't be easy. It is not supposed to be easy.

Change is scary as hell, but after all, it is what you are used to. Adversity, then some adaptation, moving toward understanding, is what you do. It's what you've done, and it's what you will do again. I know you are apprehensive about the idea of exposure, but few can do what you can, to help others. Doesn't that deserve to be explored? Is it possible to live with yourself knowing what you could have done, but consciously decided not to because of fear? That is your egoic mind pushing fear to the forefront. It is not real. How much more validation is it going to take for you to believe in yourself?

Let us not forget where you came from, where you started out: in a big pile of shit! One you made even worse through many poor choices and terrible self-destructive behaviors. You are lucky to be alive. Now fucking act like it!

It is redemption time. Time to help the universe instead of punishing it for old news and baggage. Your past is just that: the past. It is over. You are better than that now. You have been for many years. You have paid forth good, kind, karmic actions and that has served you well. You've been given success for the good you have done. It is not time to become complacent. It is time to take it to the next level. It is not time to be satisfied with what you did yesterday.

Let's go. Get ready and get your shit together! Every conscious being you help will cause a ripple effect in the universe, a ripple effect that will touch many others. Stay on course and focus. And along the way, bring yourself one step closer to your own goal of enlightenment. Nothing can ever cause you more pain than that which you have already endured. There is nothing to fear but the fear itself. Now is the time to let yourself die and be transformed, reborn into your higher self. Do not limit yourself. You can become Limitless!

(BTW, don't forget to do laundry before the weekend so you have clean underwear next week.)

Best regards,
RC

Introduction—Terminology

I would like to share with you how I have defined the following terminology so that you may better understand how it specifically relates to my writings. The following explanations are meant to clarify the meaning of these ambiguous terms in the context of this book. It is quite important to grasp what any author's definitions are, and more importantly, what they are *not*.

The Mind—Human consciousness made up of energy generated by the brain, but which exists and lives throughout every cell in our bodies. This energy radiates from within each of us; it extends outward from us and can travel through space and time.

The mind is composed of several different aspects, or parts:

The Unconscious Mind—Stores our core beliefs, feelings, default emotions, and bodily functions. This is considered the second largest part of the mind. Rarely, if ever, can it be altered.

The Subconscious Mind—Stores all past experiences since birth (and possibly before), as well as all stimuli input through any of the five physical senses. The subconscious never forgets. This is the likely the largest part of the mind.

The Conscious Mind—Our current thoughts are processed here. This is where we can create, invent, learn, dissect, and make choices—and most importantly, it is where our conscious decisions are made.

The Egoic Mind—The controlling narrator or our inner voice. It is a bridge of sorts that connects the subconscious/unconscious minds to the conscious mind. In most cases, the egoic mind brings together experiences with the emotions associated with them, and then advises the conscious mind based on those past experiences of what choices to make in the present. The egoic mind can only live in, and advise from, the past, because that is all it knows.

Awareness—The highest level of human consciousness. This is the part of our mind that is cognizant we are having a thought. Humans are one of the few living entities that are aware of the fact that they think. If one is aware of one's thoughts, then one can choose to consciously change the way one thinks. This is the highest level of the mind. It has the power to choose to change.

The Universal Collective Consciousness—An entity where all human minds are thought to become one by merging energies as they pass through a Quantum Field. Not necessarily a direct part of the human consciousness, but one's awareness has access to this structure and can send or receive information through this energetic field.

The Brain—The brain is a complex organ located in the human skull that controls the flow of information throughout the entire body, including but not limited to motor skills, vision, breathing, temperature, hunger, and every process that regulates the human body.

The brain is responsible for manifesting the mind, but the mind ultimately controls the brain.

Aura—Human conscious energy that radiates outside the human form.

Parapsychology—The study of mental phenomena excluded from or inexplicable by orthodox scientific psychology. Parapsychology is the scientific study of three primary kinds of events: extrasensory perception, mind-matter interaction, and reality associated with the human experience.

What Is *Not* Parapsychology—Parapsychology is not the study of anything paranormal or bizarre. Nor is it concerned with astrology, UFOs, the search for Bigfoot or the Loch Ness Monster, paganism, Satanism, vampires, or witchcraft.

Metaphysical—Referring to an idea, doctrine, or posited reality outside of human sense perception. Metaphysics refers to the studies of what cannot be reached through objective research on material reality. Metaphysical studies generally seek to explain inherent or universal elements of reality that are not easily discovered or experienced in our everyday lives. As such, it is concerned with explaining the features of reality that exist beyond the physical world and our immediate senses.

Intuitive/Psychic—A person capable of perceiving information not accessible through the five physical senses, and who may perform acts considered unexplainable by what are usually defined as natural and immutable laws. You must be an intuitive or a psychic to be a medium, but you need not be a medium to be psychic or intuitive. They possess different abilities.

Remote Viewing—The practice of seeking impressions about a distant or unseen subject, purportedly sensed with the mind. Typically, a remote viewer is expected to provide information about an object, event, person, or location hidden from physical view and separated at some distance.

Clairvoyance—This term comes from the French words *clair* (meaning "clear") and *voyant* (meaning "seeing"), and specifically refers to the act of retrieving information about a person, place, event, or object through extrasensory perception. There are several other *clairs* which you can read about in my first book.

Energy Being—Refers to a consciousness living outside a physical body. Some may refer to such a being as a spirit or a soul; however, I choose to avoid these terms whenever possible, as there are too many preconceived notions about them.

Mediumship—This practice refers specifically to the act of communicating between conscious energy beings who are not in a physical form (the dead) and a person (a medium) with this particular ability living in our realm.

Mindfulness—The practice of bringing one's awareness to the present moment specifically through paying attention to bodily sensations, feelings, thoughts, and one's environment, without judgment.

First Law of Thermodynamics—Also known as the Law of Conservation of Energy, it states that energy can neither be created nor destroyed, only transferred or changed from one form to another.

Dark Energy—An energetic force opposing gravity, its presence is used to explain the accelerating expansion of the universe.

Dark Matter—Matter that cannot be seen directly with the human eye because it is made of particles that do not absorb, reflect, or emit light. Its existence is inferred from its gravitational influence on clusters of galaxies and stars.

Miracle—A highly improbable or extraordinary event, development, or accomplishment that brings very welcomed consequences.

CHAPTER 1

THE JOURNEY CONTINUES

Welcome to the second book in the Awakening Series. In the first book, *The Atheist and The Afterlife: An Autobiography*, I took you through the beginning of my journey, describing my spiritual awakening and how it came to be. It was never something I sought out. It just sort of happened to me, which may be what makes this story intriguing. Did someone or something want me to be this way, and if so, why? Also, what additional obligations have I been given? I have an overwhelming feeling that I must "spread the word." That is why these books were born. I never expected I would have such an important message to share with people.

I've made a few transformations in my life, some more challenging than others. As a steadfast student of life and consciousness, I expect more of them will come. My latest transformation once again, was a spiritual one; not driven by greed or a need to get to another level of my career or finances. In fact, I left my lucrative career behind, walking away to give my all, to share this information with anyone who really wants it.

What you are about to read is based on my reality—one which is constantly changing and expanding into the metaphysical world. As a metaphysical theorist, I write as I learn, and learn as I write. Each experience, or each lesson, is like a piece of a puzzle that fits within a much larger picture. Over time, I continue to find pieces that connect and fill voids. The search for new and important pieces won't end in my lifetime, but I will explore until my last breath, and perhaps beyond. As I receive them, I look forward to sharing them with you.

The picture that this puzzle will one day assemble has begun to take form and is more vivid than ever. What once appeared to be an overwhelming task, of seeking and learning truths, is no longer that. In fact, each piece of the puzzle brings more inner peace, more stillness and calmness in a world that seems to be needlessly struggling upstream against the river flow. Too many people spend their valuable time trying to swim upstream, as I once did. I am learning that fighting the current, or anything else for that matter, simply isn't necessary.

When you stop chasing the wrong things, you give the right things a chance to catch you.

Learning and mastering the universal laws that have existed and will exist forever is the key to unlocking your full potential, succeeding without conflict, accomplishing without struggle, and achieving while in flow.

I'm beginning to understand why some folks, more enlightened than I, speak and write in poetic metaphors. Forgive me, as I just emerged from one of my daily meditation rituals. I promise to float back and forth between that state of consciousness and my usual profane storytelling, combined with what I hope will be, some enlightening surprises along the way.

Every book, of course, is written for a purpose. The purpose of the books in this series is that each of them will bring to you those newer pieces of the puzzle that I most recently discovered and explain them in their simplicity for anyone to use and enjoy. Believe me, if I can do this, anyone can. I will be reminding you of that throughout this read.

In this book, I will reveal more about my journey toward spiritual enlightenment (which I have yet to attain), to show that anyone who wants it badly enough can reach higher levels of consciousness and have all that life has to offer. This book, like the last, will take you through some of my encounters. I will discuss what I think the evolution of consciousness has been for me and what I must do to reach my next level. We are energy beings forever, temporarily limited by a physical body while continuing to evolve in this realm. We are not a body with consciousness, but consciousness within a body.

I invite you to come along with me, experience my learning process, and join me on my path. This book is focused on the concepts I have outlined and how they affect reality. There are plenty of stories within these chapters that may put most of the concepts in a useful, practical context. I hope you will enjoy the story of my journey; but more than that, I hope you will take away with you the concepts that speak most to you and use them to achieve everything you want, and more. My life's dream has always been to write a book, and now here I am, working on my second. I never would have thought the subject matter would be this amazing, but that is part of what makes the experience so rich for me, and hopefully for you, the reader, as well.

About two years or so has gone by since the publishing of the first book, and I am still not what I would consider an expert on all things metaphysical. I am a man going through his existence on earth with curiosity and a desire to learn about the secrets of the mind—not the brain, but the mind (it is very important that we differentiate the two early on). I enjoy learning as much as I can about universal laws, and putting them to the test whenever possible. That being said, I try never to write about anything I have not experienced. This book is a compilation of things I have learned from my mentors and have experienced myself. Blind faith is not something I am willing to put my trust in, and I don't expect you to either.

Take what is useful and meaningful to you from this book and leave the rest behind.

Since the publishing of my first book, I have become a teacher and private coach of metaphysics. My qualifications come from my experiences, my research, and a newly printed diploma in metaphysical parapsychology which I've hanged proudly on my wall. I am working toward my doctorate in the same. Being a spiritual life coach is something I find very rewarding. Watching my clients achieve their own individual breakthroughs and awakenings has been my passion since the release of my first book.

I chose to return to studying and learning in a big way. Besides working toward my doctorate, I have also gone to school to receive a master certification in life coaching, a master certification in Usui Reiki, and one in meditation. These formal trainings, in addition to all I have learned from my mentors, has put me on a path **to share** and **to show** how this information can be used in the practical world. (If you don't know why those two phrases are in bold type, then you didn't begin this series by reading my first book. If I hadn't experienced all that I described in Book One, there could never have been a Book Two.)

In addition to the above-mentioned certifications, I have kept up a personal study of quantum physics, reading a myriad of books and publications on the topic. I know there is always a way to bridge the gap between science and spirituality and I continue to seek them and find them, to the best of my ability. Physics at the quantum level is nothing like the basic Newtonian laws you and I may have studied in school. Everything behaves much differently at the subatomic level, almost magically. The more one understands the so-called "magic" at that minuscule level, the easier it becomes to understand the real magic we have access to in our world.

In this book I often refer to my mediumship, which is still developing. I am by no means a professional medium, intuitive, clairvoyant, or the recipient of any other label you may choose to characterize any of my various so-called abilities by. It is common for me to have those experiences and I write about them, because they are often fascinating and sometimes humorous. It is my hope that you will find these books entertaining and informative.

I do not consider myself special. Up until recently I would say that I have done nothing to be particularly deserving of these or any spiritual gifts. I was a regular guy who fought to get ahead and make a life for myself. As I mentioned previously, there was no going with the flow for me back then. It was all about the struggle. I fought for everything I had and everything I wanted to become. After many ups and downs, I eventually became what I thought successful meant. But just as I thought I'd made it, I had the first of several awakenings drop on my head like a load of bricks. My lifetime of experience has brought me full circle from atheism to being in a committed spiritual partnership with the collective consciousness and several beings on a higher plane of existence. In the first book I wrote how I got here; this second book will tell you what I've learned to do thereafter.

I describe many of my life experiences in this book, and in that respect, it bears some similarity to the previous book. What makes this one different is how much more energy it contains. By energy I mean information: information regarding things I learned post-spiritual awakening, along with actual recipes for positively transforming oneself in this realm of existence. You will read about aspects of my personal transformation and how you may wish to adopt them yourself. This world we live in is becoming less complicated than I'd previously thought. What I once viewed as an enormous, overpowering entity, with the power to dictate, has now become something with which I feel in harmony.

One of the greatest things I've learned recently is I can actually change my reality and guess what? You can too. Please, memorize this next statement. Write it down, email it, text it to yourself, say it aloud fifty times, get bumper stickers made with it. Wait a minute. Do they still make those? Anyway, do what you must to remember this. It is that important, and I didn't make you wait until the end of the book to give it to you.

One's perception is one's truth. Change your perception and you can change your truth. Change your truth and you have changed your reality.

(Did I just channel a bit of Confucius?)

I am certainly not by any means the first person to discover these truths. I'll give you an example:

I once watched an interview with basketball legend Michael Jordan. He was asked how it was that he could make those seemingly impossible three-point shots that most other NBA players couldn't duplicate. At first, he said he wasn't sure but then, he thought about it for a moment. And he said something that will stay with me forever. I will paraphrase his answer:

"You see, sometimes I go out there on the court and the basket is just a basket. But there are other times when I am out there, and when I look at the basket, I don't see a basket at all. I see a big, huge, oversized old bucket, and at those times I can't miss a shot."

Michael Jordan's perception of the basketball hoop was unlike that of almost everyone else. Such was a part of the secret of his success. He changed his perception of truth, and that altered his reality. Sounds rather simple, doesn't it? Well, it is, and it isn't. You see, for one to "see" the basketball hoop as that expanded size, one must truly believe it is that large. Regulation basketball hoops are 56.5 inches in circumference, but if one were in that "Jordan zone" or frame of mind, and, if someone were to ask how big the circumference of the basketball hoop is, one might answer 113 inches or even 226 inches. Who knows? And so, in simplicity, this is part of what made Michael Jordan so great: his ability to change or alter his perception of reality to what he wanted it to be, regardless of what it may be to the rest of us.

When you finish reading this book, I hope you will have learned how to create your own 226-inch basketball hoop and, hopefully, never "miss a shot" again.

CHAPTER 2

FIRST, YOU MUST SUFFER

Siddhartha Gautama Buddha was a king's son who abandoned a life of pampering in order to seek enlightenment. Buddhists believe that no knowledge is won without sacrifice. In order to gain anything, you must first lose everything. The Buddha walked away from his father's kingdom and wealth so he could experience the suffering of the common man. It was his belief that this is what had to be done for him to learn how to end suffering, and he eventually achieved a state of mind we refer to as "enlightenment."

Without suffering, one cannot experience enlightenment. This does not sit well with many because . . . who wants to suffer? Also, how much suffering must one do exactly? I tried to find an author who experienced his or her own spiritual awakening without suffering being a major factor in their transformation, but I was unsuccessful. The one commonality I found among them all was trauma and suffering.

At first, I couldn't understand why anyone would have to go through trauma or suffering to be spiritually awakened but after surrendering to this as fact, it became clear that the greater the suffering, the greater the awakening. Perhaps this is due in part to the duality of this scenario— certainly, going from one extreme to the other will add to the intensity of an event. My personal belief is that one must experience a sufficient amount of each and every human emotion before reaching higher levels of consciousness. Some of those emotions can only come about when tragedy occurs.

You may be familiar with David Goggins, author of *Can't Hurt Me*. In his book he tells the story of his suffering as a young man and how, later in life, he consciously chose to bring himself additional, self-induced pain. The first time I read his story I couldn't see why someone would go down that path, but now I have a better understanding.

To the best of my knowledge, Goggins does not refer to himself as awakened or enlightened, but I will. He is the only human on earth to voluntarily put himself three times through the US Military's SEALS training known as "hell week" and live to talk about it. He speaks publicly about his extremely difficult childhood and how he had to go deep down inside himself to find answers. He may not describe it in these words, but that is a form of meditation. Turning off the outside world and going inside your own mind with the intent of rising above your own consciousness is the very same direction one takes to undergo a spiritual awakening. One takes these steps when one reaches the understanding that the outside world can only give you external, temporary gratification, but your inner self, which can rise above consciousness, is where your connection to the universe lies, and where long-lasting happiness, in the form of contentment, resides.

Some folks don't appreciate Goggins because he swears a lot. If you object to swearing, you may as well stop reading this book right now, tear it up, and use it to fire up the grill. Sometimes there is no better way to explain how something is without a swear word to emphasize it. This, I promise you, is not your old-fashioned spiritual book, and I am most certainly not your typical spiritual person. I will not sugarcoat life's shit for you, nor will I tell you that once awakened all things come together in their perfect form. This book will take you through the depths of despair so as to provide you with the means of getting yourself out of there, and so far above that place that you will be free of the fear of ever descending to that level again. Furthermore, if you have had an easy, enjoyable life so far, where so many things were given to you, then I am going to ask you to put yourself through a version of "hell week," to sacrifice as the Buddha once did, so you can experience an awakening of your own.

Some Native American tribes, still to this day, have a ritual that induces self-induced suffering to cathartically bring you the answers you seek, including your purpose in this life, and/or awaken the warrior within. It is called the *Hanbleceya*, which I believe translates to "Vision Quest." I know that there are various versions of this ritual from tribe to tribe, but I am presenting here the one I recently learned.

Please note that this practice can be extremely dangerous, and is not something I would recommend although it does provide a concrete example of how self-induced pain can lead one to an awakening of consciousness.

The person who is about to undergo this ritual is brought into the wilderness to an isolated place which has been prepared by elders of the tribe and made to be sacred. Four posts are secured in the ground, creating a square about ten feet by ten feet, and a vine connects the four posts. It is usually prepared under a large tree. The person must not leave the sacred place, and no one is allowed to enter the space other than the participant. Since the space is isolated and remote, it is unlikely anyone in the physical world would attempt to enter; however, participants must do their best to not allow in anyone from other realms either. They are stripped of everything. They remain there in prayer or meditation for up to four days without food, water, or clothing. The elders leave and return on the fourth day to retrieve the participant. At that time, during the recovery process, the elders debrief the participant and help them translate the spiritual information they received during their Vision Quest.

When you think about it, this sounds remarkably similar to what the Buddha put himself through when he sat for an indefinite period under the Bodhi Tree to seek his answers.

Most of the awakened folks I know personally do not reveal the struggles that got them to where they are, and I respect their reticence. It is not easy to put yourself out there in that manner. I chose to do it again in this book for a couple of reasons. One is that most people who I interacted with after reading the first book, could identify with my traumas. They also appreciated reading how I got past them.

Sometimes, the conscious mind tries to help you survive trauma by blocking the memory out. Even if your conscious mind may not recall, your subconscious will. A scent, a word, or a sound may take you right back to that point in time and act as a psychological trigger bringing you back to relive your trauma in your present moment. Even the unfortunate events that for many years you think you have successfully repressed can return in an instant. In severe cases, someone can become completely delusional and actually believe they are reliving that moment of trauma all over again with the same people who were present during the event, only to come out of it later and realize that they were actually surrounded by friends and family. PTSD lives in your nervous system for a long time, but I am here to tell you it can be overcome.

In my first book I described my near-death experience (NDE). After publishing, I recently spoke to my mom about the incident in detail. Which was quite a shock for me because at one point she was in denial.

She and I hadn't spoken about it until after the release of the first book, some thirty years after the incident took place. She told me how she had not been allowed to ride inside the ambulance with me—instead, the police gave her an escort as they drove behind the ambulance. Every so often the ambulance pulled over to the side of the road to "work" on me. In those days, I was told, they would stop an ambulance en route to the hospital to resuscitate you by means of defibrillator paddles that deliver an electric shock to the heart. The ambulance stopped in a number of locations; my mother could not recall whether it happened two times or three. I do not understand why these brushes with death are referred to as "*near* deaths"; they are very *real* deaths, I assure you. That was when I first saw and experienced the Light. I also saw myself from above, looking down at my lifeless body in my dad's arms.

Life is a precious gift that should never be taken for granted and should be preserved at all costs. One should never risk death for a spiritual ritual, to seek answers, or for any reason whatsoever. However, that being said, when death becomes inevitable it should not be something we fear. My death changed my life, but I was lucky enough to come back, live on, and grow as a result of that change. I imagine most people are not so fortunate.

Our connection with our higher consciousness—or our "God-mind," as it was called in one of my philosophy classes—is the point at which you and I derive the power to be the co-creators of the universe we are meant to be. Using your ability to co-create using your "God-mind" is something we will explore in detail later in this book. That is one part of enlightenment. You will learn how to do this by reading this book. I am not yet an enlightened being by any means, but I have had significant, spiritual awakenings that I will share with you. But first—as I say and have experienced, and as I have learned to accept—first, you must suffer.

1.) From Sea to Shining Sea

I did not learn to swim until I was about six years old. For some reason I had difficulty wrapping my head around the idea that a person could float on water. I have always had an analytical mind that would not let go of the things I thought about. If something did not make sense to me, grasping its physical aspect was difficult. I remember it was the same for me when it came to learning to ride a bike. It seemed unnatural to glide on two wheels when all other means of transport seemed to require four. Seriously—how was I supposed to do that?

I eventually got the hang of swimming, and I really took to it and enjoyed it when we frequented the pool. About two or three years later we took a family vacation at the beach. I was excited about trying out my new skill set in a different body of water, especially one that moved all by itself. Pretty cool, I thought. On the first day out there, I was amazed at the ocean and how its waves would wash up on shore, and I recall learning how to body surf by watching some of the other kids doing it. I wanted to stay in the water all day, but eventually it was time to head back to the hotel and I was hungry. I remember that swimming made me super hungry. We returned to the hotel, ate, and went to sleep.

At the crack of dawn I awoke, excited for my parents to get up and take us back to the ocean. Once we returned to the beach and set things up, my father went to speak with the lifeguard. I had no idea why, or what they could have been talking about. I just wanted to swim. My father came back to our large beach towel and announced that the undertow was bad that day and we should all be careful.

Before I share with you what happened next, I will need to furnish you with some insight into my dad. Both of my parents came from extremely poor families. I give them credit for escaping the slums before my brother and I were born. Right after high school my dad signed up for the US Navy. He chose the military because there was no way he could afford college on his own, and the Navy would pay for school in return for about six years of his life. He took the deal. He was a tough guy growing up. He had to be, to survive his neighborhood.

As a direct result of Naval training, my father became an outstanding swimmer. He was always in top physical condition. As a kid he would cut classes regularly to go to the gym. The Navy eventually stationed him on a battleship just outside of Cuba.

This was during the time of the Cuban missile crisis—a pivotal moment in United States history. The US and the Soviet Union had nuclear weapons pointed at one another in a stalemate situation. If either country launched their nukes toward the other's homeland, the other country would have enough time to counterattack with their nukes. Everyone acknowledged that there was enough nuclear firepower to destroy everyone in both countries as well as doing so much damage to the earth that it would only be a matter of time before humanity became extinct. This standoff has been described as "Mutually Assured Destruction," or MAD.

But Russia had an idea. Since Russia and Cuba were common enemies of the United States, the two countries bonded together. I suppose they subscribed to the belief that "The enemy of my enemy is my friend." The US had previously wanted to see the Cuban government dismantled and overthrown by its own people, so they secretly assisted the civilian rebels of

Cuba who were trying to do just that. The Cuban government responded to this threat by having their own secret meetings with Russia, making a deal that would allow Russia to place nuclear bombs on Cuban soil, with as many soldiers as a Russian fleet could transport to remain nearby and watch over them. If this were done it could have been catastrophic for the United States. The island of Cuba is situated less than five hundred miles from the US. If Russia possessed nukes on Cuban soil, they could launch them so quickly that the US would not have time to respond—Russia could defeat the US in a rapid nuclear military strike and at least partially survive. Today our technology is much more advanced and capable of dealing with an attack of this nature, but back then it would have been a virtual checkmate for America.

An entire fleet of US nuclear warships—my dad serving on one of them—was stationed just off the coast of Cuba to prevent the Russians from getting through with their missiles. The Russian ships and military were already en route to Cuba.

The US president at this time was John F. Kennedy, and I do not think a single person in our country envied him having to make the decision that came next. The Russian battleships heading to Cuba with the nukes on board showed no signs of slowing down or turning around. They came full force toward our battleships—and my father. It certainly looked like we were headed for all-out war in the Atlantic Ocean. Our military alerted the Russians that we were "standing our ground," and if they tried to come within a certain radius of any of our naval vessels, they would be attacked with full force. The leader of the Soviet Union, Nikita Khrushchev, showed no signs of caring what would ensue, and his ships continued at full speed toward the US battleships. The clock was ticking, and Kennedy would have to make a call that no president wants to make.

With the Russian ships about twenty-four hours away from confrontational waters, my dad was standing night watch. At the same time, a huge hurricane-type storm with high winds was approaching the US fleet. The storm would arrive before the Russians, so the first objective was to weather the storm with our warships intact. When the storm hit, my dad was on deck. The severe winds knocked him off his post, with waves crashing violently on the side of the boat. Sailors were falling overboard, one after another, with basically no chance of survival.

As the huge ship rocked back and forth and waves came up over the sides, my father managed to make his way to a metal guardrail. With no other option, among the high velocity winds and the sheer force of the water crashing onto the deck, my dad wrapped his arms and legs around a large metal pole and literally held on for his life. There was no way to make it below deck until the storm had passed.

It took every ounce of strength to maintain his grip. The storm continued for hours. President Kennedy was updated regularly on the condition of our ships and the loss of crewmembers who had become casualties of the storm. My father continued to hold on for as long as he could, but fatigue was setting in quickly and he was fighting to stay awake. Every now and then the screams of another man falling overboard would remind him of the sheer hell in which he found himself. He began to grow more and more tired and struggled to stay awake. Finally, he was almost ready to give up and let himself be washed away and perish.

Just as he was about to accept his fate, he was slapped across the face. It was a hard slap. His adrenaline surged as someone, or something continued to slap his face repeatedly. It would not stop. He could see nothing. In fact, he could not really open his eyes, due to the seawater crashing into his face along with the heavy rains. The hitting, punching, and slapping of his face went on for hours. It seemed to worsen each time he began to nod off as he clung to the pole, fighting for his life.

Uncertain as to how much time had passed, my dad awoke with his arms still wrapped around the pole and the sun shining on his face. Completely exhausted and dehydrated, he heard someone calling his name. The other crewmembers had come to his rescue—he was one of the few who had survived being on deck that night. He told them he had barely held on all night, but each time he was about to fall asleep something violently slapped him across the face. Someone made a joke about divine intervention. As they helped him to his feet, a large fish fell out from under his vest onto the deck of the ship. The fish was dead, having gotten lodged upside down in his clothing with its tail directly under his chin. Fighting for its own life for many hours by thrusting itself back and forth trying to get back into the water, it had saved my dad's life. Every so often the water must have been so high that the head of the fish remained under water, but his tail and my dad's head were above it. It created a "perfect storm" during the perfect storm.

As a couple of the crewmembers continued to carry my dad belowdecks to receive much-needed medical attention, one of the other sailors kicked the carcass of the dead fish overboard. If he only had known just how valuable that fish was. My father believed that the unintended interventions of that fish constituted a real-life miracle. He continued to cherish that belief right up until the day he died of natural causes some forty years later. And in case you were wondering how the Cuban missile crisis ended, when Khrushchev saw that the storm did not deter the US warships in the slightest, and President Kennedy gave the Navy the order to move towards the Russian ships in full attack mode, the Russians were immediately ordered by their leader to turn their ships around in full retreat back to the Soviet Union. One small win for a man and one huge win for mankind.

Let us return to the beach on that beautiful sunny day with the warning of the very bad oceanic undertow. I wanted to get into that water so badly. My father explained what an undertow was, but I ignored his caution and went out swimming. My mom asked my dad to accompany and keep an eye on me. After swimming around for a while, I noticed that I was getting farther out to sea than the other swimmers. I heard a lifeguard blowing his whistle, though I didn't know if it was meant for me; but I did notice I was all alone, a small boy far into the ocean. I began to swim toward shore but soon realized I was not getting any closer to the beach. Something was wrong. I began to swim again straight in toward shore but I was getting nowhere fast and started to get tired. At this point I had been treading water for a while.

I screamed but no one heard me. I swam but got nowhere. No other swimmers remained in the water but me. I recall my dad was wearing bright red trunks that day. I saw them on the shore. I waved for help. I figured either the lifeguard on duty or my dad would see me. I yelled and screamed with my hands in the air, but they could not hear me. Did anyone know I was out there? I was about to panic, and if I had done so, I would have died. My heart began to race because I knew that if I just stayed still and waved for help, I would continue to move farther out to sea.

I looked at the lifeguard and waved my hands in the air again. It was pointless to scream: no one could hear me. I do not know why that lifeguard never turned his head my way. I was off to his far left and he kept blowing his whistle at someone on his right. *What the fuck?* I thought. *Do your damn job, man!* I looked back at my dad, and he was looking my way. I waved frantically for him to come get me. He was Goddamn-navy-superman for fuck's sake. *Get your ass out here!* He did not come out, but he pointed to the left. He was telling me to swim on an angle to shore. I did not understand that at the time. I was completely fucking petrified. Was no one going to come for me? Not even my own dad? The adrenaline kicked in. My heart began to race; I knew I was about to die.

At that moment something happened that I will never forget. A feeling of calmness took over my physical body. A visual of me swimming on an angle to shore came into my mind and my strength was restored. I had received a message from above. The full message I received was: *Calm down, swim at an angle, take as much time as you need, there is no rush to get yourself on land.* And that is exactly what I did. I knew I had to follow those instructions or die.

I swam very slowly to my right (my dad's left), at an angle, all the way to shore, and collapsed. Lying there catching my breath, I heard people ask if I was okay, but I remembered that I was never to speak to strangers, so I just got up quickly and began walking. I had no idea where I was or how far down the beach I had swum. It had taken me an exceptionally long time to get to shore—I had had to swim slowly and away from where my dad was standing. Not only did he not come get me, but he did not walk down the beach to follow me as I swam, not even just to make sure I didn't drown. Now I was fucking lost. The panic kicked right back in.

So I walked and walked and walked some more. Was it possible that I had swum that far from where my dad and my family were on land? The beach was crowded that day, and even more so since no one at that point was allowed in the ocean. I was getting tired again and panicking that I would not find my family. Remember, I was just a child. I kept walking and the clouds began to set in, the sky became overcast. People started to pack up their stuff and head indoors. There must have been a storm on the way—probably the reason for the undertow in the first place. I began to think that my family might have left without me. I realize today that this was a far-fetched notion, but again, I was just a kid.

I continued down the beach and although I must have found my family eventually, I cannot recall that actually happening. The last thing I remember was walking down that beach alone. That's it.

The worst part of it all was the fact that no one came for me. No one came when I was about to drown; nor did they come when I was lost. It was just me, my will to survive, and my small footsteps in the sand. I learned early in life that I could only count on me. No one was going to come for me. I suppose in a strange way this turned out to be a good life lesson, one I would need to apply from that day forward.

2.) Are you okay?

The year was 2000. It was called the year the world would end, dubbed "Y2K" by the media. I found the notion comical that every single computer would break down because their internal calendars would only go up to the last day of 1999. I remember sitting around on New Year's Eve waiting for everything to go berserk. I somehow knew that the great chaos predicted by some wasn't going to happen, but I was prepared in case it did. PTSD can make one hypervigilant, after all. I moved out of New York City and relocated to New Jersey. I was still working for the man we will call "Vinny," but I had managed to save up enough money to open a few small businesses of my own. They were successful, and I was thinking this would be the way I would transition to being my own boss, and not having to deal with the bullshit that went along with working for shady characters like some of Vinny's so-called "associates" in the bar business.

By the year 2000, my business partner and I had three brick-and-mortar businesses that were all thriving. In addition to that I was still making money working with Vinny, so financially things were good. They were, in fact, very good. At that point in my young life, I could practically purchase anything I wanted. However, a nagging thought from a familiar, friendly voice was urging me to sell the businesses. You might recall from the first book that this particular friend (a spiritual guide) always gave me lifesaving advice; even though he seemed to only reside in my head, and I rarely chose to believe he was real, he always came through with good counsel about the right things to do especially in the worst of times. Furthermore, according to him, this selling of my businesses needed to happen soon. I didn't understand. I knew this voice; I knew it had helped me previously; but, *why sell?* And why now, of all times? We were on top of the world, or so I thought. Business was thriving.

Time passed by and it was now the middle of 2001. My first child was born. I was elated. This little, tiny human was my new reason for living, my new reason to make positive changes in my life; a new reason to get as far away as possible from Vinny and that rock star, all-night-partying lifestyle. That and the fact that these people could literally hurt or kill me if they wished. Fortunately, I was always respectful and well liked, so I was more concerned with the rock-star lifestyle killing me than I was with getting whacked.

It seemed to me that the voice that was telling me to sell my business was urging me to act against everything I was trying to accomplish for my new, tiny human. If I sold the businesses, I would likely have to keep my night job. Why was this voice, which had always helped me in times of despair, counseling me to go against everything I knew was right for my family? At the time it made no sense. Since I had always trusted this voice and it had served me well, I decided to dig a little deeper and do some research. I would at the very least find out how much the businesses were worth; in case we decided to sell, I wanted to know what we could expect to get. I had a business partner back then, a near and dear friend for many years; but at first, I went to visit a business broker alone, without my partner's knowledge. The broker was one who matched up folks wanting to sell their business with others wanting to buy a ready-made turnkey business. I brought all the documents and financials over to him, then left his office and waited to hear back.

While waiting for the results from the broker, I discussed with my partner the possibility of selling the businesses. Unlike me, he didn't have a side job to depend on, and he couldn't understand why we should sell our businesses that were thriving. Hell, I didn't understand it either. I wasn't about to tell him "a little birdie told me"—a little birdie who had saved my fucked-up life repeatedly, a little voice I barely believed existed. The only thing I knew for certain was: whomever or whatever was giving me this information had never been wrong.

(By the way, and for the record, it isn't an actual voice; I have no better way to describe it than to say that it is information that comes into my head from some enlightened source.)

A week or so went by and the broker called me. He asked that my business partner and I come into his office and discuss the possibilities. At this point my partner had persuaded me somewhat to his way of thinking; but we both arrived at the broker's office anyway, to hear him out.

We walked inside the office—a nice place. It gave the impression that this guy knew his shit and could get the job done. We waited in a large conference room with a table that could seat about twenty at, even though there were only three of us present. The broker came in and asked, "So how are you gentlemen today?" I said, "We're great." Then I went on to explain my business partner's apprehension about selling before we even knew what our businesses were potentially worth.

The broker leaned forward and said, "Well, I think this may change your mind a bit." He pushed in front of us a piece of paper with a shit-load of numbers and columns on it. At this point in my life I hadn't finished college or business school and had limited knowledge of how to value a business for sale. I'd read books on how to start and run your own business, but never one about selling it or having an exit strategy. We both pretended to know what we were looking at so as not to appear stupid, but neither of us had a clue.

"Hmmm," I said. "Interesting. What do you think?" I passed the buck to my partner so he would ask the question and I could continue to pretend as if I knew something the paper was telling me.

He asked, "Which of these numbers is how much we can sell for?"

The broker said, "Oh, I am so sorry. I must have forgotten to highlight that for you." He went back into the other room for a minute. We were dying with anticipation because the numbers were all rather large, regardless of which one represented the bottom line.

The broker reentered the room with a yellow marker and highlighted one of the numbers. He then gave us back the paper. We tried to stay poker-faced, we really did, but this frigging number had seven digits. I never thought we would see a number that hefty. "Holy shit!" I couldn't hold back anymore. My partner was kicking me under the table, trying to get me to shut the fuck up, and he was right, but I simply couldn't. I felt like a little kid. My poker face was lost, never to be regained on that day. Could this estimation be accurate? Had we really built something of this magnitude?

My partner and I left the meeting on cloud nine. "Let's sign the papers," I said. "Let's sign them right now."

But my business partner wasn't ready to sign yet. I said to him, "You gotta be kidding me. Did you see that number?"

"Yes, but what will I do after the businesses are gone?"

"Absolutely anything you want," I replied.

I was stunned. I couldn't believe what I was hearing. In spite of the potential windfall, he still was not open to the idea of selling the businesses. The little voice inside was telling me that it must be done now, and the business broker was telling me it had to be done now (should anything change in the economy, that number he quoted us could change). I sat with those messages replaying in my head. If you read the first book, you'll remember the extreme importance of listening to these messages when they are repeated over and again. Things were about to change. Things were *really* about to change. I didn't know *how* they would change, but I just knew we needed to sell *now*.

Time went by during which discussions of the sale were relegated to a back burner. It was a beautiful morning in September. I was living in a home in New Jersey, just across the river from New York City. We had a beautiful view of the Manhattan skyline. My son was sleeping soundly in his crib, like an angel. We were expecting our second child. I awoke late that day, since I was still working night shifts with Vinny, to find several messages on my phone. Folks were calling to ask whether I was all right. I also noticed there was a strange and foul odor in the air. *Why would people want to know if I am all right, and what the fuck is that horrible smell?* Each person who called and left messages had called more than once that day. Something was very wrong; I just didn't know what it was. I returned one of the phone calls, and the person on the other end asked me again if I was all right. "What are you talking about?" I asked him. He said, "You don't know?"

"Know what already?"

"Turn on the television and call me back. I have more calls to make."

"Which station?" I asked.

"It doesn't matter," he said. "Pick one."

With that he hung up and I ran to the television and switched it on. This was the moment that changed everyone's life in America. It was Tuesday, September 11, 2001. After staring at the television in shock, I went to the window. I really wanted to believe that this was just a movie I was watching on TV and not real. *Please let this be some Hollywood special effects*, I thought. This sort of thing was impossible in America. I opened the window to see smoke everywhere and little, tiny objects falling from the burning towers. The smell was horrific. I will never forget that fucking smell. I watched on television as people chose to jump to their deaths rather than being burned alive. I closed the window and ran to my son's bedroom. *What have I done? What kind of world did I bring this tiny human into?* We had to get out of there, but where would we go? Where was it safe? The news reports said that there were potentially more planes coming down. I decided that the safest place was probably where we were—that's what the voice said.

Over the next few days, I turned my home into a fortress: loaded guns everywhere, food and clothing packed in luggage ready to leave at a moment's notice. I drove a large SUV at that time, and I filled it with supplies just in case we should find ourselves stuck in that car for any extended duration of time. None of us knew what would happen next. We had to be ready for anything and everything.

I think a week went by before I left the house. I was on the computer day and night trying to join any United States agency that would have me. I was too old for the military, and I was under-qualified for the FBI. That left the CIA. They seemed to accept people my age and had fewer requirements as far as schooling went—a little college was acceptable to them. I was the top age one could be to submit their application. If I waited a few months, I would be too old for them as well. I began to put my resume together. I was angry. I cannot even begin to put into words the anger inside of me. It consumed me. I had nightmares about the towers and that fucking smell! Each night I woke up in a cold sweat and ran to my son's bedroom to make sure he was okay.

As rescue workers worked tirelessly around the clock, I began receiving phone calls about the people we knew who had died when the World Trade Center buildings collapsed. I could not stop thinking about the terror those poor innocents must have endured. As angry as I was, and as much I would have liked to drop everything and fight for our country, I had a family who needed that very same protection. So I decided to stay put. I never sent in my CIA application. After a few weeks of being in shock and survival mode, I began to think of the potential consequences of this event on my own businesses and my job.

I'll never forget the first night I went back to work at the club. I was talking to a friend, and I said to him something like, "I cannot do this. I cannot be here." He responded, "You must be here. It is up to us to see that these people get some sort of distraction from this tragedy."

This was also what the NFL announced when they decided to play the football games scheduled for that next Sunday. "If we can bring just a couple hours of peace to these individuals, then we did our job," said the NFL spokesperson. They were absolutely correct. None of us were there to make money anymore. After all, we didn't know what the value of the American dollar was going to be. We were only there to help our customers deal with the tragedy, even if only for a brief time.

Our brick-and-mortar businesses basically collapsed financially. Our doors were open but fewer and fewer people walked through them. After 9/11 our seven-digit valuation plummeted to almost zero. My plan of retiring from my job in the bar business was ruined. I felt like everything I had worked for had disappeared in the blink of an eye. The voice that had told me to sell the business had been correct once again. By not following that advice, I had lost everything.

After this series of events, I resented my best friend and business partner for a long time. I regret that now. He certainly was not the cause of us losing the businesses. In those days the only thing that kept me going was my two children. My marriage to their mom fell apart soon after. Even though we had joint custody, my sons lived with me most of the time. I was now a single dad of two beautiful tiny humans who were counting on me to be a great father during one of the worst setbacks of my life.

I thought about the men and women on United Flight 93 that was hijacked on 9/11 and headed for Washington DC. While still up in the air the passengers knew they were destined to die. They had heard the news of the attacks, and they were aware what their fate was going to be. Knowing they had nothing to live for, they were going to take back the plane from the hijackers and crash it somewhere safe where the least number of people would be harmed. The man who sparked the idea to take back control of the plane said these final words to the other men and women: "Let's roll." And with that they proceeded as if they had no fear of death and no reason to care what happened to them. It was the most courageous and selfless act of any group of people I had ever heard of. And that is exactly how I felt. I had lost everything. I had nothing to lose and everything to gain.

Nothing is more dangerous than a person who has nothing to lose. I made up my mind. I quit the nightclub job, went to rehab, and went back to college to finish my fucking degree. I had nothing to lose. I had no safety net and two children I had willed into this world with every fiber of my being. They were counting on me. I had always wanted to be a father, but not one that would give up when shit got tough—I would never be *that guy*. No fucking way! I would die first, and I would die with my dignity. With that I was armed with everything I needed. I set out on this path on my kids' behalf, but what they did for me was much greater. I would have been on the road to self-destruction if not for them. By the time my kids were about three and four years old I had my degree, I was sober, and I had a real job—ironically, at one of the companies in the financial sector whose offices had been destroyed in the attacks of 9/11. There had been much turnover of their employees after the attacks, which may even be the reason I was hired.

Life was back in the palms of my hands. I could overcome any obstacle. Until I wrote these books, my children never knew a thing about my past. I completely destroyed the previous person I had been. I wore a suit to work; I made money for myself and others; my head was clear and sober. It was amazing. Everyone should have to go through rehab, whether you are an addict or not. It is an opportunity to completely tear yourself apart piece by piece, strip yourself of everything, then put yourself back together again, deciding which pieces stay with you, and which parts you throw away forever. I went into rehab a weak and pathetic person, clinging to a substance for escape and some sick form of emotional support. I had been living with bullshit excuses that allowed me to feel sorry for myself and fucked me up.

I came out of rehab living only in the present moment: I knew then that was all I had left. They basically teach you that before they will let you leave, but in a less spiritual way.

My senses returned. I could feel, smell, taste, and breathe again. Sex was amazing again. I took up reading once more. I loved reading. I did not have to worry about what I might do or say while intoxicated. I was back, and life was great again!

3.) Frankie and Heather

Vinny owned several businesses that were legitimate in nature, although many of us heard that the money to purchase these places may not have come from legitimate sources. Most of these places were nightclubs and bars, and I worked in one. Each of us had a so-called "real job" in the business for which we were well compensated. We were allowed to partake in the so-called "fun" of the establishment, but when all was said and done, our real job was to look after Vinny and his businesses, keep our mouths shut, and remain loyal. I was good at my job and respected for being that way. To the best of my knowledge, Vinny never had any of us do anything illegal. I think there were others for that.

One such person we will call Frankie. I got to know Frankie because he frequented the bar. He and I always got along. Like I said, I was respected for doing a good job. One night Frankie had a bit too much to drink—by no means an easy task for him since he had a hollow leg and was a big guy. He must have been in the bar for hours before I arrived. Anyway, I had some time and said hello to him. He called me over and put his arm around me and said to the others at the bar, "Now this is a good fucking kid right here." He said this with a drunken slur, so I was no longer comfortable even though he was praising me. We began to talk about various topics, none that I can remember except one that I will never forget.

The topic of this particular conversation had turned to guns. I had a firearm back then (legal and registered) so I told him what I had, and he told me about his weapon (I'm not sure his was licensed and registered). Then out of nowhere he said to me, "How do you load your gun?" The question seemed silly to me and meaningless at that moment. I said, "I just push each bullet down into the magazine until it is full, and then put it into the gun."

He said, "I know that, but that isn't what I'm talking about."

"What do you mean?"

He took his gun out, pulled the magazine out of it, and placed them both on the bar. He did this with the place full of people, mind you. He picked up the magazine and said, "Show me how you load it." He handed me one bullet to put in the magazine. I picked it up and began to push the bullet into the magazine.

"No, no, no. You fucked up already," he said.

"How is that possible?"

Frankie laughed at me and said, "Okay, look. The first thing you did was pick up the bullet and push it down into the magazine with your thumb. Right?"

"I'm not sure I get it."

"What are you, fucking stupid or something? Forget about it."

The man on his other side began to talk to Frankie, giving me a minute to try to understand what he was saying to me. I was looking at this frigging magazine, trying to figure out what I possibly could have done wrong. I mean, the bullet could only go in one way. I stared at that gun like it was a fucking Rubik's Cube. He turned back to me, took the gun, and put it away. "That's enough," he said.

"What was I doing wrong?"

"If you don't know, then you don't know. It's fine."

That was how those guys always spoke, with complete ambiguity. "If you don't know, then you don't know." What the fuck does that even mean?

It seemed to me that he was testing me, but for what? I had no idea. So I asked again, "What was I doing wrong?" I asked this politely, of course. I didn't want to be "shown" the correct way, if you know what I mean.

He said, "Okay, listen to me."

As if this huge man sitting next to me at a crowded bar with a loaded nine-millimeter pistol did not already have my undivided attention.

Here are the words I cannot erase from mind.

"Ray, when you fire this gun, what happens to the casing?"

"It ejects from the side of the gun."

"Correct," he said. "Where does it go?"

"It falls on the floor," I answered.

"Exactly. And now, you're fucked."

"Why? How am I fucked?"

"You still don't get it? Are you fucking stunad?"

"I guess n . . ."

"If you are ever going to do a hit, you know what I am saying? If you ever got to whack somebody, the last fucking thing you want to do is put your thumbprint on the bullet casing you are about to fire. The fucking casing falls to the floor with your fingerprint on it. You see what I'm saying? Are you going to stick around and try to find your casings? You need to get the fuck out of there. So what you got to do before you touch anything is

– 32 –

put on plastic gloves. Like the kind they wear in the hospital, you know? Then wipe everything down and start to load the gun with the gloves on. You see if you push the bullet in with . . . ."

He was still talking but I could no longer hear him. I was watching his lips move and nodding my head, but I was stunned and didn't want to move or react in any way. The voice inside me said, *Just keep yourself together, act normal, and then move away quietly.* Which is exactly what I did.

Frankie used to hang out at the bar because he had a girlfriend who worked there. Let's call her Heather. Everyone knew who Frankie's girl was, and no one dared disrespect her. She could walk around and do whatever she felt like, without fear of any repercussions. Even Vinny was intimidated by Frankie.

The thing about Heather was: she had a drug habit. Women plagued with such habits are especially vulnerable. If a drug dealer wants to be a complete dick, he can demand sexual acts for the drugs, and even after she complies, he can still charge her full price. If a dealer knows he has a hooked client, especially one who is an attractive female, he can manipulate the situation to get whatever he wants. On the other hand, there was usually more than one drug dealer in the bar, so if one of them decided to do something stupid, Heather typically had other options. Besides, who would be dumb enough to mess with Frankie's girl?

One night, at the end of a shift, Heather locked herself inside a private bathroom. No one knew why. Her girlfriends were trying to talk her into unlocking the door. She was clearly disoriented, possibly in shock, drugged up, and talking suicide. After what seemed like an hour, she eventually told one of her friends what had happened. There had been a new drug dealer in the bar that evening whom no one had ever seen before. He had taken advantage of Heather—full advantage—in the very bathroom she wouldn't come out of.

Holy shit, what will Frankie do? I had absolutely nothing to do with this situation, but I felt I needed to get the fuck out of there. Someone was sure to tell Frankie, and when they did a lot more than shit was going to hit the fan. *Should I tell Frankie?* Would he ask me why I didn't see this going down and do something about it? Part of my job included keeping an eye on things and reporting back to Vinny. I was certainly not the only one with this extra job on their list, but Frankie knew this. Vinny was nowhere to be found, and you just knew that Frankie would be furious with anyone who didn't stop this from happening. It was going to be bad.

All these thoughts raced through my head as I got my stuff together so I could leave. I had everything in the same bag I brought every day to work. I was waiting until there was no one around, hoping to leave without being noticed, looking for a moment when everyone was preoccupied with Heather or their own end-of-night-cleanup activities so I could get away. Finally, I threw my bag over my shoulder and began to walk across the main floor toward the front door. I was moving slowly at first, looking around to see if anyone was noticing me. There were two sets of doors, and between them ran a corridor in which one or more security guys patrolled and kept an eye on things. Also nearby was the person collecting the fee to get inside. At the end of a nightshift however, I never really knew who was going to be in that corridor.

So far everyone seemed occupied by something, and a small sigh of relief ran through me as I stepped closer to the door.

I was about twenty feet from it when I heard "*pop, pop*", right outside. Time seemed to slow down completely. I was frozen for what was likely a second but felt like an hour. The door was kicked open hard, and there stood Frankie. Holy shit! Disheveled and irate, he had fire in his eyes like I had never seen before, sweat pouring down his face. We locked eyes and time stopped.

Neither of us said a word. My bag began to slip off my right shoulder as I waited to see if death was imminent. As my bag hit the floor, I raised my left arm very slowly and pointed toward the bathroom where Heather was. We didn't speak. He slowly turned his head in the direction I was pointing. The bathroom was down a short hallway to my left. In my mind I was saying, *Please go. Please go down the hall. Just please go, go, go.* He turned his head and looked back at me as though he was thinking. He nodded at me in what seemed to be a friendly gesture, perhaps even a thank you from a guy too angry to speak. Then he moved down the hall to the bathroom. There was no way I was going out through the front now—I had no idea what I would find—so I turned around a hundred and eighty degrees and walked through a back door leading out to the other street. As the door closed behind me, I heard Frankie's anger erupt.

I never disliked Frankie, and I don't think he was mad at me about the incident. He had always gone out of his way to be nice to me. A few years ago, I attended the wake of a friend of mine who had passed away. At the wake was someone who knew both Frankie and me. They told me Frankie had died of natural causes many years earlier. He was considerably older than me, but natural causes sounded a bit strange. Anyway, there is this part of me that felt really bad for him. How fucked up does someone's life have to be to make the choices he had to make and do the things he had to do? I realize it may be difficult to understand how I could have a bonding moment with a person who had literally tried to teach me how to get away with murder, but I suppose in that world it was a sign of trust, loyalty, and friendship. It didn't make it any less of a traumatic moment, but I still bear some empathy toward him and the situation. Perhaps the capacity to feel that is a part of the new me, part of my awakening.

4.) The Final Bus Stop

It was a hot summer night a few years after I had gotten my driver's license. I had my car, and my friend was with me in the passenger seat. Back then we would drive around endlessly with the music blasting, up and down main streets where there might be kids hanging out, and hopefully, girls to meet.

My friend and I were driving down a popular main drag. It was a four-laned street with two lanes heading north and two heading south. We were coming up on a popular pizzeria where we thought some kids might be hanging around out front. As we got closer to our destination a large passenger bus was headed north while we were heading south. Suddenly, and without warning, the bus driver decided to make a left turn, crossing through our lane. My friend screamed, *"Watch out!"* I slammed on the brakes to try to stop the front end of my car from slamming into the side of the bus. Unfortunately, back then there was no anti-locking technology. If you hit the brakes hard enough, the wheels would lock up, and the car would just skid until the skidding came to an end—which we were hoping would happen sooner rather than later.

My car's wheels locked up and we were skidding directly into the bus, bracing ourselves for impact—I had my hands tight on the steering wheel, getting ready for when the collision took place. We skidded for what seemed an eternity but it likely was only a couple of seconds at most. You know that moment when you think a car crash is just inevitable and all you can do is brace yourself in the hope you won't get mangled up or die?

I was already thinking about what damage was going to be done to me, my car, and my friend. And then the car suddenly stopped moving. We didn't hit the bus, but a bird's feather would not have fit between the bus and my car. That is how close we came to a very serious injury, or possibly even death. After the car stopped, neither one of us moved for a good five seconds. Serious adrenaline was surging within us. The fight or flight mode had kicked into high gear, to say the least. While stopped in the middle of this main road, not moving at all, we looked over to see where the bus was going. Why would it make a turn as dangerous as that?

The bus had turned into a bus service terminal. There were no passengers on board, only a driver (who wasn't even an actual bus driver, but more of a mechanic giving the bus a test ride to see if he had fixed whatever had been wrong with it). We observed that the bus had continued driving down the long driveway into the terminal. My friend and I were so filled with anger we decided to follow the bus down that very long driveway to make sure that driver knew how pissed off we were.

We got down there and the driver was still in his seat, probably stunned and wondering how it was that our vehicles had not collided. My friend and I were even more irate. We went right up to the bus and started yelling at that guy. He was about our age or just a few years older; and he was so petrified that he locked himself inside the bus, which was probably a good move for all concerned. Too bad, though, that the story did not end there. The driver opened up one of the windows and started to yell for help, screaming as if he were being killed, in spite of the fact that, with the bus locked up as it was, we had no way of entering it.

We were about to walk away when what seemed like thirty mechanics walked out of the garage and surrounded us. Now, with the tables turned and all of his buddies as protection, the guy stepped out of the bus and proceeded to come at us along with the others. *We are so fucked right now,* I thought. We couldn't get back to my car. They had the access to it blocked off. To get out alive we would have to fight these fuckers who now bore a herd mentality, all wanting our blood. I looked at my friend and he looked at me. My friend stood a bit closer to the car but there was a group of mechanics in the way. I looked for whoever I thought was the weakest link in the lineup, and if the attack were imminent, I decided I'd go through him.

Well, my idea didn't work. I didn't make it anywhere close to that line of guys before I had a shit ton of angry mechanics from inside the garage beating on me. I managed to get a shot in here or there to persuade a few to back off. We kept trying to fight our way out of there. When a couple of them realized we were not going to be an easy take down, those few backed off a little, but some of the others just got angrier. Meanwhile, we were taking a real beating. I was getting hit from all angles. *I'm not getting out of here alive,* I thought. But it was strange because each time I was struck by a punch or kick I didn't feel the pain. I knew the damage was going to be excessive, but I guess my body was in shock. I knew each time I fell to the ground I had to get up quickly or I was finished. And then, at one point I took a blow to the back of my head, and that one was really bad. I felt myself going down. I remember being dizzy and I fell to one knee. A moment after that I heard my name.

My friend was calling me. I thought he was asking for help but when I looked up, I saw he had managed to get himself into the driver's seat of my car. The car was severely damaged, and so was my friend, but this was my opportunity. If I could get to the car, I might get out alive. But down on one knee it was hard to keep my head up. I was dizzy and nearing the end.

I heard glass breaking—it was the window of the passenger side of my car, broken by one of the mob. With everything I had left in me I ran to the car and dove headfirst through the broken passenger side window. Half of me was still dangling out as my friend whipped the car around to go back up the long driveway. The mechanics were trying to grab my legs to pull me back out of the car. I just kicked as fast and as hard as I could, held on to the seat with my hands, and told my friend to *DRIVE!* He hit the gas pedal like we were fighting for pole position at the Indy 500 and all of a sudden, he could drive like Mario Andretti. I whipped my body around, tucked in my knees, and we made it out to the crowded street.

When I look back at the choices I made, I wonder at my sheer stupidity and lack of respect for myself. Why was I placing myself so often in terrible situations? How little I must have thought of myself to put my mortality in such danger time and again.

Later in life, I mentally reframed these incidents. I did this not to minimize their stupidity and recklessness, but to find something positive to take away. If there is one thing I have learned in life, it is that if you look hard enough there is always a positive takeaway. Even the worst life events will yield positivity if you want them to and if you search for the silver linings. But you have to look for them, and what's more, you have to want to find them.

One of my favorite quotes is from William Shakespeare: *"There is nothing either good or bad, but thinking makes it so."* This will be a repetitive mantra you will find throughout this book. So profound, simple, and true.

Trauma will always offer you a lesson, regardless of how terrible it is.

The Proverbial Diamond in the Rough

You can't defeat someone who has already been defeated over and again. You can't break someone who has been broken over and again. You can't hurt someone who has experienced the worst hurt, over and again.

Consider a diamond. What does it take to become one? The process takes a small piece of rock made up of carbon atoms and turns it into one of the hardest, toughest, most sought after and valuable pieces of matter in the world. If you were to try to break a diamond with another rock, the other rock would break, not the diamond. There is almost nothing that can damage or destroy a diamond. But, at what cost? What must a small piece of earthly matter go through to become a diamond?

To start with, our little rock must go through extreme pressure at about a hundred miles below the earth's surface. The pressure must exceed 725,000 pounds per square inch. It is just about the most pressure that can be applied to any earthly substance we know of. Once this rock spends a hundred or so years under all that pressure, the earth turns up the heat. We're talking real fucking heat, deep below the earth's surface, that can exceed two thousand degrees Fahrenheit. It is only under these extreme conditions that a few carbon atoms can mold themselves collectively into what may one day become a diamond.

Even after all that, the little rock is not yet a diamond. The earth isn't done with you yet. You haven't made it out of the earth's hundred-mile depth. Remember, little rock, you are down so far below the earth's surface that the ambient temperature is two thousand degrees. No one is coming for you. No one is going to pull you out. You are on your own and the earth is not done with you yet. You must rely on molten volcanic matter to come along and push you up much nearer to the earth's surface. Volcanic matter can't break you anymore because you've been through the fiery depths of hell. You are hardened and tougher, but you must now wait and wait, and then wait some more in this volcanic mess for your ride closer to the earth's surface where, eventually, you may be found.

Having withstood insurmountable pressure and intense heat, and having waited centuries to get elevated to the surface, you think to yourself, *I've made it. I'm a fucking diamond! I am at the top, finally!* Well, guess what? No one gives a shit. Nobody wants you. Nobody wants to even look at you yet, except a small group of miners who recognize your potential and believe in you. But to the rest of the world, you're still just an ugly rock. Diamonds do not pop out of the earth looking like diamonds you see at the store.

Once the miners have excavated you and cleaned you up, you will need to be cut. And after you have been cut, you must be polished. Both of these processes will remove pieces of you. You must strip away your ugliness and bare your inner core to the world. You will lose some of yourself—but you can get through it. It is only now, once the polishing is complete, that the world will look at you. Now they will notice you. Now you are beautiful and unbreakable.

But at what cost? At what sacrifice? Think of what you had to go through to get here.

Once you are a diamond, no one can take that away from you. You will never go back to being an ugly piece of carbon again. It isn't possible. Nothing will break you ever again. You are now the strongest, toughest, most beautiful, sought-after piece of earthly matter known to mankind. The diamond is the most valuable, cherished piece of matter on the earth, and it will never be broken again. Herein lies the positive takeaway.

Are you a diamond or a rock? If you aspire to diamond-ship, you must suffer first, little rock. Then all will be yours. There is a hidden beauty in all suffering that leads to catharsis and transformation.

CHAPTER 3

EXPONENTIAL GROWTH

Generally speaking, life seems to be getting simpler and clearer. Clarity, according to dictionary.com, means "the quality of being coherent and intelligible." I began this journey without a belief in any higher power in this universe. I began without a need to search for any forms of truth. I didn't feel that I needed anything other than those emotions I harbored toward those I loved, or even those with whom I was angry. Love and anger had both driven me to successes, and therefore I felt I had everything I needed. Or so I thought.

Holy shit, was I wrong! I hadn't mastered myself . . . or anything else for that matter. I hadn't found myself nor where I fit in to the universal structure. I was able to play the game of life superficially; but I wasn't being my true self, and I had no idea what that was. Who was my true self? Here was something vital I still needed to uncover.

I do not advocate one religion over another because I think they all propound truths and fallacies. They each have positives and negatives. But they all seem to have one common denominator. They all proclaim something similar to, "God is within you," or "You are a part of God." So simple, yet so profound. Jesus said that, and also something to the effect of: "Why do you ask me these questions when I am the same as you, a part of God?"

Now, if you are the type of person who is not open to the possibility that all religions have some inaccuracies, there is no sense in your getting upset by reading any further. If you believe that your religion can do or say no wrong, please throw away this book. And remember to recycle, after all, paper doesn't grow on trees. If you do not have a recycling bin, you might want to consider using it to fix that three-legged table or perhaps use the hardcover for self-defense.

Should you choose, however, to continue on, please do so with an open mind. Remember, I was quite close-minded until I allowed for the possibility that there were things I did not fully understand or agree with just yet. I will share with you what I have found: that we are in fact all part of one Being. A part of our Creator, not separate from our Creator, but partners with Them. Just as the late, great psychiatrist Carl Jung said, "I believe we are all consciously connected through one universal collective consciousness."

This is where I believe the power of creation can be found. Since you are a part of it, guess what? You too can co-create with the help of the collective energetic entity.

Isn't it absolutely amazing to know that you and your conscious mind are woven into the fabric of the universe, making you essentially the co-creator of all things? You have unlimited power and potential, once you learn to "tap in" to this amazing energetic entity. If you can subscribe to the fact that all thoughts and words are energy, and that these words and thoughts are created by the conscious mind, then it follows, that the conscious mind itself must be made up of energy. We also know that consciousness does not exist solely in the brain. It actually resides in every cell in our bodies. We know this to be true because some people, during a near-death experience, in which they've been brain-dead for many minutes—some for as many as thirty minutes—have returned, with a detailed description of what had transpired in the room they were in while their bodies were dead. Talk to anyone who has had a near-death experience. It's mind blowing. I told the story of my own NDE in my first book. I also explained my theory of where we go when we die: that our conscious energy becomes a part of the dark energy in the universe. Again, this is just my personal belief—rather simple in nature, but plausible since science doesn't know where or how dark energy is created, even though it has proved its existence. You see it is my belief that your consciousness is what the church would call a spirit or a soul. When it is released by the deceased it must go somewhere.

Dark energy is called "dark," not in the sense of being evil, but because we cannot directly see or observe it; we infer its existence from observing gravitational interactions between astronomical objects. Just because we cannot see something doesn't mean it isn't there. Science has proven that dark energy is everywhere; in fact, what we used to believe was empty— the void of outer space—is filled with dark energy. We now know and can scientifically prove that there is no such thing as empty space. Dark energy, which fills all the spaces we once thought contained nothing, is the primary force which causes our universal structure to expand. Albert Einstein taught that if it weren't for this existing form of energy, the universe would most likely contract instead. This simple fact tells us that there must be a force or energy that we cannot see, that literally pushes the universe further and further apart. Einstein proposed this hypothesis first, and the astronomer Edwin Hubble confirmed it years later. What we also know of this dark energy is that its mass, meaning its density in space, does not change. How is that possible? Let us look at how and why this aspect is so important.

If you consider the water contained in a glass, its density would be confined to the glass which holds it in place. But spill it on the floor and the same amount of water exists, although its density has lessened. It is spread out across the floor. Why then does the universal dark energy between all things in the cosmos maintain its density as the universe expands? This would not make sense if we weren't constantly replenishing it with more and more dark energy. This in turn causes the expansion of the universe outward into space. So where is that energy coming from? Let's return to my theory. My personal belief is that it is the energy within our conscious minds which continues to live on upon the death of our physical bodies. In my theory your conscious energy becomes dark energy. Remember, The First Law of Thermodynamics states that energy cannot be created or destroyed; it can only be converted from one form to another. Therefore, the energy we know as consciousness must be converted into another type of energy and cannot cease to exist.

Upon death we become part of the universal structure. You may insert your particular religious belief as to where this place is, or what it is called, but most religions state that we go *somewhere*; and if this is the first "stop," so to speak, what comes next would be based on your interpretation of life after death.

That being said, let us return for a moment to the conscious mind. I am sure you have heard the saying "become one with universe." What this profound statement actually means is that your conscious mind, whether or not your body is alive, is part of one universal entity. When we say we must connect with our Higher Selves, we are talking about communicating with that entity, which is collectively made up of everyone's conscious minds at their highest level. Those that are living and deceased and perhaps even unborn. Levels of enlightenment can be attained from this structure—in fact, it is the source from which just about anything can be attained.

Our human experience causes us to become sidetracked by materialism and concerns regarding this earthly life. We become obsessed trying to find stimulation for our five physical senses. We tend to seek instant gratification. We then lose touch with the other aspect of our being, which is all knowing, all loving, and a part of God, the Universe, the Divine, the Source, the Light, or any other term you prefer to use to describe the Creator of all. We lose our connection. One that is all powerful and literally able to create anything, solve any problem, help all of mankind, and more. We may lose this connection to this aspect of our being by means of our constant distractions, separators, and seeking only to please our five mortal senses. In other words, stop trying to be so fucking happy and then you'll actually find true fucking happiness!

Some are so desperate to achieve this false sense of happiness, they are willing to do anything to get it. Even if that something is evil. Eckhart Tolle was asked by one of his students whether or not God created evil. (We are using the term "God" here to describe the Creator or Source of all, or the energy of the universe as a whole.) His answer went something like: imagine for a moment that the sun is the source or the creator of all things (because in a way it is, as far as the earth is concerned). All that is of this earth came to be by virtue of the energy created by the sun. That energy doesn't judge anyone. It simply makes its way toward the earth as a photon, and then merges with or becomes part of another form. The sun's energy is pure, but the form it takes here on earth changes it. That pureness can become part of a human, an animal, plant life, and so much more. When the energy takes that form, the form can then choose how to use the energy. Therefore, evil doesn't arise directly from the Source of all. When the Source is altered into form, that form can decide how to use it. That is the freewill of the form acting. Thus, evil arises when this energy takes form, and that form decides to use it for evil purposes. Prior to that it is a completely pure, non-judgmental energy intended to be proffered to everyone.

Let us consider a different example. How immensely powerful is the Internet? —a plethora of information (or energy) at your fingertips for the asking. This is my Computer/Internet analogy of universal consciousness. If anyone is going to run into Bill Gates anytime soon, please pass him a copy of this book.

Just think, you can sit at any computer and connect to any other computer or groups of computers in the world and request information from one another. You can also collaborate to formulate new ideas, and create new materials, concepts, and programs. But once you disconnect your computer from the Internet, it is limited in its behavior and the amount of information it can provide. It is also limited in the things you can create with it. But plug it back into the rest of the Internet and you potentially have available to you the "thoughts" and capabilities of all the other computers combined.

Now let us apply this same theory to the human mind. Your conscious mind at its highest level is a part of what we call the universal collective consciousness (essentially, the Internet of all minds) and as such, you may tap into its knowledge and power. We are born connected to this "Internet of universal consciousness," but over time we separate ourselves as we become conditioned and influenced by environmental factors. We separate ourselves when we think less of each other, or of a particular group of people; when we divide ourselves by political parties; when we disconnect ourselves from our neighbors by thinking we are better than they are. These degrees of separation remove us from our collectiveness. The more you separate yourself, the weaker you will become. We are powerful as one consciousness but weakened when divided.

To harm your fellow man or woman is to harm *yourself.* Therefore, everything we do to each other as humans we do to ourselves. It is that simple. We are all part of one large energy-being, which is woven into the fabric of the universe, that affects all things which contain energy. All things contain energy. We, as individuals, are co-creators of the universe. Collectively, as one, we become all-powerful and all-knowing. If you find yourself separated, you just need to return to the realization of being One, to find all that you seek and all that you can be.

If you read my first book, you will remember that near the end of it I related a story of my current mentor, whom I call "Medium Joe." You'll read more about him in this book. He really made me sweat when it came to joining his two-year mentorship program. I remember the long essay questions we had to fill out, the interviews, emails, references, and other application processes. You had to prove to the best of your ability that you were an advanced intuitive or medium. It didn't matter that I had the wherewithal to pay for his school. He didn't care about that as much as he cared about each of us possessing advanced abilities. Oh, and by the way, you also had to have experienced some form of spiritual awakening. I imagine it is easier to be accepted into Yale or Harvard University. Out of hundreds of applicants I was one of a mere dozen accepted into the program. I was (and am) honored and humbled to be part of it.

You can't buy your way into his mentorship program, and I admire him for that. Most consider Medium Joe a teacher of teachers. You better know your shit if you plan to apply. He has all the qualities of a great leader. I love, respect, and fear him. Yes, you read that right. Sometimes he scares the shit out me. I am proud to say I am entering my third year of mentorship (of a two-year program) with this great man. He has taken me to levels of spirituality I didn't know existed, and I am honored and grateful to call him my teacher and my friend. I will be with him as many years as he will have me around.

In addition to his many accolades, he is one of the very few accredited members of the Forever Family Foundation (FFF): a non-profit organization that rigorously tests folks to prove beyond any reasonable doubt that they possess the abilities of evidential mediumship. The FFF will accept only the best to be labeled as accredited members, and those members must pass their testing. As it states on their website, approximately 99 percent of all folks who try to complete the FFF testing process fail. There are (as of my writing this) only twenty-four members (evidential mediums) in the world who have passed their test and become certified. I am likely many years away from this type of certification. They use a triple-blind testing method, and they never disclose what will be expected of the medium. Their secrets are more difficult to acquire than the formula of Coca-Cola. Additionally, Medium Joe has worked for years with various law enforcement agencies to help solve crimes, find missing persons, and prevent terrorism. I think it is safe to say I have been in quite good hands with him and very lucky to have him in my life.

Anyway, getting back to that unfortunate separation from the universal collective we often experience in life, Medium Joe gave us another great analogy. Picture the ocean. Now picture taking a glass, dipping it into the ocean, and filling it up with the water. What is the difference between the water in the glass and the water in the ocean? Nothing, basically, except for the volume of water and the power it possesses when merged as one. But the glass of water, by itself, even full to the brim, hasn't much power or force and cannot serve much of the earth. The ocean, on the other hand, has the power to move mountains and create canyons in the earth. If you feel in your consciousness that you are like the water in the glass, it is time to merge back into the ocean and harness all that power again.

This is so important that I will say it again. You are a part of God and God is a part of you. You will find a similar formula in every religion. Why do you suppose that is? He or She is not a separate entity that judges you. You are directly a part of this universal structure. That means you are a part of God. Pray to yourself (your Higher Self), that which is a part of the Creator of all, that part of the Source you can connect and communicate with directly. Ask the universal collective consciousness or "Internet of all things" to find the answers you need. Ask to be shown the way. Ask to be shown your path. Ask to be given the guidance you need in order to accomplish your goals. As long as those goals are for your highest and best self, you will more than likely get them every time. (Come on and jump in. The water is perfect for everyone.)

CHAPTER 4

WHOSE WORLD IS IT?

Too many people continue to distance themselves from the universal consciousness by (what I call) separators. Separation grows each time we declare ourselves as being a member of someone else's world. For example, when we identify ourselves by a political party, our skin color, even being male or female, to some degree that separates us from others. It is our attachment to these limited identities which separates or removes us from the rest of humankind and the universe. Why this happens is because each separator or group has an opposing group. As humans we want to feel we are part of something—we need to belong—but what we tend to forget is, we already are and do. We are all a part of the universal energy structure, God, the Source, the Light, or whatever term you choose. You don't have to take my word for it. Jesus, Moses, Buddha, and many others said the same thing. Any separation from humankind that puts the group of people you have chosen to identify with, at the top of your priority list, or perhaps makes the members of that particular group more important, better than, or smarter than all others, may result in significant internal and external problems, such as, anger, and suffering—suffering that could be alleviated by transferring all of your identification to the group known as humankind.

I am not saying that all groups are bad. There are many groups that are quite good. Some focus on charity or self-improvement work, for example, all over the world, and continue to strive for the well-being of others. There is certainly no harm in that. I'm referring to the groups that suggest they are for the betterment of mankind but really are about superiority and gaining power or control.

Many (perhaps, most) people (myself included) have at one time or another been a member of more than one separator. I renounced the political party I was aligned with and became undeclared in order to remove my identification with any such political entity. When we join these separators, we are ultimately subscribing to someone else's belief system, someone else's model of the world. From each of these groups a leader will emerge from within. That leader may begin to dictate how things should be for everyone in the separator. So now you may be thinking, *So what? What's so wrong with that, if my beliefs align with that person's?* The answer is simple: to the degree that you allow that, you are living in their world, not your own. You have abandoned your world to that extent, given it up to a group to make certain decisions or speak for you. Humans so badly want to "belong" that we are willing to give up our own worlds to be accepted into someone else's.

Never let someone else's thoughts become your reality.

From the time I was in grade school, I was aware of some of the kids separating themselves into groups. I'm sure you can remember this happening when you were in school. Many kids wanted to fit in with a particular group so badly that they would do things they otherwise would never have done. You may have been one of those kids. When you had kids of your own, I'll bet you told them to stay away from those groups and concentrate on their studies. And yet, as we grew up, many of us continued to join groups which separated us in the same way, unaware of our hypocrisy and remaining ignorant of the damage these patterns can cause to humanity.

I remember an event that took place during my final year of grade school. Once a week my entire class had to walk from our school to another school ten blocks away to take a mandatory woodshop class. Most of us hated anything mandatory—typical at that young age, I suppose. The teacher of this class told us he had been teaching that exact same class in that exact same school for over forty years. My first thought was, *Wow, this guy must be really frigging old.* In hindsight, he was probably only in his sixties, but he looked like he was over a hundred and about to die any minute. Furthermore, I have never met a more miserable fucking man in my entire life! He hated his work. You could tell. He hated the fact that his class was mandatory because he would then get the kids who didn't want to be there, kids who already had a life plan that didn't include woodshop in their future. Some parents felt the same way and I'm sure that made him feel even less important, thus adding to his frustrations. A few kids (who most likely went on to a career in building and construction) loved it, but not the majority of my class. I will not reveal this teacher's name, so let's just call him "Pig Vomit."

(Credit to the King of all Media, Howard Stern, who found the perfect name to describe those who are the epitome of terrible humans we loath. Mr. Stern, please don't sue me.)

I could see and feel Pig Vomit's hatred toward us the moment we walked into his domain, and that is very intimidating for a young student. In addition, we were also in a separate building at another school where the teachers we counted on daily to protect us and keep us safe were not present. Pig Vomit would overreact to anything we did that might upset him, which was just about everything because he obviously hated all of us, every aspect of his career, and his overall fucking life. Therefore, Pig Vomit really tried to bring us down to his level. He berated us, made fun of us, and tried to embarrass us in front of our peers. Laughter was outlawed in this prick's class. It was woodshop and you damn well better take it seriously or else! I figured it out: Hitler must have reincarnated as Pig Vomit! *Holy shit*, I thought to myself, *who would marry this man? His poor wife. Does Pig Vomit have kids? Dear God, please do not allow him to have kids,* I thought.

We were living two hours a week, without a choice in the matter, in this miserable man's world. There were other teachers in the system who knew of this man and his unorthodox methods of punishment. There were rumors of Pig Vomit hitting or getting physical with students as well. Although I did not witness this, I could believe it. We all could and did.

Finally, it was near the end of the school year. This was the last year of grade school, mind you. We would all graduate (hopefully) and go on to high school, where we would never see Pig Vomit again. Woodshop took place on Wednesdays, and this was the last woodshop class of the year. Three boys got together and decided that right after this final class ended, and before we exited the building, we were all going to tell Pig Vomit, one by one, what we thought of him. The bell rang and the first "Fuck you, [Pig Vomit]!" shot from one boy's mouth, quickly followed one by one, by many others joining in. I certainly had my own collection of foul-mouthed phrases I had been saving for the moment, but before I could utter one of them, one of the girls chimed in. Not just any girl! This was the girl in your class that was the teacher's pet. The one you wanted to sit next to so you could cheat on tests by reading her paper, because it would always be 100 percent correct. The straight-A student who never got in trouble, never was late, and only spoke out loud if she was solving an equation that was two years above our grade level. I was stunned. What could possibly make her, of all people, speak this way? I paused and I thought, *This isn't her.* Why would she do this to her perfect school record? The rest of us participating certainly surprised no one, because we had that in us—but *her*?

We returned to Building One, where we usually were given instruction. By this time someone from the other building had reported the incident to our teacher and the principal. We all hated Pig Vomit so much that, though we knew the punishment was coming, we were willing to take it. Was the teacher's pet (like Molly Ringwald's character in *The Breakfast Club*, Claire Standish) going to be punished too? I felt so bad for her and still couldn't understand what had made her participate.

So, what happened, you ask? Well, for our punishment we all had to write an essay explaining that what we did was wrong, and why. We also had to include an apology to Pig Vomit. It gets worse. We all thought that since school ended on the following Wednesday, they wouldn't make us attend another woodshop class—not on the last day of school. Well, this was not the case. We had another two hours to go with Pig Vomit, where we would be asked to read our essays aloud. *C'mon man! Are you serious? Was "Claire" going to write one?*

About two days after the incident transpired, and before the dreaded last day, something wonderful happened. Pig Vomit called our homeroom teacher. Now, we'd had this same homeroom teacher for three or four consecutive years. To say that she thought of us as her own children would be an understatement. She loved us, and we loved her. Well, Pig Vomit apparently started an argument with Mrs. Homeroom in which Pig Vomit insulted her for being a terrible disciplinarian. He verbally attacked her! That morning she busted into the classroom visibly pissed off. We all asked her what was wrong, and she shocked us by saying, "I now understand why you hate [Pig Vomit]." The class erupted with joy. She said we did not have to do the essay, but we still had to go to his class for two hours and apologize. That part of the punishment had come from the principal, and she could not remove it.

So, on that Wednesday, the last day at school, we all had to be present in woodshop or receive a failing grade. An F would mean summer school with Pig Vomit. So we showed up! He made us sit in silence for two hours. If anyone so much as sneezed during that two-hour class, they would have had to go to summer school. I would rather have had my nuts stuck in a vice for an excruciating minute than attend summer school with Pig Vomit. But at one point I had to pee. *Shit. I knew I should have gone before I left Building One.*

It only took about five minutes for Pig Vomit to claim his first victim. It was the student in our class who most resembled Judd Nelson's character from *The Breakfast Club*. (Remember John Bender?) "Fuck you, [Pig Vomit]," this student said. (Oh man, summer school with Pig Vomit, that train wreck of a human? I guess "John Bender" was a glutton for punishment.) I glanced over at "Claire." She was shaking. At first, I thought it was fear, but it turned out she had to use the bathroom because she needed a tampon. She very politely started to raise her hand when Pig Vomit reminded her of the rule: no one can move or speak for two hours. I was livid! We sat there and toughed it out for the full two hours. Poor "Claire." By the end of class, she was crying and desperate to figure out a way to get to the bathroom. A small stream of blood was running down her leg, visible to everyone but Pig Vomit. In tears, she put something like a tissue under her dress and ran out. As I walked out of the class, I stared at this so-called "educator" and just shook my head at him. Throughout the entire class, I had sat in silence and thought of various ways to kill him. He looked down and away. When he eventually found out what Claire's emergency bathroom trip was for, even he felt bad. That was the last we saw of Pig Vomit. He retired shortly thereafter. I imagine his resignation was "requested, had he not retired." You see, Mrs. Homeroom was married to the Superintendent of Schools. *Justice!*

Why did I relate this story in this section of the book? Let's begin with Pig Vomit. We were forced to be a part of his world; and when people are forced into a group they don't believe in or support, they rebel; and that rebellion can become dangerous or violent. Next is "Claire." I asked her later why she had participated in the name-calling. She never seemed to have had a problem with Pig Vomit. Her answer shocked me at the time. She said she did it because everyone else was doing it. At that moment I realized she had wanted to fit in so badly that she had gone against her own morals and belief system to conform and be accepted in someone else's world. And yet—she had her own world and was going places. She was a star student and a kind person. What she didn't know was, as I look back now, I wish I had been more like her.

I hung around some with "John Bender" after graduation. We lost touch with each other a few years later when he went to prison for the first time. I heard recently that he is still serving an extensive prison sentence in a maximum-security penitentiary. I don't know what happened to "Claire," but I'm sure she is doing quite well. At least, I hope she is.

You have the right and the ability to make your own world. If your motives are pure, you can invite others into your world to experience it with you. But allow them to come and go as they please. Allow them to bring their own beliefs into your group, because in the end we are all a part of only ONE group. "United we stand and divided we fall." That is a terrific slogan, but I am not referring solely to the United States of America. I am referring to all humanity.

CHAPTER 5
REVELATIONS

Ihave taken you along, this portion of my exploration, through my
newfound spiritual gifts. Although I am grateful for them, there are
times when I have difficulty referring to them as "gifts." Being the recipient
of a message from the other side can sometimes feel more like a curse
than a blessing. The majority of the information I receive seems tragic in
nature. For a very long time I didn't understand why. The scenes or visions
I witness in my mind's eye can be quite difficult to look at and experience
at times. Imagine watching a movie that's got you emotionally off balance
and you get to a scene where you can't look anymore, so you cover your
eyes and ask the person you're with, "Is it over yet?" That is the feeling. The
difference is, when the vision is internal, I don't have the option of covering
my eyes. I'm in too deep to get out. To add to this, I also know that what
I'm watching is very real and not just a creative projection coming from
some director in his chair yelling *Action!* If that isn't enough to process, I
also have to figure out whether what I am seeing is past, present, or future,
and whether I should tell anyone.

As you may have read in my first book, I continue to learn about
these phenomena with the help of my mentor, Medium Joe. He has been
a total beacon of hope for me. If anyone can help me figure this stuff out,
it is certain that he will be the one. Learning to navigate the afterlife and
premonitions should never be done through trial and error. I have been
told that can lead one down the path of insanity. It is simply too dangerous

to take this on alone. I am forever thankful that I have Medium Joe in my corner. I hope he knows how much he means to me. Medium Joe is world-renowned as one of the greatest mediums and spiritual teachers out there. He has "written the book," so to speak, on navigating the afterlife and he is extremely well-respected in his field. People from around the world seek to get readings with him, and sometimes he is booked a year or more in advance. How I was lucky enough to connect with him is a story in itself. I wrote about it in the first book in the chapter titled *Divine Intervention*. I am honored and grateful that he saw something special in me that I did not.

Working with him I have become much more proficient at performing readings for people. Each reading seems to come through more quickly, easily, and naturally. But it all comes at a personal price. When a reading is over, I sometimes carry the emotions of the deceased for hours until they finally fade away. Furthermore, it seems the majority of my readings concern a tragic story of death, murder, trauma, beatings, violence, overdoses, accidents, or something else of a terrible nature. I often confine myself to a private room immediately following a reading, where I can meditate and be alone for a while. This inner struggle makes me shy away from readings. I do like knowing that I am helping the living and serving the dead, and I am told it is one of my tasks in this lifetime, but it takes a toll on my personal life and wellbeing. That toll may end up becoming too great for me to continue this practice. For now, I am limiting my readings to the ones I must do in class with my mentor for assessment purposes. I rarely, if ever, initiate a connection, or "link" as we call it, outside of class.

As we approached the twentieth anniversary of the 9/11 attacks here in America, I had a session with Medium Joe. He said something that day to our class I will never forget. He revealed to us that he had had a vision of those attacks some twenty years before their occurrence. He has carried the burden of that vision on his shoulders, and I could see as he recited this story that it hasn't been easy for him. This was many years before he started working with law enforcement. Do you think if he had tried to alert someone, they would have listened to him? Knowing him, he probably did try to tell someone in a position to do something about it. Do you suppose anyone back then would have taken him seriously? Of course not. This is the fucking burden we share. This is part of the reason I've said time and again, I don't know whether this ability is a blessing or a curse.

In that same session, Medium Joe told us something that gave me much-needed clarity in regard to my inner conflict: "You get what you know." Those five words shifted something. It may seem like a simple statement, but I assure you, it set in motion a monumental ripple effect in me.

"You get what you know."

When Medium Joe said that, I realized he was referring to how the messages we get from the deceased relate directly to our own experiences.

For the past year I have honestly considered never speaking again with the dead. I have become rather proficient at tuning them out when I need to. Sometimes their persistence can be disruptive, but I possess the power now to control it.

On the other hand, when I do a reading, why is it that I rarely, if ever, get the "I love you, honey!" folks from the other side? Why must I get the guy who was murdered by his business partner, or the woman put to death by her husband, or the young person who took his own life? Reading after reading, these are the themes I encounter. After a while it gets depressing, difficult, and disruptive.

It is almost as if there were someone up there directing traffic, sending all these energy beings and their issues my way. "Okay, since you are one seriously fucked-up dead guy, we will team you up with an equally fucked-up medium."

Imagine "Beetlejuice," the character Michael Keaton played in the movie by the same name.

"Step right up to the medium matchmaker! We can find a living medium for any dead person, regardless of your situation. 'Mediums are us!' Come one, come all! Big problems? Little problems? We solve them all! Get your mediums here!"

"So, you were murdered, you say? No problem. Go see Ray."

"What happened? You were beaten into a deadly coma? Go see Ray."

"You committed suicide? All right, go see Ray."

"Drug overdose? Oh, that's his specialty. Go see Ray."

"You really miss your wife and today is your anniversary? Oh, that's lovely. Let's see here. Hmm. Go see Medium Suzie."

It just doesn't make any sense that I continually get the same grim shit, while others are getting lovey-dovey shit! I want some lovey-dovey shit too! C'mon, man!

On a more serious note . . .

We are taught that when we do a reading, we must choose to serve the dead first and foremost. In order to gain the trust of those in the afterlife, we must take this oath seriously. We serve the sitter, the person we are doing the reading for, secondarily. This may sound strange since, if there is money involved, it will probably be the sitter who is paying for the service. But if one becomes the type of medium who serves the client first, one won't be a very good medium for long. Truth and transparency is of the utmost importance. We can never sugarcoat the truth or manipulate the message for the recipient, even if they are paying us a million dollars an hour. All a medium has is the truth and their integrity. Fuck with that and you are finished as a medium.

Let's go back to the statement, "You get what you know." The visions you get from the dead will be in line with what you, as a medium, are most familiar. In other words, your own experiences and knowledge. The dead can use a medium's memories as a tool to express the things they want to get across to someone in the living realm of existence. This makes the transmission of information between the two realms smoother. Therefore, if you have sessions with more than one medium, you may think that one of them is considerably better than the other; but it may be that one, according to their own life experience, is better able to interpret the data the dead wanted you to receive. They can process and understand the message better as a result of their firsthand knowledge of similar experiences.

All this time I struggled with the fact that I got messages that were unpleasant to receive and relay. I thought that was all I would ever get. Why was I mostly witnessing tragedies? Then I realized that I continued to receive similar types of messages because *it's what I know*. It is that with which I am most familiar. It is the part of the message I understand the easiest. The dead know what I have experienced in my lifetime, and they know that I can relate to them. They know I can interpret those sort of messages for them. They know I can share that information best with their loved ones and express it with the proper emotions attached.

It's what I know. Or should I say, it's what I knew?

This forced me to take a hard look at myself and my life. If I wanted messages of love, I had to love and be loved. I had to become more experienced with love. It made me aware that up until recently my life was unbalanced, with many more tragedies and traumas and much less love. I would need to create and experience more love in my life and more loving experiences if the dead were going to trust me to relay information with those feelings attached to their loved ones. Medium Joe has often said to me, "You must come from a place of love to do this work." I think I understand that now. This was the missing piece to my next level of growth and doing this work. I needed more love.

I remember reading something that Jessica wrote about me once. I found it one day, penned on a green sticky note on top of her desk. It said something like, "I will show him so much love that I will heal him with love, and I'm going *to show* him how to love himself."

Each day I will do my best to share the love that Jessica has given me and continues to *show* me.

I love Jessica. I love my kids and her kids, and they all love me. I am loved now more than ever. I love more now than ever. I love my life and I want to share my love with the people in it. I love my work, which is *to share* all that I have learned with the world, and I actually feel that it sort of loves me back.

This revelation makes me look at mediumship again in a positive light. As I inherit more love, I'll continue *to share* more love and experience more love. With real love inside me and coming through me, I will be able *to share* with a grieving person the feeling of love they deserve to receive from their loved ones. I will better myself as a man and a medium, enabling myself to receive, decode, and express loving messages.

I will experience all that love has to offer. I will be loved. I am loved. I will love.

Journal Entry, February 7, 2021—"Reading for the Reverend"

This was an "in-class exercise" with my mentor and a small group of students on video chat. It was one of my regular classes with Medium Joe. We had something like twelve students, in addition to two administrators and our mentor, on the video chat.

We were to be paired up so that we could read for one another. Basically, we would connect to someone deceased who was a loved one of the other student. The curveball that Medium Joe threw at us was that he wanted the sitter (the person who was receiving the reading) to choose who they wanted to connect with, as opposed to allowing the medium to speak to whomever they chose or whoever came through. This was a much more difficult task for the medium because we had to find and communicate with that person, and *only* that person. It is never done this way in a typical reading, and for good reason. Chasing down a dead person can create a lot of psychological anguish for the medium. The difference here was that we were reading for another medium who had the ability to bring their person forth before the reading began. In a normal reading, the medium only delivers information from whoever chooses to come forth to communicate to the sitter. That wasn't good enough for today's class. The sitter was to tell us whom they brought forth, and then we would take over from there. Medium Joe prefaced the sessions by telling us that what we were attempting would be much more difficult to do, and reminding us not to get down on ourselves if we couldn't manage it.

I was paired with a reverend we will call Janet. Janet told me she had a woman (that was all she said) and a woman appeared almost instantly in my movie screen in the two o'clock position. It actually felt as though she had been there for a while, but only made her appearance known when Reverend Janet said, "I have a woman." As the woman's image got larger and came into focus, the vibrations increased in my body. The woman took my hand and began to show me around her house, and to show me all the people who lived in it. It was a small house with many people, all family members. I told Janet I could see that her grandmother was in charge of that house. I confirmed with Janet this was her grandmother and continued. I watched the grandmother as she was telling all her kids and the grandkids what to do.

"She was upset with you in particular, Janet," I said, "about school. She is telling you now that it is extremely important for you to attend school and get good grades for your future."

Janet said that there were three generations living in that house, and then eventually a fourth generation when Janet had a child during her high school years. Janet had not wanted to return to school after she gave birth. This was the basis for the conflict I was seeing.

Janet went on to explain that her grandmother was very persistent when it came to Janet returning to school, and that they would argue over this daily. I saw the grandmother saying, "You must attend and do well in school," over and over.

I asked her grandmother to give me something evidential. Medium Joe taught us to always ask for something that only the deceased and the sitter would know. She brought me inside the house and to one of the windows. We were waiting for someone. Looking outside, I saw a lot of land with trees and grass for as far as my eyes could see. I asked the grandmother what we were looking for. She showed me a car. I told Janet, "We are waiting for a car."

Janet said, "She would wait for my mom to come home in that car almost every night before she would go to bed. Grandmother would sit by the window and wait for hours. When the car eventually pulled in, she would go to her bedroom quickly to keep the fact that she was waiting up a secret from my mom."

Janet also said that it was a small house on three acres of land. Most of the family and siblings lived there: quite a few people in a small house on a large lot. Looking out that window for her daughter (Janet's mom) was a very private secret kept between the grandmother and Janet. She didn't want Janet's mom to know, but Janet always knew her grandmother did this.

Janet obviously had a special bond with her grandmother, and I was glad I could reunite them for a short while. Afterward, I felt euphoric. Throughout the session I had been vibrating with positive sensations. Medium Joe had me tell the class about the experience. I often have difficulty remembering the details of what happens in those moments. Even a short while after, when it begins to come back to me, I must write it down or record it somehow quickly so as not to forget it altogether. I suppose this difficulty may be because during the readings I am "not all there," not consciously. Later it will come back, bit by bit, if I concentrate and continuously replay the experience over and again in my mind. It's a process I am still learning.

As we were running out of time, Janet said, "Ray, you are going to be great at this. I really mean that." I thanked her and her grandmother. I was happy with the experience. It was instructive, and it made my sitter, Janet, feel good to know that her grandmother was still "looking out that window."

Journal Entry, September 12, 2020—"Reunited"

I was in one of my all-day mentoring sessions with Medium Joe. The entire day's teaching was about how to become a better reader for one's clients. I don't have clients that I read for, and I may never have them. I don't think that is my path, but I still need to learn everything I can about this ability.

The day progressed and I learned a lot. Even with as much as I have accomplished, I continue to hold onto a bit of self-doubt regarding my abilities. I realize that I shouldn't, but I do. This occasion would be the first time my mentor was able to watch me do a reading. Medium Joe wanted to test me, and he presented me with a challenge. I was to do an impromptu reading for a complete stranger (who was not a medium) who gave me nothing more than their first name.

I was nervous, to say the least, but I knew I had to get over it, so I just moved on. We were online, as all classes had to be during the pandemic. I was to meet this woman via the Internet and perform a reading for her. I was only told her first name: let's call her "Pam." I could see and hear Pam, but I knew absolutely nothing about her. I had no idea who, if anyone, was even deceased in her family. I was told to just read whatever I got.

I took a deep breath and exhaled, closed my eyes, and began to meditate. I always keep my eyes shut so I am uninfluenced by facial expressions and so that I don't stereotype anyone in any way. Most importantly, this way I can only see the deceased, and that is who I am there for, not the sitter. It also helps me maintain concentration. And so, I went into my altered state and told her what I saw.

"I see a well-dressed man in a suit."

She said nothing, so I went on. "He seems to be holding gifts of some kind."

I paused again, trying to see more.

"It looks like the gifts are flowers and candy, but I don't think that is literal. I think he is telling me he enjoyed buying you things—many things in fact. I'm going to say that my interpretation of this is that he was a man who enjoyed buying you many things out of love and I think he was very much the romantic type."

She remained silent. My eyes were still closed, so I thought to myself, *Maybe this guy isn't here for her.*

"He is showing me a wedding ring. Did you . . ." I hesitated, ". . . lose your husband?" I was worried that I might be wrong, but I almost didn't want to be right. I didn't know what to expect.

She began to sob, and I said, "I'm so sorry. I am so very sorry."

After a moment I continued. "He was the romantic type, wasn't he? Very much so, I think. Birthdays, anniversaries, for practically any reason, he would buy you things?" I asked.

"Yes, he really was a romantic who was always showering me with gifts," she said, as she wept uncontrollably.

I felt terrible. I'm not sure why, but I did. I was apprehensive about continuing, now that I knew who this was. I did go on, though.

"I have to tell you what I am feeling. My entire body is vibrating from head to toe. There is an amazing feeling of love. This man really loves you! I'm not just saying that because he is your husband, and that should be obvious. There is an immensely overpowering feeling of love, which is rare.

I don't get this often. Certainly not like this. What I am saying is that this man's love for you is completely unparalleled in my experience. It is such a, well . . . I just wish I could pass this feeling on to you."

I felt like crying.

Her weeping continued. With my eyes closed, I could hear her blow her nose. It was true. This man loved her more than the average man loves his significant other.

"He is standing in a kitchen and making a point of showing me this. At first when I saw him it was completely dark around him but then he seemed to turn on the lights and now he is in a kitchen. I feel like I am supposed to mention that."

With that, her tears changed to laughter. She said, "Oh boy, we had a lot of fun in the kitchen. Let's just say that that was our special place in the house."

I laughed as well. "I can see his face more clearly now. He is very handsome. A good-looking guy."

She laughed again and said. "Yes. Yes, he was."

"So, I see a well-dressed, well-groomed man, but he seems kind of young." With that I was about to explain that sometimes the dead will alter their appearance and show me themselves at another period in their lives, such as when they were younger or older, but before I could say any of that, she said, "Yes, I married a man much younger than I."

"Oh, I understand!

"I see a name—it's Ben. I'm not sure why he is giving me this name because I don't feel that it is his name. Do you know any Bens?"

She said, "No, I don't know of any Bens."

I told her to just hold onto the name as maybe it would mean something later. And with that, a light bulb went off in my head. I said, "Wait! Ben is not a person, it's a thing. It's Ben and Jerry's ice cream!"

She laughed and said, "Oh my God, he loved his ice cream and had to have it all the time. He took his ice cream very seriously."

"I know! I see the packaging." We both laughed really hard.

I thought to myself, *This is getting a lot better. She is happy again.*

I then asked this man to give me something that only his wife would recognize, as evidence this was really him.

He showed me a picture of a large, older, dark blue or possibly black four-door car. I said to her, "I asked him for something that would be evidential; something only you would know about; and he showed me this car." I explained what it looked like.

She said, "Oh my God, you mean Big Blue? That was one of his cars when we first met. He and his friend nicknamed that car Big Blue and it was a running joke throughout our marriage because it was a big old jalopy, but he loved it so much."

I thanked the man and Pam, and we ended there as he had begun to slowly fade out. I couldn't keep him there any longer.

She thanked me many times over, and all I could think of was how I had been able to reunite these two folks for a good fifteen minutes. I was so grateful for being able to make someone happy, if just for a short while.

I had reached a turning point in my life. I was receiving more love in my readings. It was shortly after this reading I asked Jessica for her hand in marriage. She said yes!

CHAPTER 6

Manmade Miracles

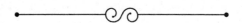

One fall Saturday afternoon I was cutting open some packages that had been delivered—they contained some basic household items, along with some health foods I usually purchased for myself. I had ordered these the day before. As I continued to open the boxes, pulling out each item to make sure I had received all of my order, my son walked into the room. We then had a conversation. I don't recall what it was about specifically, but I remember saying something to the effect of, "That is amazing. What a miracle." Just then the topic of conversation changed. He asked me what I thought about miracles, specifically whether I thought ordinary human beings could create miracles. I said, "First things first, my son. What is a miracle to you?"

"It's something that happens that's totally unexplainable and beyond the comprehension of mankind."

I agreed with that definition. As I went on taking items out of the box I had just opened, I took out one of the bottles and said to him, "Do you see this bottle of vitamin C?"

"Yes."

I said, "Five-hundred years ago, do you think that mankind would have ever dreamed that you could extract or synthetically replicate one thousand milligrams of vitamin C and place it in this tiny pill for easy human consumption?"

"No."

"But in fact, we can do this easily now, can't we?"

"Yes," he replied, with a smirk.

I went on, "I ordered these vitamins without ever leaving my house and had them delivered here. Do you think that as recently as three hundred years ago, mankind could have comprehended that happening?"

"No."

"I ordered these vitamins yesterday and they were shipped from California to New York, arriving today, in about twenty-four hours. Do you think even fifty years ago mankind could have conceived of such a possibility being a reality?"

"I guess not," he replied.

"So, by our definition, are these all miracles?"

"Yes," he said with a big smile. "They are."

"That's right. And with that in mind, let's go back to your original question. 'Can ordinary people create miracles?'"

"Yes! Absolutely," he said.

The true miracle is the inspiration we receive from above to turn thoughts like these into realizations. They aren't magic tricks. They are the inspirations and messages that come in the forms of mental pictures, signs and synchronicities, and they are happening around us each day.

At that moment his mobile phone made a vibration and a beeping sound, and I asked him, "What was that?" He started laughing. "What's so funny?" I asked.

"A friend of mine just texted me a picture. He is traveling on the other side of the world and wanted me to see where he was today. I guess, just twenty years ago, no one would have thought they could send pictures of themselves from halfway around the world in less than a second, using a handheld device that fits in someone's pocket," he said. "Just another manmade miracle I suppose."

We both laughed.

"Exactly," I said. "You got this. Now go make miracles happen for yourself."

Truth be told, as early as 1901 Nikola Tesla predicted that we would have mobile phones, but my son was on point, and I didn't want to ruin it for him. Let us not forget, however, Nikola Tesla: a *clairvoyant* inventor.

Anyone can create miracles. Everyone is a co-creator of this universe, and as such, we can all create and turn ideas into realities. Isn't that amazing? Just look around yourself. There are so many things we take for granted each day that are "manmade miracles."

We can create all that we want and all that we need. To do this, first and foremost you must learn how to manifest. I will explain how to do this. I will show you how to get all the things you really want and need. However, what you seek should be for your highest and best self, as well as for that of others. Yes, there is a catch! There are "rules." Anyone who uses this knowledge to punish or hurt others will inevitably have it paid back to them through negative karma. Don't get the idea that you should use this power to harm people. We are all one being. We are all connected through the collective consciousness of the universe. Therefore, any harm you bring to another, you will inevitably draw to yourself. There is no way around this. The same ability that allows you the gift of being able to manifest and make miracles can hurt you if you use this process incorrectly or for unscrupulous reasons. Don't mess with karma. Take it from one who knows firsthand.

Journal Entry, May 2, 2020—"Sell the Dolphin"

I was on a video call with Medium Joe, who was walking me through contacting the dead. He asked me to choose a deceased loved one with whom to connect. I chose Jessica's dad because he was one of the first I had spoken with on the other side and I knew I could make an easy connection with him. Medium Joe told me to go deeper into my altered state of mind and tell the person to come through. He had been teaching me to be firm with the dead: to just say, "*Do* this or that." A request using the word "please" leaves room for potential doubt that what I request will happen or be. It gives them a way out, and me as well. After I sent a mental query for Jessica's dad to visit, he showed up in my mind, as if on a movie screen. This is the normal beginning for me to see someone on the other side. I then entered the movie screen myself, and he and I were sitting on a park bench on a picture-perfect day, overlooking the beach and the ocean. The waves made a relaxing sound as they met with the shore. The sun was in our eyes a bit, so both of us had to squint when looking at the water below. The entire scene, as I saw it, was very vivid. (As my skills advance, I find that I am seeing things with more clarity, color, and detail.)

And so, the two of us sat on the bench, enjoying the day. I looked at him and he looked back at me. Turning his head toward me, he smirked and gave a little chuckle, and looked back out at the beach. I did the same and waited patiently. *He will say something to me. He always does.* Normally he is quite persistent with his suggestions. His eyes began to close, and I thought to myself, *Is he going to nap right now?* "John!" I exclaimed. "What's next? What do we do next?" He looked at me with the same half-smile on his face, as if to say, "Oh, you need me now!" Then he said, "You have to sell the . . ."

"Sell what?" I was on the edge of my seat, but he fell silent. Then he repeated himself. (Repetition is normal in these interactions. It's a means of helping me decode things. Sometimes I will see a scene repeat itself several times until I get the whole message. It is literally like rewinding a movie to a certain point and replaying it back to hear what the character in the movie was saying.)

Again he said, "You have to sell the . . ." With that I saw a picture of a dolphin. I immediately began to pepper him with questions, anxious to get the whole story before he went away: "I have to sell a *dolphin*? *Who* has to sell a dolphin? *Where* is the dolphin? What does *the dolphin* mean? I don't have any dolphins to sell, nor do I know of any dolphin dealers. Come on, man, help me out here. Are you kidding?"

He just went back to looking out at the ocean. I was still hoping for some clarification on Flipper and where I was supposed to find him. Obviously, his meaning was metaphorical, but he never clarified. He wasn't messing with me—he was trying to get his point across, but in these situations, words can be difficult, whereas pictures are easier. When I couldn't decipher the rest of his sentence, he provided me with a picture. Evidently, John thought that the image of a dolphin would mean something to me. Now I had to figure out what exactly that was. Remember, you get what you know. Only this one I didn't know, or couldn't remember.

At that point Medium Joe brought me out of the trance and the "call" was over, I immediately went to tell Jessica what her dad had said. Her immediate impulse was to look up the symbolic meaning of dolphins, but I explained to her that what was called for here was *my* interpretation of that image. For something like this, there can be no official book of interpretations. The dead know what a picture will mean to you and that is why they choose it. What it means to someone on the Internet may not match my definition. That being said however, if I am at a total loss, sometimes another person's interpretation will spark or lead to one of my own.

Update: May 10, 2020 (7 months, 21 days before publishing my first book)

A little over a week went by with no enlightenment. Jessica came to me rather frustrated with her phone in hand. She had been searching for the meaning of a dolphin as it pertains to the afterlife. I had been adamant that I would not take any advice from the Internet, as I knew it would not be the correct approach. However, after some back and forth between us, I agreed to look. The results of her search were, "A dolphin represents crossing over into multiple worlds."

Holy shit! Was *I* the dolphin? Did "selling the dolphin" mean "selling myself"?—or in other words, my story? Did it mean publishing the book? At that time, I had been hesitant to release the first of these books.

Now I know that if you search for the subtle meaning of "dolphin," you will get a number of different answers; but Jessica, after multiple searches, only found this one answer, thus adding emphasis to that particular interpretation.

As if that weren't enough, at the very moment Jessica was explaining this to me, one of her toddlers, who was playing a video game with her sister two rooms away, yelled out, "This could make us rich!" She was talking about something transpiring in their game, but mind you, she said this as soon as Jessica had finished explaining to me her interpretation. At that moment Jessica looked at me and said, "Do you need any more validation?" I stood there for several minutes, dumbfounded at what had just happened.

It seems that every time I entertain self-doubt about publishing, I get a message that puts me back on track.

(John, I promise you that I will "sell the dolphin"; and if, as you proclaimed, it makes our family wealthy or provides us with abundance, I promise that I will do everything in my power with those resources to spread the word and help others, whenever and wherever I can.)

Journal Entry, May 1, 2021—The Spinning Buddha and Jesus

I am putting this entry in today, but this sort of thing has been occurring for months. I seriously debated whether to include it in this book. You will understand why soon enough. This is one of those things that can be difficult to believe. I had to get up the courage to admit this was real before I could even share it with Jessica. That's how inconceivable it is.

Before I tell you this story, keep the following in mind. As you'll recall, I typically do not refer to the dead as spirits or souls. I try instead to use the term "energy beings." My intention is to respect the churches that do not condone mediumship, and also to keep this study scientific in nature. These books will always focus more on the science of post-death phenomena. Besides, they *are* energy beings. That is what is left when the physical body is gone: the energy of one's consciousness. Okay, let's move on.

Jessica and I are engaged to be married, but we have not yet set a date. However, we are living together. One of the bedrooms in our house is my home office. This is where I write. It is a corner room on one of the upper floors of the house, where I can see up and down the tree-lined street. I can also see much of the exterior of the house, the driveway, and some of the backyard. The sunlight in that room is magnificent. Perched up high with many windows to look through, it sets the tone for me to write. I set up the interior of the room with simplicity. For me, less is more. I do not like clutter because it reminds me of work yet to be done, and to write well I need to temporarily ignore other types of unfinished business.

I set up my desk with a gaming computer because of its power and speed. I have double monitors to spread out the pages of my book electronically on the two very large screens. I have a professional microphone and webcam for my work and some extra space on my desk with copies of my first book I need to sign—a task I keep putting off for some reason. (When did I become someone who autographs anything? I digress.)

Anyway, back to my desk. I have the original picture that was drawn by Medium Joe of Jessica's dad, which I wrote about in my first book. I also have a picture of Jessica and her dad smiling together. I have an autographed baseball by former Yankee superstar Joe DiMaggio (BTW - he has much nicer handwriting than I do). I have many of Jessica's original paintings, which I adore—not just because they were made by the woman I love, but because they are genuinely awe-inspiring. Jessica never painted professionally a day in her life, until one day she ordered painting supplies and was completely inspired to paint on canvas. She now has a collection of about twenty-five pieces that we are beginning to catalog.

Again, back to my desk. I have a statue of Jesus meditating. It was one of the most difficult statues to locate and purchase. It is easy to find a statue of him standing, or on the cross, but try to find him meditating and you would think it was taboo or something. Jesus meditated as much as the Buddha did, but you would not know that if your only impression of his teachings comes from the mainstream denominations of Christianity.

Anyway, returning to my desk again. I also have a statue of the Buddha—meditating, of course. Many Buddha statues depict him as overweight, but my statue is truer to his life. I understand that in many eastern civilizations being a little overweight suggests that you live in abundance, but that is far from an accurate portrayal or resemblance of the Buddha. The true story of Buddha is that he walked away from the riches of his royal father and mother to go out into the world and experience suffering firsthand. He went without food for as long as possible, and would only eat once a day that which was offered him by strangers. He became quite thin as a result of this practice. There is a story in fact, that the Buddha lost his life by accepting food that he knew was spoiled. He ate it because, it was, that which was given to him, and he did not want to offend the person who gifted him the food. The Buddha was older and frail at this time in his life, and his physical form simply couldn't get passed the illness that spoiled food created.

Perhaps, let us return to my desk, ... again. The Buddha and Jesus statues are placed to my right, facing me. They are set back near the wall. The desk is large and L-shaped, and the part the two statues are on remains untouched by anyone or anything. The point is that anyone would have a difficult time reaching out to handle them even if they wanted to, including myself. Yet you can see them easily, as nothing obstructs their view. They are not in contact with anything on the desk either, except the Buddha sits on top of a rectangular wooden desk organizer, which has a built-in analog clock. The clock no longer ticks or tocks, but it is a very nice piece. He sits there because his statue is a bit smaller than the one of Jesus. I purposefully placed them in this position so that they would remain undisturbed and untouched. I put some thought into it when placing them because we have young kids in our home, and I did not want the statues to be used as toys. They are both sacred to me. (As are the kids, of course.)

The Buddha sits with his left knee at three o'clock and his right knee at nine o'clock. Jesus sits on nothing but the desk itself. His piece is much heavier. One morning as I entered the door of my home office with my coffee in hand, I greeted Jesus and the Buddha as I normally do. But the Buddha seemed different that day. I could not figure out why; something just felt different. Nevertheless, I went on with my day. I did my early morning work from home and then drove to my office. That day I coached several clients. Two of them had tremendous breakthroughs. I was very happy for them both. Upon returning to my home office, I walked in and noticed something was even more "off" with the Buddha statue than it had been earlier in the morning, but now it was easier to see what it was. He had turned ever so slightly to his right. His right knee had moved a little past nine o'clock.

I stared at him for a while to see what may have made him move. The kids were still at school, and my office door had been closed all day. I asked Jessica if anyone was in the house, and she said no. She wasn't even home all day.

Two days went by, and I had another great day coaching: different clients, different breakthroughs. I came home once again, doing my usual routine, to find that the Buddha had moved slightly more to his right. His right knee was now at the ten o'clock position!

"Jessica, who was here today?" I asked.

"Just Lucy, the cleaning lady."

"Oh, thank God. I thought I was going crazy."

Maybe Lucy had gone into my office to clean. She almost always skips my office unless I ask her to do it. This is probably due to the fact that I'm usually working in it when she's here. Just then I went to throw something in the trash can and saw that it was full. My first reaction was I couldn't believe Lucy hadn't emptied the garbage. The second was, "Holy Shit! She didn't empty the garbage. The door was closed, so she probably thought I was in the office and didn't clean it." I was back to crazy-town again.

The next day there was no change, his knee remained positioned on the ten. Jessica and I had been working for months on sealing the deal on a local yoga studio, we were looking to open soon. The following day, we got confirmation that the place was to be ours and we signed the lease. I got home to find the Buddha had moved again. Now his knee was past the ten o'clock mark. I began taking pictures to document this phenomenon and asked Jessica to come into my office. Keep in mind that no one goes in there. It is the one place in the home set aside strictly for my use. Besides, there is nothing for anyone else to do in there anyway.

I told Jessica the Buddha statue was moving, that he was turning to his right, and it seemed he was doing so after I did something good. Jessica didn't believe me. "You're probably doing something that moves him without realizing it." I thought, *Maybe I am crazy.*

The next few days nothing happened—no movement from the Buddha. A week went by without any change in position. Then, on about the twelfth or thirteenth day, I came home to find the Buddha's knee over the eleven o'clock mark. "Jessica, come here quick and look!" She ran to the office and saw the Buddha. "Holy shit!" she exclaimed. When Jessica curses it's a big deal, so now I knew I wasn't crazy. She frantically looked under the desk as I had done many days earlier. We checked under the room to see if there were any potential vibrations emanating up from below, but the office is directly above the garage, and we use that space exclusively for storage. I don't think we have ever used for its purpose of parking our cars in it.

She and I were dumbfounded. A few days later I got my first public speaking engagement—and the Buddha had now turned completely sideways. It seemed clear that my doing good things for myself and others, resulted in the spinning of the Buddha. I have many pictures tracking his movements. I realize these occurrences may be difficult for anyone to accept: at first they were for me too.

One day I came home with a feeling of anticipation as I felt I had done a really good job helping my clients. Since I had reached the point where I was measuring my successes now based on the Buddha's movements, I couldn't wait to see how much he had shifted that particular day. I got home, ran into my office, and with excitement looked to the Buddha for his feedback, but he was back in his old position looking directly at me, as he had been when I first placed him there. My heart sank into my stomach. In the distance I heard the noise of a vacuum cleaner coming from a bedroom across the hall. *Oh no*, I thought. "LUCY!" I yelled and ran to the room with the vacuum. There she was, frightened by my scream.

"Did you clean my office today?"

"Yes. Did I not do it well?"

I hadn't been able to get this woman to clean my office for months, and *today* she decided to clean it? C'mon man! I was really upset but all I said was, "Actually, Lucy, you did a wonderful job in there and I just wanted to tell you how much we appreciate you."

The following morning I walked into my office, coffee in hand, and looked over to pay my respects to the Buddha and Jesus. The Buddha hadn't moved at all, but the statue of Jesus in meditation had shifted slightly to his left. We were back in business! Oh yeah!

Since then, both statues continue to move. They change direction: sometimes turning right to left, and sometimes left to right. The Buddha has even moved sideways on more than one occasion. I reset them periodically so that it is easier for me to scan them for guidance. It means a great deal to me when they move, as crazy as that would seem.

So, would you like to know how this could happen, from a scientific perspective? If so, read on. If not, and you are happy with just knowing that your work here on earth can be acknowledged from above, then you can go right ahead and skip to the next chapter.

The way this happens is pretty simple. Here is how I learned this.

I was in class with Medium Joe one evening when someone in our class, on the video chat asked Joe, "Can spirits move things?" His answer was, "Of course they can. They are energy, and when energy enters a room and leaves a room, that energy can be passed to any object in the room and move it slightly." He explained, "It wouldn't be a big movement, but a small one is absolutely possible."

I suppose, when you think about it that way, it makes sense. Just as when air enters the room in the form of wind, the energy from the wind can be transferred to something in the room and move it. Similarly, an energy being can transfer energy to an object and move it slightly.

Update—September 2021

Jessica purchased another statue of the Buddha as a gift to me. It is beautiful. It's much heavier than the first one I told you about. When placing this one, I put him far from the others, just to see what would happen and to make sure my self-doubts were unfounded. I even made it more difficult for this one to move by nestling him up against a solid surface.

Well, it was Jessica who first noticed it when the new Buddha moved. The doubt is "out."

CHAPTER 7

COMBINING CONSCIOUSNESS

Jessica and I continue to evolve as a couple, but also as individuals with our own respective abilities. Jessica has always been an empath and intuitive in her own right, and now as I grow and enhance my own abilities and competencies, she grows with me. The more time we spend together, the more we blend our conscious minds. This blending allows her to make use of my connection as a type of antenna to the universe. I also receive the enhanced benefit of using her increasingly exceptional connection. As they say, two heads are better than one—or in this case, two conscious minds blending and working together.

By working with my mentors I continue to grow and expand my capabilities. The interactions I have with them are nothing short of spectacular. They are so blessed with uncanny abilities. They have decades of experience over me, and a more complete understanding of each type of phenomenon. Through continued contact with them and being allowed into their world, I am able to blend with their competencies and consciousness, which, even if for only one hour at a time, advances my techniques and takes me to higher levels after each session I've spent with them.

Combining consciousness and energies with others is something we all do without realizing it is taking place. I am not just referring to people who are intuitive, psychic, clairvoyant, or have medium-like capabilities. This sort of thing happens to everyone. Therefore, one of my rules to becoming limitless (see *The Atheist and The Afterlife*, chapter 35) is to remember that you are the sum of your peers. Surround yourself therefore with family, friends, and colleagues who have accomplished great things, or those you believe will accomplish great things in the future—people you admire for their drive and determination, or for their happiness, love, and positive outlook. This will inevitably merge your consciousness with theirs and dwell in a positive state of mind. Their energy will combine with yours, and yours with theirs. This osmotic sharing happens naturally.

I'm sure you have friends who are successful, happy, loving, positive-thinking go-getters whom you admire very much. And then there are those folks you may love but who lack motivation or are negative about most matters, bringing their drama with them and slinging it around— the ones who tend to say, "That will never work." And of course, let us not forget the ones who want to tell all the things that are going wrong in their lives.

It is so important to not subject your consciousness to negative people and their conscious states too often. The truth of the matter is, as you reach higher levels of consciousness, you may not want to see them as much anymore. I don't mean to be hurtful, but you will feel differently about having them around. You'll grow to be more in tune with the energy of others and their positive frequencies. The negative ones may also hold you back from your own happiness. It's not that they consciously intend to do this, but they likely will do so inadvertently. Since this process happens naturally, you cannot stop or prevent it.

Here is what you can do. Seek to limit your exposure to them. I cannot begin to tell you how important this is to your own growth, success, and happiness. Keep in contact and close proximity with those you admire, respect, love, and wish to be more like. Combine your consciousness with theirs as often as possible. Allow their energy and thoughts to blend with yours on a higher plane. This will automatically happen through exposure and interaction, or sometimes even just by thinking about that person. You don't have to do anything except be mindful and present. You certainly need no additional psychic or intuitive training to do this.

I have had folks challenge me on this philosophy and rebut me with, "I don't let other people affect me, only I affect me." I'm sorry to say that this statement is at best only partially true and that is the latter half. You see, the entire universe is made up of one universal collective consciousness and we are all part of it. Your higher self or your awareness, connects your consciousness to this entity, and it is within that consciousness that you truly realize your own individuality. At the higher levels, we all blend together as universal energy beings, but we also blend on smaller fronts as well. We are each greatly affected by those we live with and see daily, especially as children growing up in our families.

Unfortunately, this can be a terrible thing for some. On the other hand, it may be, for others, a huge advantage. That being said, as you grow older you will of course gain more freedom to decide who will help shape your future. You will get to pick your own people to interact with. This is one of the ways in which you can and will affect your own future. You can gain a significant competitive edge of which many are unaware. Remove the baggage, the drama, the negative beliefs, and the people who bring theirs into your life. It's fine and natural to still love them and be kind to them but put some distance between you and them. Limit conversations, whether in person, on the phone, or electronically, and gravitate toward those who will help lift you with their energy, not inadvertently hinder you from moving forward on your journey.

Learn to see people for what they are, not who you want them to be.

If you want to be the best at something, find a way to acquaint yourself and communicate with some of those people who share a similar mindset. Otherwise, you will have a much smaller chance of becoming one. You are looking for folks who match energetically to you. You will feel it and know it when you have. The same can be said for happiness, love, or any other worthwhile goal. If you want to live a more spiritual life, spend your time with more spiritual people. Get rid of those friends who want to suck the life out of you because they don't like their own. Remember this very important statement:

Environment trumps will over time, every time.

I recently was in a worldwide online class with about thirty or so other students from almost every continent. I was paired up to work with this guy from Rwanda. He asked me if I had ever heard of his country. I said, "Of course." He was impressed. He sent me the address of the university he attends so I could look it up. He was quite proud to be studying structural engineering at this particular Rwandan college. The class he and I were taking was about how to overcome self-imposed limitations. I asked him what he was planning to do after graduation. He didn't really have an answer. The reason, he went on to explain, was that although he will be a highly qualified engineer, his specialty involved the construction of very large, high-rise buildings. He went on to explain that such jobs were limited where he lived. Rwanda is not especially known for its large buildings—or any major buildings for that matter.

I could tell by speaking with him that he was quite intelligent. I could also tell that he was in no rush to graduate, for then he would have to apply his degree and knowledge to making a living. I asked him if he planned to come to the United States. He laughed and said, "I would love to, but I can't." I waited for a reason, but one didn't come. I told him that, in the States, we are likely to need many more graduates with his skill set, as the real estate market here was growing rapidly, especially the need for high rise properties.

"No one in my family has every left Rwanda."

"Okay," I said, "what is preventing you from being the first?"

"I don't know."

He really didn't. I asked him different variations of the same question. His only answer to me was, "No one else has done it." Since within his environment it was a rather large accomplishment to complete college and get a degree, he had chosen simply doing that as his goal: to be the best in his world, or his environment. You see, no one he knew personally had left the country to pursue a dream. Some people he knew, at the very top of their respected careers, had accomplished the acquisition of a degree. Therefore, his self-limiting belief had been derived from his environmental influences. He was willing to accomplish the same goal he had seen others do, at their highest level, but he did not consider himself good enough to *surpass* them. However, I am happy to say that, after our conversation, when we returned to the main room with the other students to discuss progress, he changed his goal. His new goal was to never allow his environment (or the people within it) to dictate what he could or could not accomplish in his life.

Your mind is constantly being hit with all sorts of information, from various sources, that bypass traditional senses. Your objective then is to slow down; be present; identify the experience, the source, and the message within it. Then decipher what to do with that message. This happens to everyone, just not in the forefront of the mind; and most people don't recognize it consciously. But it is still absorbed and stored in the subconscious. *Your subconscious mind can be your best friend or your worst enemy.* (More on that a little later.)

Let's look at how else we can combine or blend our consciousness for our own good and that of others. There is so much energy out there in the universe to tap into. Remember that information is energy. Speech, words, sounds, and thoughts are all forms of energy.

Tapping into the universal collective consciousness of all things is like having all the knowledge of the Internet, and much more, accessible by your mind. How do you perform a search in the collective consciousness? You meditate and ask. How did people, thousands of years ago, obtain answers to their greatest mysteries, before the invention of the Internet? They unlocked their minds through meditation.

This is a far more powerful tool because you have access to virtually everything and everyone in this way. Do you think, if you could ask the god Osiris, you could get the answer to how the great pyramids of Giza were created? Or, maybe you would prefer to ask the Irishman where Jimmy Hoffa is. But on a more serious note, whatever you need to know, manifest, or change is out there (or in there) waiting for you. It is not always easy. Contacting Osiris might prove as tricky as getting the cable guy to come out and fix your television between 2 and 4 p.m. next Friday—but it would be worth the wait, don't you think?

Learn to meditate. It will change your life.

Journal Entry, July 16, 2020—"Random Madness"

After a long day, Jessica and I decided to meditate together in bed. I did some breathing exercises with her, and we entered an alternate state of consciousness rather quickly. I decided to open the doors to the universe and invite anyone in who wished to speak with me. (This is something I rarely do.) The first thing I saw was a small girl, just under ten years old, with short blonde hair—a beautiful child too young to be on the other side. She wasn't sad or unhappy. She approached me with open arms as if wanting to hug me, so I touched her hand. It was one of the first times I had ever touched anyone in another realm. It felt so strange and it blew my mind. I tried to speak to her, mind to mind (telepathically), but it didn't seem that she knew how to do this yet. So I just continued to speak to her and made her feel welcome, letting her know she could talk to me anytime she was ready. She smiled and stayed around for a while. Then I moved on.

The next thing I saw looked like a putting green on a golf course. There was a man standing with his back is to me, playing golf. He had white hair and was wearing a bright blue shirt. For a fraction of a second I also saw Jessica's deceased father, who often brings other deceased friends to meet me when they need something or want to send a message to someone in my realm. I tried to open communications with the white-haired man, but he seemed to be having a little difficulty with it. The man began turning his face to me so I could see more of him. He was an older man, and not in particularly good physical shape. He had some type of paper in his hands. I asked him what the paper was, but he did not answer. I tried several times to figure out what he wanted, or at least what was in his hand, which I thought might be an envelope.

Still in trance with this man, I asked Jessica if her dad had played golf. She said yes, he'd had regular golfing buddies that he usually played with, and she named two men. Neither name meant anything to me, but I stayed with the man in my vision for a while to get him to connect so that I could get his message. However, like the young girl, he had trouble speaking to me. I was fully open and communicative, so I'm not sure what, if anything, went wrong. I also saw the letters JR. I mentioned this to Jessica, and then I moved on.

I had one more interaction with someone who I believed was the mother of a man I had recently met. We were business associates and he had told me the story of his mom's passing, asking me to keep an eye out for her. I said I would, and here she was. However, the message she left me with wasn't one I was prepared to deliver to someone I had only met a few times and with whom I was discussing going into business. Her message to him was, "You must stop what you are doing before you hurt the ones close to you," and, "I know you know better, firsthand." She didn't reveal to me what he was doing, for which I was glad—it was none of my business. I did not feel close enough to this person to deliver the message. This is a challenging struggle that comes up frequently. What information do you give to whom, and when do you give it? I hope to obtain these answers soon so I can navigate these waters with more confidence.

I emerged from meditation and shared everything in detail with Jessica. She tried to remember her dad's golfing friends to see if we could accurately figure out who had been playing golf with him in the vision. She had two guys in mind and looked up the first one on Facebook. The man and his son had the same name, the son being Junior, or "Jr." for short. The most recent post from Junior said something along the lines of, "Dear Dad, if you can hear this, we miss you and we love you." The photo on the post was of an older man sitting in a chair on the grass outside in a bright blue shirt, with a full head of white hair and a newspaper in his hand. It was the one-year anniversary of his death, and his son, Jr., was paying respects to his dad. *(Well kid, your dad heard you and acknowledged—he loves you right back.)*

It turned out that other mediums had told Jessica about the ten-year-old girl. Jessica had once suffered a late-term miscarriage of one of her pregnancies with her ex-husband. The child was a female and would have been turning ten years old if she still had been alive. Jessica began to sob uncontrollably as I told her the child was fine and not unhappy at all.

"That is why she came to me—to let you know this. The child is fine and knows how to find me."

Journal Entry, July 23, 2020—"Ray-Ray"

One evening Jessica and I were going to bed, but as we tried to fall asleep, we both felt uneasy about a presence in the room. This was not an uncommon occurrence for us, and we usually just ignored it. But on this night Jessica was receiving more and more indications of additional activities around us. Her abilities had been growing continuously over the past couple of years we had been together. I remember the day we went to my first retreat. After a full day of activities, I said to her, "This year your abilities will grow exponentially." She looked frightened—reasonable I suppose, since she had been a full-time witness to my transformation. This shit can be scary as hell.

That particular night, each time I was about to fall asleep, I woke up with my body shaking hard. Have you ever had a dream where you felt like you were free falling from a high place, and then right before you hit the ground you suddenly awoke with one big shake or jump? That is what this felt like to me, but I wasn't dreaming. After it happened a third time, Jessica asked, "What is happening with you tonight? Are you all right?" I told her I was okay. She then placed her right hand on my chest as we lay next to each other in the bed. We both became sleepier and began to drift off, but just as she was falling asleep, she jumped the same as me, and again a few minutes later.

"What's happening?" I said. "You have this too?"

"Not exactly. I tried to take this feeling away from you to give you some relief, so you could get some sleep. I guess it worked." Apparently, it had transferred over to her—now I was no longer shaking or jumping, but she was.

She and I have been able to heal one another's energy and pass feelings back and forth—that aspect is nothing new for us. We have also experienced annoying energy beings visiting us in the evening at bedtime as well, but this particular being was rather unusual.

I was getting quite angry at this "thing" in our bedroom who was making it impossible for me to sleep and was now affecting Jessica's sleep also. If anything hurt Jessica, I would kill it! Even if it was already dead!

I took hold of Jessica's hand and said, "We need to meditate. I'm going to throw everyone and everything out of the room." I've been able to do this before. I can usually get rid of uninvited guests, if necessary. Some can be stubborn and annoying, but it can be done. Jessica agreed, so we began to delve into a deep meditative state.

Now before I continue this story, you need to know that just a few days prior to this evening's events I was on the phone with Medium Joe, explaining that I was passing through a significant dry spell. I hadn't been receiving much of anything for several days, and I thought something was wrong with me. Even when I tried to initiate a link and connect to the afterlife, I simply couldn't. It was unusual for me to have such a long dry spell, but Medium Joe said that it could happen to anyone, even him.

"So I guess I'm not broken then?"

He laughed and said, "No, Ray. You're not broken."

That made me feel better. Medium Joe told me to meditate for ten minutes a day to center myself, and while doing so I could welcome energy beings to visit me when and where I chose. This was not a new exercise for me—my first mentor had taught me a similar technique. I practiced this for three days, and this night was the end of the third day.

After meditating with Jessica, we lifted ourselves out of it just enough to say good night and drifted off into a relaxing sleep. I was sure that we had cleared the room and would be able to sleep peacefully though the remainder of the night.

I couldn't have been more wrong. What transpired next scared the shit out of me! Jessica and I had been lying in bed asleep for a while when I got up to use the bathroom. As I returned to lay down in bed, I heard someone whisper very loudly, "Ray-Ray." I literally jumped up with my eyes wide open, ready to fight the fucker in our room. I didn't recognize the voice at all. Jessica was still fast asleep, undisturbed. My adrenalin was pumping. I was shaking, in complete fight or flight mode. I began to search the room for whatever or whomever had spoken, prepared for what I thought at this point was an intruder. I grabbed the nearest weapon, which at this time was a Smith and Wesson knife on my night table, and I began to look around the room, the hallway, the bathroom, and so on. No one there. *How can this possibly be?* I thought. I heard it again, loud and clear: "Ray-Ray." I searched the room and other parts of the house a second time, but since Jessica continued to sleep and remained unaffected, I began to calm down, realizing what must have happened.

Very few people have ever called me Ray-Ray during my lifetime and this voice did not sound like anyone I knew. But I realized that someone who must have known me well enough to know that I used to go by Ray-Ray in my younger years was trying to communicate with me. However, I was so pissed off at having been scared like that, I had no interest in trying to figure out who it might be. I had to go back to bed; my schedule called for me to get up at the crack of dawn. I tried to relax, and eventually I fell back asleep—but the night was not over.

In the medium world this type of phenomenon—when someone receives just a word or phrase from an energy being in a different realm—is called a "word drop." It is not something you actually "hear" with your ears—if it were, Jessica would have heard it as well. It is a telepathic transmission of information that enters the mind and is interpreted as sound. Since I now realized what this was and that it could not hurt anyone, I relaxed and eventually fell back asleep.

The next day Jessica told me that she had heard me talking in my sleep—as though I were pleading and almost crying—and it woke her up. She said I had been moaning like I was in physical or emotional pain, begging someone to: "Please stop!" Jessica is one of the very few people who has ever seen me in real pain, —both physical and emotional. I don't allow myself to be broken down or brought to tears by my pain. So it surprised her to hear me speak as though deeply depressed, using words I typically would not have chosen. Was the cause an event from my childhood? Or was someone or something speaking through me? I had no recollection of saying anything in my sleep, or anything else about that part of the night. It was then, however, that I shared with her what I did remember.

I recalled, after falling back asleep, the feeling of a strong presence pushing down on my heart. It felt, as I lay flat on my back, like a large, heavy, object was sitting on my chest. I didn't feel that I could get up or shove it off me. It became hard to breathe. I awoke in a state of fear. That "thing" continued to push on my chest. I opened my eyes wide but there was nothing to see—only feel. I was beginning to panic. This was way outside the norm of anything I had ever experienced.

I held my breath as I pushed with everything I had to get it off me— then let out a huge exhale of air. At the same time, I had pushed my body upward until I was sitting in an upright position, holding onto my calf muscle on my lower right leg. I continued to sit there motionless, catching my breath, trying to make sense of what had just happened. My movement had woken Jessica as well and she asked me if I was okay and did I have a leg cramp? I could see why she asked me that—it appeared that way and would explain why I had been talking in my sleep and holding my leg as though I were in pain. She said that I replied with, "Yes, but I am fine," and then went on to say, "I'm sorry if I scared you." Moments later, strangely, I repeated myself and said again, "I'm sorry if I scared you." Jessica found this choice of words odd because she said I hadn't scared her, so to apologize for that twice was strange. Also, why did I say I had a leg cramp when I didn't? Jessica went on to say that at that point it didn't sound like me speaking at all. It was like another voice was coming through me. She said I then lay back down and returned to sleep. We did not discuss any of this until the morning.

Later, I discussed this with one of my mentors, who told me that this is one way of an energy being showing me how they had died. I had recently had two friends pass away—one of whom used to call me Ray-Ray. They both died while in the hospital of massive heart attacks in their sleep, but they were both originally hospitalized for reasons not related at all to heart problems. To this day I still have many unanswered questions about that night.

Journal Entry, May 14, 2020—"Look Here"

I was in a webinar class with Medium Joe and other students, learning about remote viewing. After he explained what it was and what it wasn't, we practiced controlled environment exercises. These were designed to see how far along our abilities had progressed and how to improve upon them.

Medium Joe had a caller on the phone who said, "Hello everyone, my name is Jane." (Not her real name, of course.) After hearing her voice and first name twice, we were supposed to "remote view" her, to look through her eyes to see what she was seeing, feel what she was feeling, hear what she was hearing, and so on. We had exactly seven minutes to do this.

I placed myself in a very mild altered state of consciousness. I had begun to use a crystal paperweight from my desk to help me focus and enter trance. I guess you could say that this was my version of a crystal ball. Looking into any shiny object will give you the same effect. (Medium Joe once used the shiny metal of a chrome bumper on an older car for this purpose.) Anyway, I wasn't sure what to expect, so I just went for it. In my mind's eye I immediately saw the room she was in and began to write down everything I "saw" or "felt":

I wrote the following:

Blue and white sweatshirt; a prominent picture on the wall; a nice view; a love seat with a pattern on the fabric; a cat; a white windowpane; neutral colors; a red-hued point of interest; two trees; a porch; a rustic style exterior, bright with natural light entering; white cabinets; a cup of tea; a large, multicolored, outdoor-themed painting (significant); a location in Pennsylvania.

This wasn't overly detailed, but not bad for a beginner (if I say so myself).

To check our accuracy, Medium Joe showed us the images that Jane had texted him during the exercise. In the pictures Jane had on a blue sweatshirt with white writing, and the prominent picture on the wall and the view were combined. She had large pictures of the ocean and beach on her walls, and she sat on a sofa with the pattern I had seen. The windowpanes were white, as was most of the décor in her home, including the cabinets I had mentioned. One wall however was painted a shade of red, and this one wall had a large oil painting on it that was very colorful and abstract. Out her window we saw two trees. The place was bright. She had a cup containing some liquid, but I didn't find out what it was. She was in Pennsylvania. The only thing missing was the cat. Jane said she had a dog. I doubted myself for a moment, but two other people chimed in and said they had seen a cat also. I knew if two or more of us in the class saw the cat that it must be there. I went back to the photos of Jane's home and found a photo on a table of a person I could only assume was someone important to her (perhaps a relative or significant other), and they were holding a cat.

We did this with another subject and the results were almost as good. This subject was a male. In this instance I was able to describe the man much better than his environment.

There was a third subject as well, but by that time I was too exhausted to do another. What I had been asked to do required a lot of energy. Remember, all we had to go on was, "Hello everyone, my name is _____."

That day we had one final test, which was twofold. There was a disposable razor, and a small plastic pencil sharpener—the kind a child might bring to grade school. We were asked to focus on one of the two items for five minutes to see whether we could move it or change its temperature. The starting temperature of the razor was 77.7 degrees, and the sharpener, 78.3 degrees. Our instructor had a device to test temperatures. At the end of five minutes, neither of my items had moved at all, but the temperature of both items had changed by about 0.4 and 0.6 degrees, respectively. Nothing especially dramatic, but like I said, by this time I was exhausted, as were others in the class.

Journal Entry, May 15, 2020—"The Kids Are All Right"

Late one night while Jessica and I were in bed, and her two small children were in their bunk beds, Jessica heard a noise that startled her and asked me whether I had heard it. I admitted I had not. Jessica said, "Well, this is your department," by which she meant it was up to me to get out of bed with some sort of weapon and check the house. I said, "All right," but didn't move.

"What's up? Why aren't you going?" she asked.

"I'm looking."

"Looking at what? The ceiling?"

"No," I said, "I'm looking around the house. I don't have to get up to see around the house anymore; I can see everything from here in my mind."

I did not see or feel that there was any danger. There have been other times when things have gone bump in the night and I have sprung into action like an alpha dog, but it didn't feel necessary this time.

Jessica asked, "What do you see?"

"Well, the children are fine and asleep. One is sleeping sideways on her bed." We laughed. "The other is not in view, but I can feel that she is there, sleeping soundly too. She may be rolled up in a little ball under the covers in the corner of her bed, just barely out of my view." I went on to explain there was nothing inside or outside the house to worry about at the moment. They and we were all safe.

Jessica said, "I'm going to check on the kids."

I waited. She returned a minute or so later and said, "Well one of them is sideways and the other . . ."

"Curled up in the corner under covers?" We both laughed. I said, "It's really kind of crazy, isn't it?"

Ever since the class about remote viewing, I knew what to look for and how to switch on my vision, so to speak. Remote viewing has proven to be one of the easier things for me to do. Originally, I thought it would be hard; but then I realized I had actually been doing it for some time, just not recognizing what to look for in order to distinguish between what might be a passing thought in my mind and what could be a moment of clairvoyance. Now that I can distinguish the two, it has become easier and much more fun.

The following day I texted Jessica in the afternoon and asked her to call me. She wrote that she couldn't at the moment; I was going to ask why, but then I just looked for myself and saw that she was in a private meeting with someone at work. I respectfully turned off my remote viewing, as it was the proper thing to do, and said, "Never mind. I see why."

"Talk later. Love you, Babe."

CHAPTER 8

ENERGY, FREQUENCY, AND VIBRATION

Before I began my spiritual journey and quest for the answers to universal laws, if you had told me there was a way, I could attract the things I want, I would have said you were completely out of your mind. When I was growing up, we always had a significant need for money. I thought the way to acquire it was to push my way through life and fight for everything. Society teaches us that we must go to school, get a job, save our money, then retire and die—and possibly repeat. Let us look at who are the major players giving us that advice. Who originally said that this was the way to live our lives and make money? I do not mean, who said this to you the first time, but from where does the idea originate? It is the employers. The folks who are now, or were, in power, and who own the companies that they want you to work for. They are the ones who invented this strategy for you. This is because they need employees. A boss is not a boss if he or she has no employees.

So then, you may ask, what is the problem with that advice? Simply put, your boss did not become the owner of a large company by following his own advice. He used the laws of vibration and attraction to get where he is, and now he is telling you not to follow in his footsteps, but to work for him instead. That is typical, hypocritical human nonsense. This is not to say that all employers are bad people. I certainly do not mean that. In fact, I was an employer of hundreds of people over the course of my career. As hard as it was to let a great employee go, I had to accept it so they could get themselves to the next level of their lives. I never had the preconceived notion that someone was going to work for me forever. I thought that attitude was selfish and wrong. I told my people as early as their first interview that if they wanted to, they could learn everything there was to learn about my business, but that in three years, they should leave. They should have the knowledge at the end of three years to go out and stake their own claim in the world. I preset their exit strategy: learn as much as you can, and then leave.

Let us now take a closer look at what your boss did to create a successful company. He may have worked for a competitor for a while before branching out on his own, but that approach isn't necessary. He used a different formula to find success.

There are two universal laws that you need to understand to attract anything to you. One is the law of attraction, and the other is the law of vibration. It is important to mention that these laws are not limited to acquiring wealth. They can be used to do or obtain anything you want— even love. There really are no limits to what can be done with the knowledge of how to utilize these two universal laws.

We will look at the law of attraction later in this book when we get into how to specifically manifest things into your reality. For now, let us look at the law of vibration, how it works and why. Without the law of vibration, the law of attraction could not exist, because the law of vibration drives the law of attraction.

Nikola Tesla once said, "If you want to find the secrets of the universe, think in terms of energy, frequency, and vibration."

Tesla was probably the most underrated visionary of all time. I realize I'm going off on a tangent here but if you read my first book, you know the question I've hated most is: "How do you know that?" The answer is:

I have no frigging idea how I know things; I just receive the information. Tesla would say something similar when he was asked. He was shunned and ridiculed for it. I have the luxury of the Internet to verify much of the information I get from the Universal Collective; Tesla did not. He also never doubted himself the way I often doubt myself. He was a genius who possessed intuitive abilities, which made him an amazing human. I am not at that level, but I feel I can understand him a little better and can relate on a smaller scale. A much smaller scale.

Tesla tapped into the collective source of all information, just as many of us today are as well. Anyone can tap in, to some degree if they want to. You just need to learn how to do it, and then practice. I firmly believe this. That doesn't mean you will be a great inventor because that takes a certain level of genius, which Tesla had.

Of course, I am going to show you how to do this. That is, after all, why you purchased this book, isn't it? Let's get back on topic.

Thanks to quantum physics we know that the energy within every atom in the universe vibrates. We also know that similar vibrations attract one another. Science has also proven that vibration and frequency affect humans. "How?" you ask? Keep reading; we are only scratching the surface.

Let us break this down. The law of vibration states that absolutely everything in our realm of reality is vibrating. Even solid items vibrate. Right now, I am standing on a wooden floor. If, in fact, the floor is vibrating, why do you suppose I don't fall through it? The answer is that the particles that make up the wooden floor are vibrating very slowly—so slowly in fact, that the floor remains sturdy enough to allow me to walk on it. If you took a small piece of this wood and cut it up into its smallest possible pieces, then viewed one of those pieces under an electron microscope, you would see the particles of the wood move or vibrate. Things vibrate because everything contains energy. Energy exists in everything. Solids vibrate the slowest, while air vibrates much higher, and light vibrates amazingly fast. You and I, as humans, contain energy as well. Our thoughts are made of pure energy. In fact, I have read that about twenty watts of electricity runs through your brain to make it active. Vibrations will affect your mood and your emotions, and your moods and emotions can change your vibration. The beauty of this is that it really doesn't matter much which one comes first. So, you can use vibrations to change your mood or your mood to alter your vibrations. Either way, it works.

The Winfried Otto Schumann resonance study and the Heinrich Rudolf Hertz scale of vibration, when used together, show us how vibration affects human emotion.

Inanimate objects and matter have a lower and slower vibration, whereas most living things have a higher and faster vibration. Depending on the size of the living thing, the larger it is, the faster the vibration within. The vibration of a small cell of bacteria is slower than that of, say, a fish, and both are slower than that of a human. The following are averages. Bacteria vibrate at 77 KHz–900 KHz, a small fish may vibrate at 1000 KHz–1300 KHz, and humans anywhere from 1520 KHz–9460 KHz. The wide range listed for humans reflects that we possess and embody, at different times, a wide range of feelings and emotions.

Each human emotion has a unique vibrational frequency. These emotional vibrations range from higher and faster to lower and slower. When you are laughing and having fun, your body's vibrations are lighter, higher, and faster. When you are tired and sick, your vibrations are heavier, slower, and lower. You know when you feel energized, inspired, and loved, you feel "high"? Conversely, when you are negative and depressed, you feel sluggish, lower, and heavy. "I'm down today," is a statement with which we are all familiar. This is because vibrational frequency will influence your consciousness, which will in turn affect your emotions. Certainly, being around happy people, and pleasant places and things, thus merging your energy with theirs, will have a most positive effect on your being. Try looking at a bunch of beautiful flowers in full bloom and then tell me you don't "feel" that doing so has raised your energy and made you feel better or happier. Visit a museum and look at some amazing works of art and tell me whether you "feel" the energy placed on the canvas by the artist.

To understand this a little more, let's take a look at Cymatics. Cymatics is the study of wave phenomena, especially with regard to sound and its visual representations. It is the study of visible sound and vibration. I am sure you have seen the experiments whereby a pile of sand is poured on top of a metal tin placed on top of a speaker, and when sound or music is played through the speaker, the sand makes beautiful symmetrical shapes depending on the frequency of the sound. Change the frequency and you will change the pattern. If you have never witnessed this phenomenon, take a moment now to pause, look up online, and watch a video on Cymatics.

Cymatics provides evidence for the fact that everything we perceive as solid is actually continuously vibrating, each "thing" at its own specific rate, called a "prime resonance frequency." Any object free to vibrate on its own tends to do so at a specific rate which is called the object's natural, or resonant frequency. The earth's natural frequency is known as the Schumann Resonance and is the very pulse of the earth, measuring in at 7.83 Hz. In other words, left unaffected by any external forces (such as lightning, earthquakes, etc.), the earth will naturally vibrate at 7.83 Hz. Early experiments to find the human body's natural, fundamental, resonant frequency, showed it to be about 5 Hz. However more recent experiments have shown average readings of 10 Hz. to 12 Hz. Although, I suggested that higher is better, not necessarily when we are talking about one's prime resonance or a person's resting state. This is a natural starting point. Is it possible that, over time, our lives have become more stressful?

If my prime resonance or starting point is 5 Hz and your natural starting point is 10 Hz., then you are out of alignment with the universe and will have a more difficult time aligning your frequency with the intention of attracting. The good news is, this can be corrected.

In the context of humans or animals, prime resonance can also be described as the frequency of vibration most natural to a specific system or organ, such as the heart, liver, or lungs. All cells emit sound as a consequence of their metabolic processes. Our cells exchange information and regulate bodily functions through the sending and receiving of specific frequencies. This signaling precedes and regulates all biochemical actions. When these natural frequency signals become scrambled, so does our body's ability to self-regulate and maintain a healthy function.

The Law of Resonance states that the rate of the vibration projected will harmonize with and attract energies with the same resonance. For example, love is a connective energy, whereas fear is a separative energy. Those emotions create different vibratory frequencies that are amplified through our electromagnetic field. Our electromagnetic field creates what some may call an "aura" or energy field. Scientists have discovered a phenomenon called "sympathetic resonance" or "sympathetic vibration," whereby one vibratory body responds to the vibrations of another to which it bears a harmonic likeness. Therefore, we know that like frequencies attract; but it is even more important to note that one's vibration can have a great effect on another person's vibration. The lowest emotional frequency is thought to be that of shame, while the highest belongs to peace. Anger, hate, jealousy, and judgment all emit lower vibrations, while gratitude, compassion, joy, and trust emit higher ones.

Unfortunately, destructive frequencies can entrain our thoughts toward disruption, disharmony, and disunity. They also stimulate the brain, causing a disharmonious resonance. Therefore, taking control of your own frequency and learning to adjust it can literally change your life. This is why it is important to seek to keep people around you who have a peaceful vibrational energy or "aura." (Unless, of course, it isn't peace you are looking for.)

I recommend taking a look at Dr. David Hawkins' Life Energy Chart. He created this chart so folks can see and measure the differences between one feeling or emotion and another, giving each a number or value from lowest to highest. At the top of the chart is enlightenment, which he hypothesized has the highest frequency, and therefore gave it a value of 700. That level comes with the greatest expansion of energy as well. For joy he applied a value of 540, which is still quite high and expansive. His value for anger is about 150 and begins the fall toward contraction. At the very bottom, and the worst state of mind one can have, according to Hawkins, is guilt or shame, with values of 30 and 20 respectively. Yes, oddly enough it is much better to be angry than guilt ridden or shameful. When I first thought about this I found it hard to believe, but then I reflected on the type of people who commit suicide more often—is it those who are angry or those who feel guilt and shame?

Since we recognize the extreme importance of our vibration and how much it influences our emotions, let us look at some ways to raise our emotional vibration.

Foremost, become conscious of your thoughts. Another way to say this is: become conscious of your own consciousness. Everything you think, say, or feel can, and most likely will, become your reality. Find something beautiful and focus on it. Meditate, and be grateful. Practice acts of kindness. Exercise and get your blood pumping. Be mindful of everything you consume. If it isn't good for you, do not allow it into your body. Everything you put into your body (including but not limited to food, drugs, alcohol, vitamins, supplements, and so on) most likely will impact your vibrational frequency for the duration of time the item remains in your body. There are no exceptions to this. If you eat the eggs of a chicken who is treated poorly on the farm, you ingest the natural energy of the animal, which in this case would be the traumatic and negative energy associated with it. If you eat the eggs of a happy, free-range chicken, you will ingest that happy, positive energy. Again, there are no exceptions to this rule, so please be conscious of everything you consume.

I think it goes without saying, but intoxicants will lower your vibrational state significantly for days after their consumption. This lasts until the half-life of the item is removed naturally from your cells in your body and brain.

In addition, try to limit interactions with other sources of negative energy. This would include those sources we watch on television, the movies, the Internet, and social media (celebrities, politicians, gossip, the news, etc.). There is absolutely no exception to this rule.

Limit exposure and conversations with toxic people, even electronic conversations such as email and texting. This is because it is the thoughts and the information that carry the vibrations. Exceptions for those who want help, and who ask for our help, should always be granted. It is those folks who don't want to change or better themselves that we must leave behind.

This is part of self-preservation. It is not being mean or evil. You were not put on this earth to absorb the troubles of others and carry those troubles with you as you go through life. Like I said, we always make exceptions for those who ask for help. That is much different than a negative person who sees nothing wrong with negativity or self-destructive and self-limiting behaviors.

By now you are most likely putting this together for yourself, but just in case, here is a recap of the most important themes we've covered thus far.

We now know that energy is inside of everything. Everything is made up of particles that vibrate energetically at different speeds. These particles vibrate in waves (string theory), at various frequencies we cannot see, in the subatomic world. Frequency is a measurement of vibration. The higher the frequency, the faster the item is typically vibrating. Thoughts are made of energy, and energy vibrates. Energy, frequency, vibrations, and human emotions are tied together directly.

All words are thoughts. All thoughts are things. All things have their own vibrational frequency.

There is one more piece to this puzzle that is most important. *This is the big one.* This is going to tie it all together for you—it did for me, anyway. Similar vibrations at the same or similar frequency are attracted to one another, almost like strong magnets. Match your frequency to that of the things you want, and you can get them. They will be attracted to you because you will be emitting the same frequency. This is where the laws of vibration and attraction meet harmoniously. Through meditation you can change your body's frequency—also, through your thought and speech patterns. We will delve deeper into how to do this in a later chapter.

We can measure the body's frequencies because human beings are made up of electromagnetic (ELM) energy. Our ELM energy vibrates or pulses. With every pulse, your ELM energy broadcasts and attracts. Your energy field transmits your vibrations and magnetizes other similar vibrations into your energy field. You are constantly broadcasting your own energy outward and attracting similar energies and vibrations to match your own.

With a satellite dish, the direction you turn it in determines what comes into the dish. The same can be said of your energy field. What you attract into your human energy field are vibrational energies similar to what you emit. Simply said, that which you put out there you get back. I'm sure you have heard this statement before, but now you know that not only is it real, but it can also be backed up by scientific data.

The more you understand yourself and your personal uniqueness (who you are, and more importantly, who you are *not*) the stronger your vibrational signal and message will be. When you cast a strong message into the universe, your chances are much improved of finding (or being vibrationally attracted to) similar people and things. People who are like-minded and like-spirited, and the things you wish to attract to yourself, will begin to appear.

There is new research in the area known as the "unified field theory" which suggests that the unifying force underlying everything may be consciousness. This idea has been introduced, or perhaps reintroduced, recently by a doctor of theoretical physics named John Hagelin. Hagelin, who earned a PhD in physics from Harvard University, feels strongly that this is the case.

The initial unified field theory was originated by none other than Albert Einstein. It was the final project he was working on, right up until his death on April 18, 1955. A puzzle left unsolved by the world's greatest mind. I should mention that Einstein did not necessarily suggest that the unifier was consciousness which unified everything. That part was Hagelin.

Whether that theory is proven or not, there is no denying that consciousness plays a key role in the transference of energy, and therefore possibly creation itself. Albert Einstein also bequeathed to humanity the teaching of E=MC squared: that is, energy equals matter times the speed of light squared. In other words, energy can become matter and matter can become energy once again. It is a never-ending cycle of transference.

Consciousness can certainly move stuff around. I apologize if that statement is lacking in scientific vocabulary, but I have seen the truth of it firsthand, through my own efforts. I think most scientists would agree that the human conscious mind is made of energy which vibrates and is measurable.

And so, I am sure you are asking yourself: How do I match my frequency with that of an inanimate object? Think about it with conviction and passion! Meditate on it until you become one with it. You become it, and it becomes you. You visualize it (using all sense perceptions), and you make it be so, always thinking and speaking in the affirmative tense only! You will feel when your energy aligns with it. Remember: thought patterns, speech patterns, and meditation are keys to the law of attraction. We will delve more deeply into this shortly.

Journal Entry, August 15, 2020—"Find the Fish"

On a beautiful Saturday at 6 a.m., the morning sun was shining through the windows all around us and onto our bed. *It's going to be an amazing day,* I thought as I woke and looked over at the most beautiful human being I have ever met. There was Jessica sleeping peacefully. I knew that she had awoken about an hour earlier, even though at the time I had been asleep. She had woken up thinking to herself what a wonderful night's sleep she'd just had. She was contemplating whether to get up for the day when I said out loud, "It's because of the rain." Jessica smiled and went back to sleep. She knows my abilities don't turn off just because I'm asleep—I still know what's happening around me. Awake, asleep, or in a meditative state, it doesn't matter. She and I are so connected and consciously evolved that we can almost communicate entirely telepathically. Because she wanted me to sleep well, she decided to go back to sleep herself, knowing that if she got up my mind would awaken too.

The night before Jessica had fallen asleep before me, I believe at around 10 p.m. I stayed up for a while lying next to her in our bed. I wanted to sleep but I had just had two energy beings visit me. One was Jessica's grandfather. He was holding a mounted green fish in his left hand and pointing to it with his right hand. He continued pointing to the fish as if it were something important. When I later relayed this information to Jessica, I explained that we would have to figure out what the green mounted fish represented, as there were no words coming through. One thing was certain, Jessica's grandfather was making it clear that we needed to find the green fish. I told Jessica that I wasn't getting anything else from him and that I needed to move on. There had been another energy being around me all week, following me since Monday. I knew I needed to speak with that one, so I began to distance myself from Jessica's grandfather; but as I did so, her father showed up.

Her father joined her grandfather and was quite animated and adamant that we must find the fish. Now, since both of them were making a very big deal about this, I decided to stay in contact with them and concentrate. I knew that fishing had been one of the shared pastimes of

Jessica, her dad, and her grandfather. The three of them used to go fishing together on a regular basis. So the image of the fish was telling me that there was something of importance regarding which the three of them were connected. A fish is a type of reward that someone may receive after going fishing. I began to focus on that for a moment: the fish had value—a monetary value perhaps. I was getting closer. *Perhaps the green hue of the fish represented money.* That felt right. I was sure then that I had it. They wanted her to find some money they had left behind.

After I relayed this information to Jessica, she reminded me that she had received a letter that indicated there was money for her to claim. Initially it looked like a scam, and I told her to throw it away. The company that sent the letter was offering to locate the money for a 20 percent commission of whatever was found. I knew that if, in fact, there was money out there, we certainly did not need this or any other company to get it for us. I'd asked Jessica previously if I could give this letter to my mom. She had recently found money held in my family's name, and I thought it likely that she would know how to find this other money too. The state in which we reside has something like a lost-and-found fund which holds money when the state cannot figure out how to get it to the rightful owner. Any bank account can be seized by this fund after seven years of inactivity. It is up to the heir to contact the state to retrieve the money—a catch-22 situation, because if the heir doesn't know it exists, how can she claim it? The state won't come looking for you, that's for sure! They will gladly just "hold on to it" for you.

Well, my mom was able to locate something that the state was holding in the name of Jessica's dad. We thought at that point the mystery was solved, but as we looked a little deeper, we found that there actually was no money in her dad's name. However, Jessica's dad was named after *his* dad and when we inquired, we found that Granddad did in fact leave behind unclaimed money when he passed away. Now it all made perfect sense. "Thanks, Pops," Jessica said. We had found the fish. It was much appreciated, and at the time, much needed.

The second visitor I had that night was a woman. She had light-colored hair. She came to me upset about something. Her arms were straight out as if she were holding a tray and offering me something from it. There was no tray. Her hands and her arms were actually empty. Something was missing from her arms, and with that it hit me. She had lost her child. *Oh no, not this*, I thought to myself. I felt so badly for her. I continued to stay with her, wanting to help.

The woman was deceased, obviously, so if she'd lost her child, that would mean her child was still alive. This mom became increasingly more emotional as the vision went on. How could I figure out who her child was? She started showing me a visual. At first it looked like a blob of clay that needed to be sculpted, and then it began to take shape and grew rather large for a child. That is when I realized her child was now a full-grown man, middle-aged in fact. I waited for more. The man was slightly on the heavy side. As I watched the clay morph into a human form, his face began to take shape. Suddenly I felt like falling over. I not only saw his face; I recognized him. I was very close with this man. He was my true friend, one who had taught me so much. I remember him telling me stories of being transported as a child from city to city and having to live with different family members after his mom had died at a very young age.

This man has done so much for me. I have said to him many times, "I wish someday I could repay you." Although this may have been my chance to do so, I had to be certain of the information I was being given. I couldn't just call him and say, *Hey, guess who I spoke to last night?* She would have to revisit me again so I could be certain I was correct. As of this writing, she has yet to do so.

CHAPTER 9

AMAZING SPACE

I f you read my first book, you will know that when I began this journey, I was told I needed to get back to astronomy. *Get back?* I didn't understand this statement. I liked the subject of astronomy in school very much and was always fascinated by the universe, but I just didn't know what to "get back" to. Things always seem to fall into place whenever I follow the advice of those who are guiding me. A few nights after getting this counsel, I came across a streaming web service that specialized in space exploration and science documentary films. I thought it looked interesting and explored the channel and the shows they aired. I found titles about the universe, but I also found some about the conscious mind and the scientists who study it. Here are some of the key take-a-ways.

In order to understand the creation of the conscious mind, one must comprehend how the universe itself was created.

It used to be that, to me, the universe was this enormous overwhelming concept, but as I began to observe the connections between the cosmos and the human mind, the universe seemed to get smaller. It became a simpler place, easier for me to comprehend than ever before. The universe and I are now one. We are part of one another, never to be separated again. This universe we live in is alive. Its energies connect us all in this realm of existence, and in the other realms where energy beings dwell without form. The space between one planet and another is alive, filled with dark energy and dark matter. Although you and I may see nothing, thanks to some of the greatest scientific minds who have ever lived, we can prove undeniably that this is true. The universe is alive!

I used to joke about the Buddhist idea of becoming one with the universe. In fact, it was the butt of my jokes often as a young man, but— holy shit, do I get it now! The Buddhists were onto something really big. I do not advocate one specific philosophy or religion over another, as I think they all have something to offer. I also think they all contain fallacies and shortcomings as well. However, if you strip away the dogmatism in most religions, you'll find accurate concepts in accord across traditions. I have said many times in my writings that religion and my theory of the afterlife can coexist in harmony. That is, if you want them to.

Your consciousness is made up of energy. About twenty watts of electricity runs through your brain, and one hundred watts runs through the entire human body when at rest. So where does it go when you die? Energy in any form cannot cease to exist. We know from science that energy cannot be created or destroyed, it can only change form. We know this to be scientifically true, and yet some people continue to believe that, once the body dies, consciousness is the only form of energy that can cease to exist. That would certainly defy the First Law of Thermodynamics, which has been proven by so many, beyond doubt.

Let us examine this a little more.

You have just read two scientifically proven facts. First: that the "space" between all things isn't empty but very much alive. Alive, with what scientists refer to as "dark energy" and "dark matter." Second: that energy must transform and cannot cease to exist. Let's add one more scientific fact to the mix: we know that the universe is expanding rapidly, yet the density of space remains a constant. For this to be true, we must acknowledge that some type of energy (perhaps dark energy) is continuously supplemented and added to space, thus forcing the universe to expand. We can't yet answer scientifically where the energy contained in the human consciousness goes when the body dies, nor can we prove what keeps refilling the empty space of the expansion of the universe with dark energy. Perhaps you have drawn the same conclusion I have?

I believe dark energy is the energy extracted from the conscious mind when the body dies.

Death is said to be the beginning of the process whereby human consciousness becomes a part of, or "one" with the universe. What I am saying here is, when the human body dies, the energy that once made up your consciousness is released into the void (space) and becomes a part of the dark energy that permeates all of space. Enjoy the simplicity and beauty of this theory. You aren't dying; you are transforming. You will become part of the universal energy structure and remain in many ways very much alive.

This is my personal theory of where we go when we die. I have written about this in greater detail in my first book, *The Atheist and The Afterlife— An Autobiography*, published in 2020.

Given that hypothesis seems to be gaining some traction, I decided to include a new theory in this book. In the next chapter I will present you with my theory of the creation of our universe. (I can see you smiling.)

Journal Entry, November 16, 2020—"Officer Bob"

It was during my daily routine in my office on a Monday morning that the phone rang as it typically does, but this time I answered before my assistant could pick up. This in itself was unusual as I rarely, if ever, answer the phone. On the other end of the line was a policeman we will call "Officer Bob." Upon hearing him tell me his name, his rank, and the unit he was with, my mind immediately began to race: *What is this about? What's happened to my kids? Who got hurt?* All the bad shit a police officer would call anyone about began to run through my mind.

He said, "Hello Ray, I am with the Police Officers Association (not the real title) and our president asked me to give you a call and see if you would be interested in giving a small donation in return for some advertising space in our annual newsletter." What a relief. A request for a donation I could handle.

I asked several questions about the advertisements offered and the typical donation amounts. I typically give to these types of organizations once a year, so I listened. I asked that he send me more information via email and told him that I would think about it and get back to him. I usually give to various local police organizations every year just before Christmas, but I didn't know anything about this particular organization, or Bob for that matter, so I decided to check up on him and them. I found the webpage of the organization and looked up the president to give him a call and verify that Officer Bob was on the up and up.

Bob continued to call me every other day to see whether I was going to send a check. I didn't want to tell him I was waiting to make sure his was a legitimate organization, so I dodged his calls until I heard back from his boss. Let's call him "Chief Smith." Smith told me about the organization and what they do for the community, so I thanked him for the return call and waited for Officer Bob to get back to me to commence the deal. I made a donation that year and the next few years through Officer Bob each time, as he called me annually. He would come by my office to pick up the check, and he gave me membership cards signed by the president of the organization.

Year after year I got to know Officer Bob a little better. We only spoke once a year, but I began to look forward to our annual chats. In October of 2020 Officer Bob once again called me as he normally would, to chat and get my donation, but something about this phone call was different. The words that were spoken were much the same as any of the previous years, but the very second, I heard his voice and our energies blended I could feel deep vibrations within me. Deep and low vibrations usually mean something bad is on its way. I asked Officer Bob if everything was all right, and he began to open up. Things were *not* all right in his world. He had just lost a few friends who had passed away as a result of the COVID-19 pandemic dominating our country at the time. He also implied that things were not great at home. I was shocked that he was willing to share this information with me. We weren't that close, but it sounded like he needed a friend, so I listened. I closed my office door and we talked for a while. The whole time he spoke to me I saw in my mind's eye a black cloud of smoke I had to push away in order to see his face. When I see a black cloud like that it always indicates a death of some sort, and he seemed really upset about the things that were troubling him. I let him speak until he was done. In the three or so years I knew him, this was the most we had ever communicated. I have had several police officers as friends, and my experience is that they don't easily open up to anyone. It is completely out of character for most police officers to express themselves in that manner, especially to a relative stranger, so I knew he had to be hurting badly.

I went on to express my condolences and spoke of some of my own frustrations with the pandemic. I wanted to say, "You're not alone," but in actuality I had no idea what he was going through. Before our phone call ended, I asked that he send me the paperwork I needed to fill out and place the advertisement. I explained that my donation would be a bit smaller that year since my business had been down some due to the pandemic. He understood and we said goodbye. I remember making a mental note to follow up with him when he came in to pick up the check. I wanted to make sure he was okay. I could see that depression was taking him over. This was a very difficult time in America, but if you were a police officer or a first responder, it was even more so.

One thing I knew about Bob was that he was extremely persistent. I could almost set my watch to the exact time and date he would call me each year to get my donation, and the same would be true for every follow-up call as well. He never stopped calling or emailing me until he had the check in his hand. In fact, he was so persistent that I never bothered to write down his phone number.

That year neither a phone call nor an email came. In fact, there was no communication whatsoever until November 16, 2020, when a completely different officer from the same association called to "pitch me" on buying his advertising. He said, "You came very highly recommended, and the chief would like to know if you want a shield for your car." I said "Sure," but what I wanted was to hear from Officer Bob. I agreed to the donation and this new officer came to pick it up. I was certain in that moment that what I had foreseen in the form of a black cloud had come to pass. Nonetheless, I had to ask. "What happened to Officer Bob?"

"Oh, yeah. Bob died."

"I just spoke to him recently. What happened?"

Hesitating for a moment, he said, "I think it was a heart attack or something. It was very sudden and unexpected."

I knew he was lying to me, but I also knew that technically it was none of my business. I was just some businessman who donated once a year. I asked no more questions and thanked the officer. A few days later an article showed up in my newsfeed about a record number of police officers committing suicide that year. I never even knew his last name, but I knew for a certainty that Officer Bob was one of many to which the article was referring. I have seen him since in the afterlife. He is always smiling now, but I can't help but wonder if there was something more I could have done to help. I guess we all question ourselves when someone takes their life, even when there is nothing anyone could have done.

Journal Entry, December 17, 2020—"Here We Go Again"

I was on a video conference working with my mentor, Medium Joe, and a few other students. The class was from 7:30 to about 9:30 on a Thursday evening.

Medium Joe told us what our exercises would be for the evening so we could meditate and prepare for the testing we were about to receive. We began with an exercise in which he showed us a picture he had drawn. After looking at the picture for ten seconds, the picture was taken out of view, and we were to go into an altered state and tell him what we saw, who we saw, what had happened, and so on. The challenge was to share the impressions we got from the other side without allowing them to be mixed up with our own thoughts and interpretations.

The first picture Medium Joe held up was that of a hammer. Everyone agreed it was a hammer, except for me and one other person. I saw the hammer clearly, but as much as I wanted it to be a hammer, the universe insisted that this was a baseball bat. There was no question I was looking at a hammer, but the energy being I was working with obviously wasn't okay with that. He wanted me to perceive that the hammer was a bat, and so I just went with it. The hammer had the number 12 on it.

My energy being transported me psychically to Yankee Stadium where I sat in the twelfth seat of the twelfth row on the third base side. The stadium was completely empty—he and I were the only ones there. The being stood to my right while I sat, and I asked him why we were there, especially since the picture I had been shown was obviously of a hammer.

"This is *your* consciousness," he said, "Do you really want to make it a hammer, or would you rather be here in this beautiful place? Why do you want it to be a hammer so badly? Who would want to go to work and build shit when you can be in this amazing place?"

"Okay, I get that. But why here?"

"Because YOU need to look around more and be more present." He began to show me very slowly the exquisitely green grass, the perfectly round pitcher's mound, the flawless white chalk lines down the third base side. The point was to find the beauty in all things and relax.

"Slow down," he said to me. "Take it in and enjoy it. It can always be a hammer later."

"Oh, now I get it."

If you haven't guessed already, it was Jessica's dad who was my visitor that day from the other side. When he was alive, he had owned a construction company and had loved the Yankees. I am, admittedly, a bona fide workaholic. Therefore, his overall message to me was: "All work and no play is no way to live." He was also telling me to slow down more often, look around, and appreciate the things I have. I certainly did appreciate the blessings in my life, but recently had gotten sidetracked with work, books, education, and life in general. If you recall from my first book, I found solace listening to the Yankee games on the radio in my difficult times as a child. The message was now clear.

"I will do it," I said. "I will slow down, appreciate the things I have more intentionally, and enjoy them." I thanked him and we left the ballpark.

Journal Entry, January 23, 2021—"Crash Course"

In this particular exercise we were to enter an altered state with a starting point chosen for us by Medium Joe. Mine was a car crash. That was all the information I was given. From there I had to connect to someone on the other side and get the rest of the story from them. We would then recite what we saw aloud to the class and see if this vision I was receiving was for any of them.

I saw a man in a white T-shirt and blue jeans who looked like he was from the time period around 1968. He had Elvis-styled hair. He was familiar with the male driver and the woman passenger in a blue car that was hit by a brown car. The woman died as a result of the crash. The man loved her deeply. I didn't get around to figuring out if he was the driver because I was cut short: the information wasn't streaming fast enough. However, someone in class knew the people I was viewing, the year, the man, the car, and the description perfectly. My classmate said the woman did indeed die, and she was the love of his life. She began to cry. The man had sincere regrets and missed her so much. It seemed as though he felt he was at fault for the accident. Whether he was or not, that is how he felt about it.

My interpretation of this episode was that the man was apologizing to my classmate for the way the accident took place, and he was showing us all the sorrow and regret he felt for having this happen and not preventing it, or possibly for causing it. Once the message with the apology was shared, I felt a huge relief pass through my body.

When I take on someone else's message from the other side, I must sit with it until I deliver it. Their emotions can sit with me for hours after the connection is broken. Due to the nature of what I saw I found it difficult to stay present for the rest of the class.

CHAPTER 10

My Theory of the Creation of the Universe

Allow me to preface what I am about to say by making it clear that I am not a scientist, astronomer, or physicist. This theory came to me while I was researching an unrelated topic. The concept seemed to me to be completely logical, and perhaps you'll agree.

I am, admittedly, a theoretical physicist wannabe. While Jessica can't wait for the Dave Matthews band to come back to town and perform live, my own dream is to score tickets to the next Brian Greene and Sean Carroll doubleheader, speaking event.

Yeah, so I've got that going for me.

I was thinking one day about the formation of our universe—or of any universe, for that matter. (How do you spend *your* Sundays?)

I think our universe may be one among many in existence. That may be a topic to elaborate on another time, but in this hypothesis, it makes it easier to understand my idea about how our universe came into being.

Scientists postulate that there is a black hole at the center of each galaxy in the universe. Andrea Ghez and Reinhard Genzel were awarded the Nobel Prize in 2020 for their confirmation that there is, in fact, a black hole in the center of our own universe. This discovery adds to the possibility that each galaxy may have a black hole at its center, or core, as well. For a long time now, many astronomers have ascribed to this idea.

The big bang theory continues to raise questions, one of which is: How can the explosion caused by two tiny particles crashing into each other have enough power, force, and impact to create an entire universe? Well, my question would be: What if the two particles were the ones located at the singularity region, or the very bottom (or nadir) point, of a black hole?

There are two primary parts to a black hole: the *singularity*, and the *event horizon*. The event horizon is the "point of no return" of a black hole. It is not a physical surface, but a sphere surrounding the black hole that marks where the escape velocity is equal to the speed of light (escape velocity is the speed an object would need to travel to be able to escape the gravitational pull of the black hole). This is where particles and matter enter into the black hole. Everything enters and nothing ever leaves—or does it?

At the very bottom of a black hole, as described by general relativity, lies a gravitational region called the singularity, where the space-time curvature becomes infinite. When particles reach the singularity, they are crushed to infinite density and their mass is added to the totality of the black hole. Before that happens, these particles will have been completely torn apart by the growing tidal forces in a process sometimes referred to as "spaghettification." (Yes, that is a real scientific term.) Basically, it means everything is ripped to shreds, vertically stretched and horizontally compressed, and brought down to its simplest and smallest possible form— pulverized into a single, tiny, subatomic point.

Black holes suck in everything that gets near the event horizon. Even light cannot pass by a black hole without falling prey to its gravitational pull. The hole continues to pull in more and more matter over millions, even billions of years, sucking up and destroying everything that comes its way and ripping it to shreds. (Reminds me of someone I dated many years ago, but that is a topic for another time.) At the very bottom of a black hole lies its singularity: a point the size of a subatomic particle, containing all the mass and all the power of what the black hole vacuumed into itself, including stars, planets, light, and anything else around it. Now we have a subatomic particle with the power of an entire universe within it.

Imagine, if you will, a garbage truck. A garbage truck is essentially a supersized trash compactor. The garbage goes into the back of the truck and gets crushed down into a smaller form so that more garbage can be added into a small space. The garbage of an entire city can be placed into a few garbage trucks and then compacted down into a tiny piece of junk, which is then hauled away to a landfill. The garbage must be compacted significantly to make it as small as possible, increasing the density of the landfill.

That being said, here is my theory on how our universe came into existence. (Somebody please prepare and engrave that Nobel Prize.)

Let us say for example that two of these points (or singularity regions) of mass collided on the other side of space-time, causing an explosion so great and powerful (a "Big Bang" event) that it created a new universe on the other side of the fabric of space. For this to occur, two black holes must exist for billions of years, acting like trash compactors (that naturally know how to recycle, I may add), their individual points of singularity protruding through the fabric of space until they collide with one another, exploding and releasing all of that matter and energy, enough power and material to create a brand-new universe on the other side of the fabric of this one.

Two black holes collecting materials from this universe, their singularities growing in mass, density, and energy, pushing against the fabric of space, stretching until they meet one another in a very unlikely collision on the other side, would create an explosion great enough, and contain all types of matter in its smallest possible form, to create another Big Bang.

This doesn't answer the question of how everything began in the first place because, if this theory were true, it would have taken two other black holes with points of singularity regions to collide to create the universe we live in, but I think it may show us how two subatomic particles might have enough energy and power to create a universe.

Now, don't get all up in arms; this is just a thought experiment on my part. (Or—dare I say it?—a Nobel Prize-winning theory?)

Journal Entry, The Morning of May 16, 2021—"The Second Message"

It was a picture-perfect spring day when Jessica and I were taking our two younger children to visit (Jessica's mom) their grandmother. We had an early, quiet dinner together.

After dinner Jessica and I took the children to a park nearby the house in Westchester County, New York. (Why am I giving you the location and the exact day? Because I truly hope that what I am about to share with you was seen by others and documented somewhere.)

Once arriving at the park, we observed other families with their children playing all around us. It was a Sunday afternoon, sunny and warm, not too hot. In fact, the temperature was just right. The sun was directly overhead, beaming down rays of warmth that felt so peaceful as they shone down upon us. Our kids ran off to play. Jessica and I sat on the swings, from which we were able to keep an eye on our youngsters. As I sat there, I was looking around the park at all the people, mentally checking them out. I was still in the habit of hyper-vigilance, so I was scanning the immediate area for any "stranger danger." Meanwhile, Jessica was swinging like a child back and forth next to me, saying, "Look at me!" I laughed. I love that childlike quality in her.

She continued to swing back and forth, leaning back all the way to be able to look up at the sky, just like the toddlers twenty feet away on the other swing set. Jessica is so beautiful, and I love watching her smile. She complimented the beauty of what we were seeing. Suddenly she stopped the swing and said loudly, "Look!" Startled, I immediately went into self-preservation mode. I jumped off the swing, looking around, looking for the kids—they were fine—scanning the park. Everything seemed to be fine. Jessica pointed up to the sky and said, "Oh my God, can you see it! Can you see it?"

"See what?" I said.

With my pepper spray in one hand and my Smith and Wesson Black Ops Tonto Folding Knife in the other, I was casing the joint for who or what I needed to destroy. (Yes, I know what you're thinking, but like I told you, I am a work in progress.)

"In the sky. Can't you see it? Look!"

As I began to realize that I had nothing to worry about, I squinted up to see what had Jessica so excited.

"All I see is the sun, and it's blinding me. What am I looking for, Babe?"

"Look at the circle around the sun. Holy shit! It's a rainbow. There's a circular fucking rainbow around the sun!"

In my first book I shared a story in which Jessica began to swear as she recognized that a certain message in the snow was that of a lotus flower. For Jessica to swear, it is always a big deal. Now, just like the lotus flower, I had no idea what a circular rainbow was or even if it was a real thing. I would have to look it up, but first, allow me to share with you the visual.

There was a perfectly symmetrical circle surrounding the sun. Even though I could see it, I didn't understand its significance. Nonetheless, I appreciated its beauty. Jessica told me to take a picture, but I had left my mobile phone at the house, and apparently, so had she.

She said, "I will run back to the house and get a camera. This is unbelievable! We have to document this! You watch the kids, and I'll be right back. We have to get a picture of this," she repeated.

"Okay, I'll be right here."

As I waited, I began to push one of our children on the swing set. "Higher, higher, *higher*," she said.

"No, no, *no*," I replied. "Any higher and you'll be upside down."

"Higher, higher, *higher*," she intoned again. Just like her mom.

Jessica was taking a long time to get back to the park, and I was wondering if I should head back to the house with the kids. As I called them over with the intention of taking them home, I saw Jessica in the distance with a phone in her hand and a big smile on her face. I smiled back.

"Is everything okay?"

"Yes. Everything is just fine. I went into the house and got the phone, and then my mom and I went outside the house to take pictures of this miraculous event. I got a great shot of it by lying down in the middle of the street."

"So, um, you lay down in the middle of the street to get a picture?"

"Yes," she said matter-of-factly. "Then we looked up this, circular rainbow thing, on the Internet to find out how it forms."

It turns out that these types of circular rainbows are called "haloes." They perfectly encircle the sun, or in some cases, the moon. Although not an uncommon event itself, what is uncommon is to be able to see them from earth. They are usually only witnessed by airline pilots or passengers in flight. They are more easily glimpsed at higher altitudes. We all know that rainbows in general are somewhat rare and beautiful, but a halo is even more so, and to see a halo from the surface of the earth is nearly impossible.

In order to see a halo, the angle between you and the sun must be precise. Some haloes can be seen at forty-six degrees and others at twenty-two degrees, but either way, the words "exact" and "precise" are the operative terms here. Additionally, the light of the sun must pass through ice crystals suspended within very high, thin, wispy clouds at equally precise angles. It is interesting to note that there is no way to predict when a halo will show itself. The last halo like the one I've described that I could find online (as of the date of publication) was recorded on August 31, 2015, in India.

It is difficult to express the magnitude of this event—even I, who sometimes consider myself a writer, cannot find appropriate words to do so. There it was, in all its beauty, directly above us in the sky. Simply put, it was one of those magical moments I will never forget.

Journal Entry, April 20, 2021—"Happy Birthday"

A few days before I composed this journal entry it was Jessica's birthday. I often struggle when it comes to buying her gifts. I guess when it comes to Jessica, I want whatever I get for her to be perfect. I know that nothing can be perfect, but I really do try to put some thought into what I get her. I tend to frequent a certain store that sells jewelry and places each purchase in a signature blue box with a white bow. By now I expect you've figured out which store I'm referring to. (Sorry: no plugs in this book.)

Most guys are familiar with this store because we know we can't really go wrong with this particular brand. Women know this store because as soon as they see the light blue box their eyes widen like its Christmas morning, and they are five years old again.

For this particular birthday I purchased Jessica a gold and pearl necklace. I considered this gift exceptionally nice because this year I was inspired to give her something that came from the sea. Jessica loves the ocean for its peace and tranquility, and as a result of her fond memories growing up with a family house near the beach. Her dad had a boat and as a kid she loved to prop herself at the tip of the bow, like Rose in the movie *Titanic*.

However, upon opening the gift I could tell right away that she didn't love it and it was going back to the store in the same pretty little light blue box it came in, minus the bow (which had become a toy for one of the many animals running around our zoo-like premises—if I were a betting man, my money would be on the cat making off with it).

I put the necklace back in its packaging and placed it on one of the bookshelves to the left of my desk in my home office, where I do the majority of my writing. It is important to mention that when I bought that necklace, I felt it was the perfect gift, so when Jessica didn't like it I was sort of shocked. I remember browsing the store' s website, and when I saw that particular piece of jewelry, I knew it was the one I was supposed to get her. I left the box on the shelf for a while, not ready to return it to the store. I recall feeling strange at the thought of returning it.

One day while writing I began to sense the high vibrations I often feel when there is another presence in the room with me. I also saw a black line shoot across the wall, making its way over some of the artwork and paintings Jessica has made for me over the years. A peaceful, calm energy being entered the room. I looked around briefly but paid no more attention to it and went back to my typing. I felt the presence again to my left, where the box containing the necklace was on the bookshelf—except the box wasn't there. Or at least, at that moment I couldn't see it.

I got up and went to the master bedroom where Jessica was about to take a shower. I asked her whether she had changed her mind about the necklace and decided to keep it, because I didn't see it on my bookshelf. She smiled and shook her head a little sheepishly. (I could tell she felt badly because she knows I always put thought into buying her things.) I asked if she had moved the necklace and once again, she said no. With what must have been a perplexed look on my face I walked slowly back to my office, dumbfounded.

When I entered the office door, I looked again for the box. And it was right there, on the shelf where I originally placed it! *What the fuck had just happened?* I've often been asked if the dead can move things. The answer is yes, but minimally—the remnants of their energy in the room can slightly move the position of an item. But this was very different—it had disappeared from my sight.

I sat down in my chair to begin writing again when I felt that same presence return to the room. I closed my eyes and went into a mildly altered state to see if I knew who this energy being was. It turned out to be a woman, and I knew exactly who she was. In my first book I wrote about meeting Jessica's deceased grandmother. The evidential identifier she gave me was a family heirloom she wanted to give to Jessica. If you remember the story, Jessica was the only one of all the siblings allowed to play with Grandma's jewelry. And so now I headed back to the other room with the necklace in the box. I knew what I had to do. Sticking my head in the shower, I asked Jessica, "When you used to play with your grandmother's jewelry, what pieces did you play with most often?"

"The pearls. Why do you ask?"

"That's it!" I exclaimed.

"That's what?

"This necklace isn't from me; it's from your grandmother, and she will not let me return it to the store. I will buy you something else. This is from her." And with that, I handed her back the box. She shut off the water and came out of the shower with an open-mouthed stare and a tear running down her cheek.

"Are you sure?"

"Yes, my love, I am absolutely certain."

As I was explaining what had transpired, one of Jessica's young daughters entered the room all dressed up. She had on a beautiful dress with her shiny little shoes, and she had tried to put on make-up all by herself. It was one of the cutest things I had ever seen: this beautiful child just decided she wanted to get all dressed up with nowhere to go. She looked adorable.

"Do you like my dress?" she asked.

Jessica and I told her how beautiful she looked. Then Jessica said, "Look at her little dress."

"I did. It's adorable."

"No, really, look at the dress. Look at the *pattern* on the dress."

The dress was a light shade of pink with white strands of pearls on it.

"Like I said, Babe. I am certain."

CHAPTER 11

THE PURPOSE OF HERE AND NOW

Many people seem to think they must find their purpose in this life. I believe this may be a topic we over-think, for the answer typically, is quite simple and right in front of us. You see, *your purpose will find you.* In fact, at this very point in time you are most likely fulfilling a part of your journey, even if your current situation is unpleasant. Each step you take forward, will lead you ultimately to a place of fulfillment. I hope every step you take is one of beauty and wonderment. Even the hardships that transpire can be a helpful positive experience, as they are often the events we learn from the most. Use them to learn, grow, and evolve. I had to experience many difficult things to really understand them.

Some folks feel that they are less important than others. Perhaps they think that if they can't do something as dramatic as curing a dreaded disease, or saving the planet, their individual purpose isn't that important to society. That way of thinking is so very wrong. Each of us can serve the universe and ourselves at the same time by doing things that may seem small, but which may have a tremendous ripple effect of which you're completely unaware of. Making good choices each day is paramount to your own development and evolution as a conscious being, in this life and beyond. Those same choices will affect everyone around you as well. So please choose wisely.

We are here to deal with the obstacles that show up in our lives, and when those have been overcome, we can then move on to our next level of consciousness. It works the same way both here and in other realms. I have my guides and various energy beings with whom I communicate. I don't know why they chose me, but nonetheless, I am grateful. I feel compelled to utilize this ability to try to help others find the same. It would seem that each time I help someone significantly, I am granted something positive in my life. That's karma baby.

Putting others before myself gives me the ability to gain higher knowledge. That is perhaps my path of evolution. Yours may be similar. You may be in a different place in your own evolution, but regardless, we are here to help each other, and through doing so, we also advance ourselves. That is our most purposeful endeavor. We must master our realm of existence to get to a higher one. Mastering this realm of existence has nothing to do how much success you receive in this one. It certainly has nothing to do with materialism.

Whether it be something small like helping someone change a flat tire or something larger like helping someone overcome grief due to a major loss, it doesn't matter. The so-called "size" of the problem you help someone solve is irrelevant. It will not change your return on investment as far as karma is concerned. The universe will grant you things for everything you do for the benefit of others, both large and small.

So what about when we help ourselves? Is that a selfish behavior? This is a question I often get. The answer is, "No, it's not." The burdens you carry don't affect only you but others as well, including your loved ones. We may think our problems are solely our own, and are only negatively affecting us, but the fact is, you are also hurting someone who loves you, and perhaps far more than you are hurting yourself. So, helping yourself is not selfish. Self-care and making yourself better is not selfish. When you better yourself, you indirectly help others with whom you come in contact, especially those who love and respect you.

Through combining consciousness or blending energies with others we can pass forth our happiness. "When you smile, the whole world smiles with you" is an old song lyric, but its message is very true. Whoever wrote it understood the meaning of combining consciousness. Try this yourself: walk through your house with a miserable look on your face and watch the other members of your family bring you their negative shit. Wake up the next day happy and excited, and watch them gravitate to you with good news. You will gain this ability to lift up others if you display positive behavior and attitude toward everything. This phenomenon is virtually universal.

By "doing for yourself," I mean helping yourself become a better person, taking care of yourself, and tackling the challenges you face in your life. I do not mean taking a vacation. (Not that there is anything wrong with a vacation, but that is not what I'm referring to here.)

The choices you make daily will determine the outcomes for you and those you affect. For example, if you have the option of taking on a problem of your own today and getting one step closer to resolving that problem, but instead of seizing this opportunity you decide to take the day off and go to the beach, some negative karma may come your way. An intentional lack of willingness to propel yourself one step forward ultimately harms those who love you and are influenced by you. Your own problems are to some extent the problems of everyone who cares for you. I am not suggesting you should never go to the beach or do something you enjoy, but generally speaking, if you bypass an opportunity given to you by the universe you will have a harder time getting a second chance, and the difficulty you are avoiding may only get worse, not only for you but for others around you.

Self-care helps others who care for you.

Taking care of yourself will lead to a more fulfilling life and will serve others indirectly. So then, what must we change to achieve inner happiness and self-love? Let's begin with some key factors.

No one can ever love us more than we love ourselves.

When I first received that statement, it resonated deeply with me. You can actually put a "stop limit" on being loved by others, simply by not loving yourself enough. I had heard the statement, "You can't love someone else unless you love yourself," but this takes it to another level. Over time, the more I've put this concept to the test in my own life, the more I've seen its validity.

This principle can be applied to success, finances, or any other metric by which one can measure oneself. You won't be given more if you believe your value or worth is what you already have or receive.

People do not rise above the image they have of themselves.

Here is another self-imposed "stop limit." If you think you are unworthy of something, that perception will become your truth. If you define yourself as "I'll never be wealthy," "or "I will never be healthy," then that is your truth. You set the limits for yourself.

It is possible to change these mindsets.

The human mind is programmable, and the subconscious mind will continue to run the program it was originally given until it is overwritten with another one. We will delve deeper into this concept in a later chapter.

Before you get too down on yourself, remember your original programming didn't start or come from you. Once you were born into this world, your subconscious was programmed with the beliefs of the others in your environment. And then you were sent on your way. Each of us is capable of retraining ourselves and re-parenting ourselves.

Journal Entry, June 5, 2020—"Meeting Vic"

I decided I was going to work on my life coaching certification. There were thirty-two students in the class, myself included. Classes were online through a video platform, so everyone could see one another. This was an important factor because we did exercises where we broke up into smaller groups of two or three and practiced coaching each other.

One day I was in a group of three students. We had to choose who would coach first and everyone was apprehensive, so I jumped in. (That's me in this latest portion of my life. As a young person I never wanted to be the one who went first. In fact, I would sit in the back and try to go unnoticed and never be called on in school. Now I am the complete opposite—I jump into the water without knowing the temperature because I know I won't die, and besides I am aware there are things far worse than death in this life.)

The student I was coaching was named Vic. During our greeting he said something that nearly knocked me off my chair. He was a veteran who had fought for our country and had needed an operation that was quite serious. In the midst of the operation, he died on the operating table, saw the light, and then returned to his body.

In all my studies I have been taught repeatedly this one golden rule: there are no coincidences! There was a purpose for my meeting Vic on this day, although at the moment I had no idea what it was.

In my last book I told a story of how I died and came back, how I hovered over my own body deciding whether I should go into the light or return. Since then, I had been searching for another person who'd had the same experience. It was my intention to compare notes and find out if their experience matched mine. It took me over twenty-five years to find Vic. Is it a coincidence that I found him around the same time I was writing these books? The timing of our meeting could not have been better as I entered this new chapter of my life. He gave me the validation and the courage to tell this story without fear.

I learned that Vic went further into the light than I had gone. He may have been dead for a longer period because in addition to the same things I had seen, he recounted more. I do not know the exact length of time either of us were dead, because there is this thing about death: one minute in our realm may seem like hours on the other side. There is no concept of time in the afterlife. Time is manmade, or at least man-perceived. I have had two out-of-body experiences, and in the second one I was gone for what felt like an hour, but when I returned to my body, I found that I had missed only a very small portion of the television show I had been watching.

Vic and I exchanged contact information. I will write about our conversations in upcoming books.

Journal Entry, June 24, 2021—"Rocking Out with My Glock Out"

Jessica decided to go visit her mom for a couple of days. She took the children with her because I can barely be entrusted with the care of the animal kingdom we have living in our home, let alone tiny humans. I was unable to go on this multi-day visit anyway because I had work: clients to see, paperwork to do, and hopefully some writing for this new book as well. Of course, I would miss them all because I love them, but on the positive side I would have the entire house to myself for two nights and three whole days. I was a little excited about that and here is why.

Would my female readers like to know what we men actually do when you go away for a few days? (Men are going to hate me for writing this.) It isn't what you might expect. You're probably thinking we're going to invite the guys over for a poker night or go out to a strip club and come home late. No frigging way would I waste a perfectly good night all alone with that shit.

Jessica left in the afternoon while I was still at the office—I wouldn't be home until about seven in the evening or so. We said our goodbyes by telephone, and I told her to text me when she arrived so I would know she'd made it there safely. I finally finished up at work, and within minutes of getting home I got the text, "We made it. I love you."

"I love you too," I replied, and with that it was official—I had the house. Me, only me! I was not inviting anyone over and definitely not leaving to go anywhere.

This was a rare event: like a fucking lunar eclipse. First things first—I removed all articles of clothing. Fuck clothes. I hate them. I made damn sure to walk into all the rooms that I could never be naked in. Then it was off to the kitchen—time to make food, anything I wanted. I could make a peanut butter and Swedish fish sandwich if I wanted. No one to judge me. But then I thought, *Why make anything at all? Everyone delivers food now. I will order food. A lot of food. Any food I want.* I grabbed the phone and went out to the deck (which happens to be another place I am not allowed to be naked) and ordered an obscene amount of take-out of which I planned to take one bite of each item and then discard the evidence. Okay, so food was on the way, and I had about an hour or so to kill. Then it hit me: I could watch anything I wanted on any television! Now, this was the life!

I found the latest John Wick movie: the most violent, good, old-fashioned revenge film I could find. The kind where someone does something bad to the good guy and then the good guy goes around and kills every bad guy in the film. You know the type. Food arrived about midway through, after about ninety-three bad guys had met their violent death for pissing off the protagonist. I told the delivery person it was best to leave the food on the doorstep and go. I didn't want him to be alarmed because another place I am never allowed to be naked is on the front porch, and this was my chance. I opened the door as the delivery man was pulling away, waved to him, and grabbed the food. I brought the plethora of edibles to the living room, and I was now naked on the couch watching the bad guys get blown up and shit, yelling at the television, *"Kill him!"* while eating no more than one bite of every delectable item on the Chinese menu. Life was good!

By the time the movie ended I was sick of the food, so I headed back to my home office with the big screen computer monitor, and I am not ashamed to say, I fired up the porn. I could kick back, relax, and rub one out without fear of being caught by anyone! I was living the dream!

Scrolling through the various porn clips to decide which to click on, I heard a big thud. Now that was strange, but it could have been the dog, the cat, the birds, the hermit crab, or the fish—*wait a minute, not the fish*. Maybe a groundhog tried to get into the garbage cans just below the window? Anyway, I ignored it and continued on my XXX movie hunt.

Then I heard it again. Now I had to go inspect. I walked around, checking every nook and cranny of the entire house with a huge bottle of pepper spray in one hand and my penis in the other. It was at this moment I began to realize just how big this fucking house really was. I had just recently moved in after I proposed marriage. Jessica had bought the house without me. If this had been my house, I'd have finished this security check very quickly. My house had no garage; I didn't have several bathrooms to decide where I was going to take my morning piss; I didn't have any guest rooms or extra bedrooms that had been turned into storage facilities with stuff we never use. *A game room? Who the fuck has a game room?* I was lucky growing up to have games, let alone a room designated for them. Then I searched the back yard, which had its very own back yard, and then there was the gazebo overlooking the swimming pool. *Ooh, I thought, I could watch porn in the gazebo! I'll save that for next time she goes to her mom's. (Note to self.)*

I was thinking: *I must pay attention, just like in the movie,* I was hunting bad guys in my compound. After a while I was convinced that there were no bad guys and I returned to my office with my big . . . ah . . . computer screen.

Okay, where was I? Looking for porn. Just as I got back to it, another noise in the hallway grabbed my attention, right outside the room I was in. I went out and took another look. Usually when I walk down the hall, nine times out of ten the dog will follow me thinking she can go outside, running past me under my legs to the back door. I felt her push past me as usual. I was about to look down and tell the dog we were not going outside right now, for literally a handful of reasons, but when I looked down there was no dog. *Oh shit, not now. No way; not now, go away- fucking dead person! This is a once-in-a-lifetime lunar eclipse. Go away!*

I sat back down at my computer, and it inexplicably shut down. I had not touched it. All I had done was sit my ass back down in my office chair and the computer switched itself off. I turned it back on. Moments later, the lights went out. Not in the entire house mind you, like your typical power outage, just in that one room I was in. The lights came back on quickly (about a second later) and I saw the ever-so-familiar black lines that shoot across the wall when I am being paid a visit from the other side, followed by some familiar vibrations—and I now knew exactly who I was dealing with. This could be the work of only one dead energy being: one who loves to break my blue fucking balls.

"*What the fuck, John?* I'm not cheating on your daughter. I'm watching porn. Do you seriously have nothing better to do?"

This was now getting weird. I know what you are thinking, *now it's getting weird?* I was beginning to lose the enjoyment, and so I gave up, and climbed the stairs to the bedroom. John was fucking with me, I knew. I could "feel" his laughter. He never did this sort of thing when Jessica was here, and I thought I knew why he was messing with me. Not that long ago I had gotten really pissed at him for the last message he had given me, because when I relayed it to Jessica, she got angry with *me*, even though I was just the messenger. So I'd been refusing to speak with him at all since then, and very effectively (or so I thought).

I headed up to the master bedroom which basically has a "his and hers" everything. Upon entering the room, the first thing you see is the master bed. If you're facing the bed, Jessica's side is to the right and mine is to the left. Therefore, her nightstand is on the right and mine on the left. The bed itself is usually neat with nice covers and pillows, both the kind you can sleep on, and the don't-dare-go-near-as-if-they-were-radioactive show pillows. We also have something called a duvet—I call it a fucking blanket.

Upon first glance at Jessica's nightstand you will observe a small replica of Mount Everest made up of various lotions, creams, and potions that keep her looking twenty-nine years old forever, along with several bottles of drinking water from all around the world—Poland Spring, Deer Park, Pellegrino, Evian, Voss, and Fiji to name a few (you never know which country may quench your thirst on any given evening I suppose)—plus several types of bubbly water with just a hint of fine flavoring, should the need for sparkly flavored water arise; tens of thousands of different types of vitamins (one for each part of her little body, including but not limited to her eyes, hair, toenails, and skin); a cell phone charger or two, plus the phone, of course; the iPad and its charger; a few other chargers of things we may have had years ago; a notebook for those middle-of-the-night, must-remember thoughts; the most recent bouquet of flowers from me (whether wanted: dead or alive); a photograph of us; and some mala beads, crystals, eyeglasses, two flashlights, and a massager-thingy that she supposedly uses on her "back" (I'm sure that is *exactly* where she uses it). In the midst of, and protruding through this marvelous, creative structure, held together like a Jenga puzzle, is the lamp which emits a soft glow of light just like a tall tree in the forest up on a hill as it seems to touch the sun.

I have a nightstand also. My nightstand, as you already know, is on the left if you, once again, are facing the bed (where you obviously have no business being in the first place). It has items on it too—a mobile phone, eyeglasses, a book, and one weapon of choice within arm's reach. (I remain a work in progress.) That comes to a grand total of four items and a lamp. You can actually see the base that supports my lamp, and the color of the night table as well. On this particular evening my book of choice was *The Art of Happiness*, authored by His Holiness The Dali Lama; and I slept with my Glock out.

Get your mind out of the gutter. I said "Glock." That was not a typo. A Glock 26 is a sub-compact, semiautomatic 9-millimeter handgun. This one was fully loaded with a ten-round magazine, and I also had two additional fully loaded ten-round clips, ready to be fired (just as much of course, as my other thing that rhymes with Glock was ready to be fired, but thanks to Jessica's dad neither one of those damned items were going to be fired on that completely ruined, lovely evening). My dream-night alone had turned into a nightmare!

CHAPTER 12

HIGHER LEVELS OF CONSCIOUSNESS

For anyone to achieve enlightenment, one must experience all emotions on the spectrum, many times over and again. You must experience sheer happiness and bliss. That seems to be an easy one. Most people have done so by finding a way to make it happen for them. I guarantee most often, the ways folks reach extreme happiness are actually artificial and, in some cases, unhealthy. They just think they are happy. Probably because someone told them what should make them happy. Perhaps buying an expensive car for example. Once you own and drive the car for a while, the bliss wears off and then you need a better car to achieve this state of happiness again. Try this with anything that makes you happy. I'll venture to bet that most of them don't give you any life long-lasting happiness. Does marriage make you happy forever? Of course not, but we are told it is supposed to. We are told that our partners are supposed make us happy. Are you fucking kidding me? No one is responsible for making someone else happy. It cannot actually be done. Many get divorced because they think that marriage is supposed to make them happy. The truth is, only you have the power and control to make yourself happy, sad or experience any other emotion. Divorce is usually quite traumatic. The marriages that make it forever, are the ones where each party is content. So, what does it mean to be enlightened? It means to be content for one thing. You'll never see emotions swinging from one side of the pendulum to another in an enlightened state. All nature lives this this way, somewhere in the middle, harmoniously, or else it dies.

Enlightenment is state of being at peace with all things. A state of contentment with being a part of all things. It is that feeling of oneness, or state of flow, whereby nothing is either good or bad. It just is.

This may be tough to swallow but you and I were not put here to be extremely happy. Too much happiness leads to the idea that you're supposed to be happy all the time, and that's impossible. This doesn't mean you can't experience being happy. It just means never expect it to be sustainable. The good news is neither is trauma or sadness. They will end eventually as well. If you are one who is always chasing happiness, you will never be happy for any length of time. The more anyone chases happiness, the more saddened and depressed they will eventually be. If you are often saddened, it goes without saying, you will not achieve a state of happiness. However, somewhere in the middle, which I call contentment; this is where true happiness lies. If you could remove ninety-eight percent of all your pain and suffering, isn't that by default a form of happiness? Suddenly, contentment just started sounding pretty good, didn't it? You don't have to chase happiness any longer when you learn to remove your sadness.

Can higher levels of consciousness be attained through experiencing trauma?

Let us examine trauma a little more closely. We learn things very quickly from trauma and suffering. To protect ourselves from a traumatic event while it is taking place, our minds may choose to disassociate from our bodies. At the time of the trauma, we may wish to escape our reality so badly that we push our minds to find another, more bearable place outside of our bodies and outside of our current existence. Even if our bodies must surrender to the traumatic event, or perhaps even realize death, the mind is so powerful that it can take you away from what you are experiencing. It is in these moments that it becomes possible to "break through the veil" that separates our realm from another.

Eckhart Tolle speaks quite candidly about his own experience before becoming enlightened when he felt suicidal. For me, the most memorable part of his story was the point at which he said, "I hate myself. I want to kill myself." In that moment Tolle wondered whether the fact that there was a "he" wanting to kill "himself" meant that there were actually two people or entities within his mind. He began to think, if so, then which one was he really? Which one had the ability to enforce change? Which one was the master of his destiny, and furthermore, where did this other one come from? That was the very beginning of his revelation. In order for "him" to hate "himself," there must have been a separate entity within deciding to think this way.

I was working recently with someone rather young who asked me why he'd had to go through so much trauma at a young age. If karma is real, what could he possibly have done at such a young age to deserve the traumas he faced? I paused for a few moments to see if he had his own answer to this question before I chimed in. I felt he knew the answer, but perhaps he needed to hear it out loud.

"Let's look at what changed in you, after the traumatic events." I asked him if he felt he was a different person as a result of those traumas.

"Absolutely yes."

I asked him to describe in what way he had changed. He looked confused for a moment, so I continued, "Is it safe to say that because of those traumatic events, you are now more motivated to achieve your life's goals?"

"Yes."

"And is it safe to say that you are closer to being fearless as you engage this process because you know for a fact that if you could live through that terrible shit, nothing can be as bad as that and take you down?"

"Yes."

"Is it safe to say you now have enough anger inside you, that you are able to tap into and use as the driving, motivating force behind your efforts, and therefore you will not let anything stand in the way of accomplishing your goals?"

"Hell, yes!"

"Are you going to do what you set out to do and achieve those goals?"

"You better believe it."

"So then," I said, "Did you get anything positive from those traumatic experiences that helped you evolve from the person you once were into the person you are now?"

He nodded vigorously and gave me a huge smile.

Before you take the attitude of "Why me?" I encourage you to adopt the attitude of "Try me!" You see, it's like they say: whatever doesn't kill you makes you stronger. Truth be told, it doesn't actually matter if it kills you because you'll still have the benefits in the afterlife. Nevertheless, the idea is correct. Each and every trauma you have gone through in your life has helped you evolve into a stronger energy force. You have become less fearful, more motivated through anger, and you could handle more than the next person because you actually did handle more than the next person.

Look at those who have had everything handed to them in life. Do you think they have the power and passion to go out and accomplish the same things as someone who came from nothing and had to fight and experience failure and pain in order to succeed? There is nothing more empowering than overcoming the worst shit life can throw at you. If you have done that, you are stronger than the rest. Now act like it!

Never allow yourself to play the role of victim. Fuck that! You are not a victim. You were given those traumatic events to make you stronger than others. You are more evolved and empowered by your experiences, the good and the bad. We learn and grow in tremendous leaps and bounds through exposure to the latter. We all must experience our share of good and bad in order to become enlightened beings.

I am sure I've said this before, but the one common denominator I've noticed among all advanced evidential mediums is that we all have endured repetitive traumas. And that, my friend, is certainly no coincidence. Surviving trauma is a blessing, not a curse.

I recently learned a little about Navy SEAL training. For those who do not know, the SEALs are an elite task force with very few members. They have one mission: to destroy their target by any means necessary. They are trained killing machines. If your name is on their hit list, you are going to die. It's simply a matter of when.

Many soldiers and sailors aspire to be part of this elite group, but most cannot withstand the training. In order to drop out of Navy SEAL training you must remove your helmet, walk to the center of the training facility where there is a large bell, pick up the mallet and ring the bell. All these steps are required by the rules and regulations because they want to make absolutely certain that you want out. How many trainees do you suppose ring the bell and tap out? I have read various statistics and the lowest rate

I could find was 85 percent. The highest report stated 99 percent ring the bell. Even if the higher of the two numbers is exaggerated, the point here is that the overwhelming majority cannot make it through the training. Let us look at what this training consists of and a theory as to why these percentages are so high.

Aspiring Navy SEALs must go through a six-month training and selection process that is broken up into three phases. The infamous "Hell Week" portion happens at the end of the first phase and lasts for six days, during which students run more than two hundred miles (often while holding boats above their heads), swim relentlessly, do hours of physical training with heavy logs, and go through many other grueling tests. Getting little more than four hours of sleep throughout the whole week, they are constantly wet, cold, and sandy. They are fed eight thousand calories per day, yet they still lose weight. Broken limbs, muscle contusions, lung injuries, and blackouts (from swimming underwater for long periods) are not uncommon. Deaths also may occur.

Are the soldiers in great physical shape the only ones who make it through this process? Does one have to be as powerful as a superhero? The short answer is no. When SEAL Team instructors were asked why the dropout rate was so high, they said the primary reason had less to do with physical abilities and capabilities, and more to do with mental anguish. The Instructors admitted that the training was ninety percent mental toughness, and that was the reason most could not make it through. The instructors pushed each trainee to his psychological breaking point to see exactly where that was.

Why do you suppose the military puts such a premium on psychological toughness when it comes to being part of an elite military group? It is because they realize that physicality is not as important as your mental capacity under stress and duress. They deliberately subject these soldiers to trauma after trauma for weeks on end to see what they can endure psychologically. To figure out which of these guys are the best, their instructors put them through their worst.

The troops that succeed begin as sailors and evolve into SEALs after about a year of the most traumatic experiences of their lives. Think about it. Maybe you, in your personal life, are like a Navy SEAL.

Journal Entry, May 19, 2020—"You're the Boss"

Jessica and I were exhausted and about to fall asleep. We both have difficulty sleeping at times (you would too if you were being visited regularly by strange energies), but this was one of those rare occasions when both of us were ready to fall asleep almost immediately. But when we shut off the television, Jessica heard a scream. She asked me if I'd heard it too, but I hadn't. She had been hearing a few "word drops" here and there as of late and I knew that this too must be related to that; it's not unlike the dead to scream if they get frustrated trying to reach you, but it's scary and annoying. I had been down this road many times and I always took care of it right away; if any energy being wants my help, they had better never scare me or anyone I love. If they break that rule, they are fucking dead to me. (Okay, poor choice of words—they are banished for life. Damn! That won't work either. They are banished forever from communicating with me and from ever receiving my help.)

Jessica was almost shaking with fear. It's a horrible feeling when you are new to this and still trying to figure out what is happening. Was the scream something that originated in the house or in another realm? After the scream she heard a high-pitched sound on one side of her head—I am also familiar with these sounds, which are definitely from the other side. This is typically how my guides contact me and try to help guide me to navigate life. Once I explained that what she was hearing was coming from a guide, Jessica calmed down some, but she was still freaked out over the "word drop" she had heard. She was scared and I was pissed off.

My heart was racing with anger, but I very calmly said, "Jessica, you are the boss of them. You make the rules. These energy beings do not." This is our world and as such, humans make the rules in our realm of existence. They are the visitors and if they are unwanted guests, we can throw them out. I decided to enter an altered state, to cross over and communicate and ream out whoever was there. I took an angry breath and dove into an altered state where I could see both realms.

"Jessica," I said, "there is nothing here anymore."

"Well," she replied, "apparently you are the boss, because you just made everything stop."

You may have experienced a word drop or these sounds I referenced. They are not uncommon. In fact, many times when I explain what this phenomenon is, the person I am speaking with will remember an occasion when this has happened to them. If you have, you will not use your ears to hear them, only the mind. All five physical senses can be experienced using your sixth sense, which is consciousness. Everyone has this ability. In my first book I explained why the sixth sense was removed from the early medical journals. It was during the early 1400s and the church was considered all-powerful and all-knowing. They didn't like the idea of people being able to communicate with anyone or anything on the other side. So they pressured these early scientists to remove references to this from their textbooks. How did they do that? By killing those who resisted, of course. Anyone who crossed the line was called a heretic and burned at the stake.

After three hundred years of killing people who went against the church, science gave up and held on to only five of the six senses.

Journal Entry, September 25, 2020—"Jessica, You're Glowing!"

Jessica and I went to a resort in upstate New York for a few days. This particular place was nicknamed "Little Tibet" because it had that look—like old Tibet when the Dalai Lama lived there.

The place was so beautiful: trees and mountains in the middle of a valley, a yurt, a sanctuary, a swimming pool, indoor and outdoor yoga, fresh foods from the garden grown on the property, Buddhist symbolism everywhere, and real hiking—not the type where you walk an easy dirt path, but up a mountain over a waterfall and down to the pond. The resort had its own well for water, a spa on the property, and all food was vegan.

It was said that the resort was built in a crater made by a meteorite that hit that spot millions of years ago, and that once you got on the property, your energy would change as it took in the energy of the surroundings.

It was a Friday evening, about 7 o'clock, and we had just taken showers and sat down to rest. Jessica and I got into a deep conversation regarding the Buddhist culture and manifestation. As the conversation continued, Jessica was sitting on the edge of the bed, and I was in a chair at the desk which I had turned around to face her directly. She was explaining to me her thoughts on manifestation . . . when it happened.

I began to blink continuously because I felt that something was wrong with my eyes. I was looking at Jessica but seeing something unexplainable. I continued to blink, and then tilted my body and head to my left, and then to my right. I could tell at that point that Jessica knew something was up. I blinked harder and faster to get whatever it was out of my eyes. *This is completely impossible*, I thought. We had just come back from dinner, so I thought—were those *magic* mushrooms we had eaten?

Radiating from Jessica's body was a light pink and white glow. It extended three to four inches and completely surrounded her head, shoulders, arms, and down to her waist. I was moving about to see if it was just a shadow, but each time I moved it was still there. No matter what I did the light remained. It was beautiful. I interrupted her and said "Jessica, you're glowing."

"Oh, thank you," she said. "It's this new cream I purchased from . . ."

"No, not that!" I interrupted. "I mean, I can see your energy. I can see your aura."

I had heard about this phenomenon but hadn't experienced it firsthand until now. It was amazing. I was looking at her energy in the form of light! All of us radiate energy. It isn't typical to see energy. For example, you typically cannot see the radio frequency signals that go from your mobile phone to the nearest tower, or the WIFI signal from your modem to the computer, but we know they are there. I think if we were to continually witness all the energy around us it would be overwhelming.

CHAPTER 13

MANIFESTATION THROUGH MEDITATION

Have you ever seen or heard folks chanting during meditation? Chanting makes the vibrations of the sound of the chant run through your body and mind and out into the universe. The spiritually engaged brain vibrates at the frequency of the earth. This can be incredibly powerful. You can likely find videos online where folks are chanting at different frequencies. Frequencies are measured in units called hertz. The higher the frequency, the faster something is vibrating. You will find that different frequencies may make you feel differently. Find the frequency that sounds and, more importantly, *feels* right for you. Make it a part of your meditation practice. It will make a considerable difference.

I will be the first to admit I had no idea why people sat around like a lotus flower on the floor, with their eyes shut, chanting sounds. That was until my mentor made me try it. ("Wax on, wax off," as Mr. Miyagi said.)

Sometimes I just shut up and take the advice of my teachers without question. They have proven themselves to be correct time and again. I am certainly not one to argue about the secrets of the universe. Remember, not long ago I was the idiot atheist who accidentally discovered that there is an afterlife.

In this instance my "Mr. Miyagi" was Medium Joe. He said that, to manifest the things you want, you must begin meditating and chanting with the primordial sound of "AH" and the universal sound of "OM." This is not the only way to manifest things, but it is likely one of the best. "Do this for at least ninety days," he said. I will now share with you this wonderful, amazing, process, and later in the book I will explain how it works.

For now, just take it in and start practicing these techniques. I promise you this is the greatest gift I or anyone can give you. This is how to create your own life's experience. I use this myself every day. I have taught it to hundreds of people who have found success with it. There is no better gift than giving people control of their lives. You really can have it all. You just have to know exactly how to ask for it. Due to its immense importance, let me repeat that: *You must know exactly how to ask for it.*

I am going to assume you already know how to meditate. If you don't, then please refer to my first book and the chapters on meditating. Then return here and read on. I am going to give you techniques to add to your meditation. To do this most efficiently, I suggest getting two soundtracks ahead of time and having them nearby. You might store them on your smart phone and listen using headphones, but that is optional. You need one track with the chant of "AH" and a second track with the chant of "OM." Play these recordings during your meditation times and chant along, or just be quiet and listen, feeling the vibration of each chant as the sounds move through your physical being and then out to the universe. Being able to alter your vibrational state is the key to unlocking the door to the laws of vibration and attraction.

Here is the process. In the morning, the first thing to do upon awakening is meditate. It doesn't have to be the very first thing you do, but it is best to meditate before you start the day. You can practice for five minutes or thirty minutes, with the latter being better of course, but please try not to skip it. I realize that having time in the morning may be difficult. Even if you can only meditate for two minutes due to time constraints, that is better than nothing. It must be done with consistency to work successfully.

Never think that because you cannot dedicate a half hour to this process it is better to skip it. That is not the case. Shorten the amount of time you practice, if need be, but do it. It will set the tone for the rest of your day.

There is also a meditation to be done in the evening. This one may be easier to dedicate more time to, as you will likely have more time to plan it. This may be done just as you are getting into bed to go to sleep. It may even help you sleep better, and you may find that you prefer it to picking up an electronic device to see a social media post of what your friend had for dinner.

This is a twice-a-day meditation process: once in the morning and once in the evening.

Remember how I mentioned that my mentor taught me to give this process ninety days before expecting to see results? Well, my first manifestation came much sooner than that. Some of the folks I have taught this to have had results come sooner as well. However, as this is the way I was taught, this is the way I will pass it on to you. Of course, individual results will vary, and nothing is guaranteed. Let us begin.

Step one is the attitude of gratitude.

First things first. After several deep breaths, begin listening to the soundtrack playing the chant of "AH." Again, you may chant with it or just listen to it. Feel the sound go through your body. You are changing your frequency through this practice. After just a little while we will go into what I call "the attitude of gratitude." To do this part, say aloud or to yourself all the things you are grateful for—you will have plenty to choose from. Even if you hate your job, be thankful and grateful that you have one. Even if you hate your car, be thankful you have one to get you around. It can be anything. Find the positives.

For example: I am grateful for the roof over my head; I am grateful for the food I have to eat; I am grateful for my loving family, and so on. Don't worry if you forget something. You can always add it in later if you want or even tomorrow. Nothing bad will happen if you forget something. It doesn't work that way.

Step two is stating what you will manifest.

For the next few minutes return to the chant of "AH." By now you'll be breathing more slowly; repeat a few more AHs. You can go back to listening to the sound AH in your mind or chant it aloud. Feel the sound going through your body once again. By this point you have already changed your mood, your mind, and your frequency for the better. I have yet to meet anyone who has completed their attitude of gratitude and found themselves in a bad mood. I don't think it is possible.

Then begin to think and say what it is you want to achieve, or have, or what it is you wish to manifest. You can also say things like, "Show me the way," or "Show me the path to get what I want." When I am in a deep meditation, I will often ask the universe to show me how to do something. "Show me the way to achieve what I want." If you don't know what you want, you can ask to be shown what is best for you. "Show me what I should be manifesting at this point in my life." Continue to listen to the AHs in the background, and you will now begin to manifest.

When I have asked for money, I typically say what I will use the money for. I don't know if this makes a difference but I feel better when I say I need this money so I can help more people. This way it doesn't seem to be about greed. Unfortunately, bad people can and will manifest bad stuff. But karma will catch up with them later.

So, what are the rules, or what is the catch?

There really aren't many rules at all. However, there is one rule that if you break it, you will get the opposite of what you seek! Therefore, please pay close attention. Do you recall earlier I said most people do not know how to ask for things?

You must speak or think in the affirmative tense when you ask for anything.

The universe does not speak English, or Spanish, or Italian, or any other language. It speaks in vibration, using the visuals you see in your mind when you think or speak. The vibration that emits from you when you picture something in your mind is converted into vibrations and sent out of your being into the world. Like vibrations attract one another and unlike vibrations repel one another. Are you starting to see how the law of attraction works scientifically?

Here is an example. Let's say you are having money problems and during the manifestation portion of meditation you repeat, "I don't want to be in debt." The problem here is that the universe doesn't understand the terms "don't want." The visual message you are sending out only involves *you* and *debt* (which may look like a pile of bills in your mailbox or whatever image comes to you with the word "debt"). The universe will receive only the visuals translated through vibration—the picture of *you* and the picture of *debt* combined with the vibration that those pictures create—and guess what you are going to get? More debt would be on its way to you.

Never ever ask for what you do not want!

How should you ask for money? Try this: "I want an abundance of money." Now the visuals are *you* and perhaps a pile of *money* or however you visualize currency or wealth. Maybe you see it as a large amount in your bank statement. The point is you cannot ever tell the universe what you *do not* want. It will never work, and you will only get more of what it is you do not want.

Another example is, "I don't want to be sick anymore." Can you see the problem with that statement? Change it to, "I want to be healthy." Or better yet, "I will be healthy." Another one may be, "I don't want to be overweight." Change that to, "I want to be in great physical shape." Or "I will be in great physical shape." Your speech and thought patterns will determine the outcome of your life! Begin to fix these patterns through meditation and you will take notice of the effects. Additionally, use this technique with all of your thoughts throughout the rest of each day and watch your entire life change.

If you believe it, your mind can achieve it.

Here is another very important rule: whatever it is you ask for, it must be conceivable and believable to you. For example, I personally would not ask for one billion dollars because I cannot fathom what one billion dollars looks like, feels like, or what I would feel like if I had it. I have no experiences connected to that much money, or anyone who has that much money, and therefore it is not something believable to me. This may not be the case for someone else. Money is relative. If I am going to ask for a certain amount of money, it must be a number I can relate to or know what it might feel like to have. You need to be able to envision yourself with it, believe it can be real, and use all your senses to experience it in your mind. You will use your sixth sense (consciousness) to recreate the other five physical senses in your mind. If you can do that regularly, whatever it is you are seeking is most likely believable to you and therefore possible for you to have. You can work your way up to one billion dollars in believable increments, if that is really what you want.

Let us say you have a job that pays you $100,000 dollars a year. You know what having $100,000 dollars feels like because you have experienced it. It is fathomable to visualize it. So now perhaps you would like to have that $100,000, but in one lump sum. You have experience with that amount of money already, but now you are saying, "I need one year's salary in one lump sum right now." That is easier for you to imagine while engaging all your senses.

Please do not get the impression that this practice is limited to money, because it isn't. You can manifest love, health, happiness, goals to be accomplished, a new job or career, what you want Santa to bring you, and much more. I use money as the example because it is an easy concept that everyone can understand and relate to.

Allow yourself ninety days to receive your manifestation.

I mentioned earlier that your manifestation could present itself in ninety days or sooner, and that individual results will vary. Don't expect a bag of money to fall out of the sky. This isn't magic. You will be shown the way to get it or achieve your manifestation. It may not come within that time frame. Perhaps what you seek is too big to come in ninety days. Don't get upset or give up, just alter it a little to make it easier. Some things come in pieces—like that office chair you ordered from Ikea—and others come already assembled.

In addition to achieving goals or getting what it is you want; you should probably have a fairly good reason for getting it. This is not a law or rule that must be followed. However, it is morally important to keep this in mind, especially when asking for money: Will the money be used for a noble cause? Are you going to start a car collection with the money, or feed the hungry? You are allowed to have a car collection, don't get me wrong; but it would be best to have a positive spiritual reason attached to your request, like feeding the poor, donating to a shelter for the homeless, helping to fund a cure for something dreadful, donating to some cause, and the like. If you are planning to ask for money so that you can do something destructive with it, I advise you to take this book, tear it to pieces, and use it to line the bottom of your birdcage. Use it to collect bird-shit, because that is exactly what will be coming your way if you get the money—you will get plenty of other people's shit. It will be attracted to you, and it will find you. Karma is everywhere and it is inevitable.

Most of the wealthiest people on the earth created businesses that served two purposes: one was the business aspect, or the mission that was based on money or profit; the other, however, was more "spiritual" in nature, more virtuous. A successful business should have both a financial and a spiritual mission. For example, Microsoft made the personal computer easy for everyone on the planet to use in their home; as a result, people all over the world were suddenly empowered and enabled to start businesses from home, create environments for people to learn new things, even in remote areas, or communicate with one another in a simple-to-use, nearly limitless environment. This made Bill Gates one of the richest men in the world, as he should be, but he also changed mankind for the better. That was the spiritual side to his business. If you can create a business that gives people what they want and at the same time changes their lives for the better, then you have manifested a livelihood with both a financial and a spiritual mission.

Don't get greedy using this formula.

I promise you that greed will be met with negative karma every time. I know of some very wealthy people who are extremely miserable. Money cannot buy you happiness, but changing the world for the better using your money can.

So, why the chanting and what is it for? Let's break this down.

The Primordial Sound of "AH"

The power in the sound of "AH" comes from the various names which have been given to the Creator of All Things, such as God, Jehovah, Allah, Brahma, Yahweh, and so on. Different religions and cultures have fashioned various words for the "Creator of All Things," but you will notice that they all contain the sound of "AH." It is the sound of creation.

"AH" is an extremely powerful sound for achieving higher levels of consciousness. It is used for the manifestation of goals. Think of what you wish to have or to manifest in your life—love, wealth, abundance, peace, joy, or happiness; focus on this goal during your meditation and repeat your goal to yourself in between chanting the "AH" sound.

Make this your morning meditation. Upon waking, begin your meditation with an attitude of gratitude by thanking the universe for everything you already have. Follow this with the "AH" chant and finish up with what it is you wish to manifest. Lastly, make your request, "Please show me the way to get what I want or need. I need this now." Then, I often close my own meditations with the statement. "So it is said and so it shall be." This final statement I learned from Dr. Paul Leon Masters, who wrote much of the college level curriculum for the University of Sedona, where I studied. This was for him a very important statement to close with, and so it is for me as well.

Remember that you are the co-creator of all things. If you don't believe me, read on. I will show you.

Next up:

The Universal Sound of "OM"

The power in the sound of "OM" manifests peace within and around you. OM is considered one of the most sacred chants in existence.

The sound of OM should ideally be combined with feelings of gratitude and thankfulness for the good in your life. In between chanting OM you may thank the universe and express your gratitude. Once you have done that, return to thinking of and visualizing your manifestation in between the chants of OM, the same as you have done with AH.

In the evenings, before bedtime, begin your second meditation using the chant "OM." This meditation may last longer than your morning one as you will probably have more time to do it. We begin the same way, with an attitude of gratitude, thanking the universe for all that it has given you thus far.

Then go into your "OM" chanting for a few minutes. In between the chants tell the universe what it is you want to manifest. You can also manifest for others in this way as well—there is nothing wrong with that. After you have asked for what you want, remain in meditation for a time. By now you should be very relaxed, and it is likely that you will not want to leave this meditation for a long while. It may help you fall asleep also.

Two meditations per day—one in the morning upon waking and the other in the evening before going to bed. Do this for ninety days. After the first one is completed, the results will likely come quicker as you continue to practice. This exercise is extremely powerful. As the co-creator of the universe, you have the right to make changes to it, especially when it is for your own life. Use it for good and enjoy!

Neville Goddard tells a really great story about manifestation. He had gone to Barbados for several speaking and teaching engagements. He did not know how long he would remain there, so he purchased a one-way ticket for himself and his family. The primary form of transportation in those days was a boat or a large cruise liner.

Then he got a call to return to America for something essential, and he had to get back rather quickly. He went to purchase a ticket, only to find that there was a two-year waiting list. It was explained to him that even if by some remote chance someone canceled, there was a list of over a thousand people waiting to travel from Barbados to the States.

He returned to his hotel room, sat in a chair, and meditated. He pictured himself boarding the ship to take him to America. In his mind he saw himself going up the gangplank. He did this repeatedly, up and down the plank, handing the man the tickets for himself and his family. He knew that the mind must see things repeatedly to manifest them into reality. And he used all five senses as he visualized: he felt the railing as he climbed on board; he smelled the sea air as it entered his lungs; he saw the morning sun in his eyes. The very next day he received a message in his room that a ticket for him and his family had become available—would he like to purchase it? Someone had canceled. He bought the ticket and returned to America.

He later found out that the woman who had purchased the ticket had cancelled because she was too afraid to go to America. What was the reason for her fear? It doesn't matter. Maybe in her universe it wasn't time for her to go to America. Then what made the cruise liner offer the ticket to him instead of the more than one thousand other people? Was it simply an error or some form of universal intervention?

When he got to America he went to stay in a hotel in New York and was visited by his two brothers. They wanted to see the musical *Aida* and asked if he could arrange two tickets for them. But the play had been sold out for months in advance and there was no way to get tickets. His brothers were extremely disappointed because that was the main attraction they wanted to see in New York.

Understanding how upset his brothers were, Neville Goddard returned to the chair in his hotel room and told the universe he needed two tickets to the show. He told the universe the tickets weren't for him. "This is only to make my brothers happy. I do not have to go see the play, so just two tickets will do." He visualized his goal again and again, the same way he had for the tickets from Barbados.

The night of the play, he and his brothers decided to go by the ticket booth just in case. There were three lines that led to the teller windows. He said, "Just for fun, let's see what happens if we try to get tickets." He got in line behind an exceptionally large, tall, muscle-bound man who asked for two tickets to another show. The teller handed the tickets to the man, who paid the teller with two one-dollar bills. The tickets were ten dollars each in those days. The teller asked the man where the rest of the money was, but he said, "I gave you two ten-dollar bills." The teller said, "No, you didn't," at which point the man began to walk away. Neville Goddard yelled at the man in front of everyone in line, demanding that he get back there and pay the teller correctly at once. "I saw what you did," he said. This huge guy could have leveled him with one punch, but for some reason, the man paid the eighteen-dollar difference and went on his way.

Then the teller asked Neville, "Can I help you?"

He said, "Yes. I would like two tickets to the show *Aida*, and I would like them front and center in the first couple of rows, please."

The teller said, "Yes sir, coming right up." He handed him what were arguably the best seats in the house. Neville happily gave them to his brothers to enjoy.

How did this happen? Well, each theater that is "sold out" always keeps on hand a few tickets for the VIPs who show up at the last minute, such as actors, directors, producers, celebrities—or even the President, if he feels like seeing a show. Even though Neville was a complete unknown at the time, he was a very important person to that teller on that day. You see, the teller would have had to pay the eighteen dollars out of his own pocket—which was close to a week's pay back then.

How does manifestation work? Let us dive in.

To make this concept work to your advantage, use your conscious mind to repeatedly feed the subconscious imaginary information so that the subconscious thinks it is real. Since our perception of reality is our truth, eventually our truth becomes our reality.

Your perception of your reality will overpower the reality of your perception every single time.

You may want to pause here and reread that once more.

Example: To the man who only has a hammer, everything he encounters begins to look like a nail.

You may ask, "How does this perception migrate from inside my mind into the physical world?" This is the good stuff. I get really excited when I explain this.

Part of your consciousness is integrated into the universal collective consciousness and is part of that oneness or the singularity of all mankind. It's that huge Internet of all consciousness that is connected by energy, frequency, and vibration. This is how you know you are co-creator of the universe, because you are connected to its source: energy. This totality of energy is often referred to as God, the Universe, the Source, the Creator, the Light, and so on. You are connected to that which many refer to as our "God mind." The "God mind" term was coined by Dr. Paul Leon Masters. It is perfect to explain this concept.

In different philosophical beliefs this "God mind" is given different names, but it is in essence the same thing. Remember, all religions have told us, "God is within you, and you are a part of God." This statement is literal.

Take this information and enjoy your life. Go out and co-create. This is the so-called "secret" some may not want you to know because it is so powerful, and people covet power for themselves. Most religions know this truth already, or at the very least, knew it at one point; but they would rather keep this information to themselves so they can appear to be the distributor of this power, telling you to complete their specific rituals to achieve certain desired results. Folks then thank the religion for their good fortune and look to its leaders as the beneficent authorities who protect them and allow them to be redeemed and blessed when they only need to thank themselves and the power of their own minds. I am not suggesting anyone abandon their religion. I would never do that. If you like it, keep it, but you can add this understanding to your life and be truly happy. No religion can deny the fact that God is a part of you, and you are a part of God. Now tell me, how awesome is that?

The Side Effects of AHs and OMs

While *en route* to your manifestation goal, and thereafter, other things may begin to come into your life, typically in the form of synchronicities. Since you are raising your frequency to be able to speak with the universe and communicate on that level, other things may begin to fall into place. Answers to questions you have been seeking for a very long time may seem to appear out of nowhere. Life overall may seem to be easier to figure out. The world, which perhaps you viewed as this large, out-of-control place, may seem to get quite small and manageable for you. Problems become easier to solve. You may find you have less anxiety, anger, and other unwanted emotions. It may seem that, more often than not, everything comes together for you as planned.

You will find yourself in a flow state more often—it is one of the most wonderful feelings. You will fall in love again with yourself and the world.

Journal Entry, March 18, 2021—Thank You . . . *More Please*!

I woke this day like any other; getting up while it was still dark outside, before sunrise. Made some coffee and greeted the day. Everyone else lay asleep in their beds. It was a peaceful morning, and yet I was met with unrest as I made my way outside: a pain in my chest; the sound of loud, disturbing light language in one ear; and a premonition I could not piece together. That is one of the most annoying feelings I get—when a vision is trying to make its way through to me, but for some reason, it cannot. Furthermore, I knew this one was serious in nature. I felt like the blockage was on my side—I had been feeling clogged for a few days and realized I needed to remove the blocks. Such energy blocks can be caused by a variety of factors, including just the distractions of everyday life.

Jessica and I were also transitioning at this time: moving in together, creating and merging our businesses, purchasing a yoga/meditation/wellness center, and telling the world about the first book which was recently released—all this while I was writing the second book, studying metaphysics in school, and working with my mentors. It was exhausting, but thrilling at the same time. We were so happy and excited for the future and continued to work diligently to make all a reality.

I decided to have an energy clearing just as I described in the first book, which has the power of realigning my energy, connecting me with my higher self, thus allowing energy and information to flow freely to and from my God mind.

My spiritual clearing was to be done in the early morning, but I had forgotten that this was the day. I sat at my desk to begin my workday when my phone beeped. The clearing was about to begin. This type of energy healing does not require the subject to be in the same location as the healer. I was delighted, because if anything could get rid of this feeling and give me some much-needed clarity, it was this. I paused what I was doing, put on some meditation music, and went into a trance-like state. Exactly twenty minutes went by. I looked at the clock and it was like a light switch had been turned on and I could see with all the clarity I needed. I felt as though a weight had been removed from my shoulders. I wanted to climb up on my desk and jump up and down—except then people would know for sure that I am insane. Once this dreadful blockage was removed, I was off to the races. Jessica and I had much to do, and it required some money to proceed.

We were manifesting things faster than ever before. I remember one time needing a certain large sum of money quickly to pay for some of the things we were doing, and I had to pay my typical year-end tax bill as well. I did my usual manifestation meditations, morning and night, telling the universe point blank, "I am creating something to help others, something big, but I need your help and I need this money now, please." Three days later I received a package in the mail. Before I tell you, what was in the package, I must first mention that a few weeks earlier I had given all of my annual financial records to my accountant for the purpose of preparing my year-end taxes. He typically calls me when he is finished and lets me know how much I will need to set aside to pay the annual tax bill. I appreciate that he lets me know in advance so I can get everything in order. This year, however, I had not heard back from him, which was quite unusual.

That being said, let us return to the package I received in the mail. I opened it; it was from my accountant. The letter inside said that I was to receive a refund. This must have been the reason why the accountant hadn't called me back—I didn't have to pay anything as I was due this refund. This doesn't usually happen to me. In fact, I can't remember the last time I got money back for overpayment. The letter went on to say that there were going to be two different refunds coming, one from the state and the other from the federal government. When I added the two amounts together, can you guess how much it was? That's right! It was just a few dollars more than the exact amount I had asked for in my manifestation meditation— something like twelve dollars and some cents more, if memory serves. I fell to my knees. I was completely overwhelmed with emotion. There simply was no denying that those monies came as a result of my asking the universal collective for them.

Jessica and I had discussed that if we were to make enough money to be comfortable, we would begin taking on as many pro bono clients as we could. We especially would like to help the younger generations. The younger people we have worked with have absorbed these concepts easily and embraced them without prejudice.

I thanked the Universe for everything—and I do mean *everything*. I had much to be grateful for. Jessica and I practiced our meditation for manifestation regularly, both in the mornings and in the evenings. During this particular meditation I again asked for more money. I had an unexpected need for $4,000 relatively quickly. About a week went by when I saw an unusual deposit in my bank account. I had been given $4,200. It had come once again from the government, and again it was slightly more than I had requested in my meditation.

The funds were used as planned to help build the businesses and promote the books that will hopefully help people. I meditated again and was extremely grateful for these funds. It still wasn't enough for me to quit my day job and dedicate myself full time to this new venture. So I called on the universe again. The next day we had a meeting at work. In this meeting the president of our company reminded us that we were considered independent contractors and not employees. Therefore, we qualified for a loan dedicated to help us through the difficult financial times we all had been experiencing because of the pandemic sweeping through our country. The best part of this loan money was that, so long as you used it for payroll expenses, you were not required to pay it back. Well, of course it was to be used to pay myself what I had lost the year before.

The pandemic was also the reason I qualified for the previous tax refund I had received, and the other $4,200 given to me as part of the economic stimulus package put into place by our country's lawmakers at that time. We were extremely thankful for this relief money because during the pandemic our businesses were shut down for months. We had no way of recovering from that, had the government not stepped in and helped. I received the tax refund, the stimulus check, and the forgivable loan I did not have to pay back. The irony here is that each amount of money I received was always just a few dollars more than the number I requested. There are no coincidences!

There is one more part to this story. I had wanted to take advantage of a marketing opportunity to help advertise the book launch, but by now money was tight. The cost was about $2,000 and so I was contemplating putting it on a credit card and paying it off. I was thinking about asking the universe again but had gotten so much recently, I wasn't sure that would be the right thing to do.

I was thinking about this, one morning at my day job. I was literally in the bathroom, when my mobile phone rang. It was my accountant. I thought, "Oh shit, here it comes. They want the money back." I waited until the very last ring before I answered.

"Hello Bill, how are you?"

"I'm great. And you?"

"I am well, thanks for asking."

"Are you sitting down? I have something to tell you."

"Oh yes, I'm sitting down, all right." (Right on the toilet bowl but he didn't need that information--neither did you, I suspect!)

Fuck! Here it comes. I just fucking knew it. I wonder how much I'll have to give back.

He said, "In my fifty-plus years as an accountant, I have never had this happen to any client."

Why am I not surprised in the least?

"I just got a call from the IRS."

Oh shit, this is worse than I thought.

"What is it?"

"They wanted me to tell you that due to a very recent change in the tax law they owe you at least another $2,000—and they will get that additional refund to you in the next few weeks."

I was speechless.

"Are you there?"

"Um, yes," I replied. "Is that it? Is that everything?"

"Yes, that's it—can you believe it?"

"No, no I cannot, but I'll take it! Thank you. Thank you! *More please!*"

Journal Entry, May 22, 2021—"The Hits Just Keep on Coming"

One Saturday after leaving my full-time day job permanently, to begin my new career as a metaphysical and spiritual life coach, I was seeing some of my coaching clients at our office. As one of my clients' sessions ended, she began to walk out the door to a hallway that leads to the elevator. A delivery service had left a few packages just outside our door. When my client was leaving, she said, "Did you know that you have some packages out here?"

"No, I didn't. Thank you. I'll be right there to get them."

I picked up the boxes and moved them into my office and noticed that one of them was not a typical brown box with minimal writing on it, but rather a bright blue and white box that was kind of heavy. The labeling on the outside indicated that the box contained a currency counter. I had never ordered such an item. In fact, none of our businesses are set up to accept cash as a form of payment, only credit and debit cards. I looked to see whether it was addressed to myself or Jessica. The latter was the case, but I had no idea why she would have ordered it.

After seeing my last client of the day, I headed over to see Jessica at the yoga studio. As I stepped into our newly furnished and decorated studio, I was floored by its beauty: attractive works of art, flourishing plants, and even a gong imported from Nepal. You could just submerge yourself in the peaceful and tranquil ambiance.

I walked in and complimented Jessica on the amazing job she'd done setting up the studio. If I had handled it, the colors likely would have been limited to blue, black, and white, and the decor probably would have consisted of a picture of the Buddha and a phallic-inspired spot of art. (Don't judge me. I am, as I said, a work in progress.) Anyway, good thing I'm not in charge.

I told Jessica I had to run back down to the car to grab the packages that had come to our office. As I was walking out, I asked her, "Why did you purchase a cash counting machine? We rarely accept cash as a form of payment."

"What is a cash counting machine?" she said.

"It counts cash, like the machines they use in banks, and it's for when there's too much cash for anyone to count by hand."

"Oh," she said. "Why did you order one of those?"

"I didn't. I thought *you* did. It has your name on it."

"I never ordered it."

"Who would send us a cash counter, that we don't need, to our office that doesn't accept cash as a form of payment? Not to mention this is a really nice one—it probably cost a lot of money. "

There was no return address. We couldn't even tell what company shipped it to us. There was no receipt in the box either. We just stared at each other for a good three minutes. Jessica's toddlers were nearby and when they sensed that Jessica and I were both stirred up and completely perplexed they dropped everything to ask us what was going on.

Jessica said, "Oh nothing. Ray just got some more material to write about in the next chapter of his book." We all just laughed.

CHAPTER 14

THE LAWS OF ATTRACTION AND VIBRATION

xplaining how these laws work will require a small understanding of physics. As I have said, I am not a physicist, but I will do my best to explain how the laws of attraction and vibration actually function at a subatomic level.

For me to accept the laws of attraction and vibration as fact, it was necessary for me to learn about a Nobel Prize-winning physicist named Peter Higgs. His discovery would become known as the "Higgs field" and without its subsequent substantiation on July 4, 2012, I would not have become convinced that these laws exist. For these laws to exist they require an electromagnetic field, the Higgs field, or some other Quantum field. Thanks to Peter Higgs we now know the latter exists.

The first thing you'll need to understand is how matter interacts with the world. All matter is made up of atoms, and atoms are made of electrons and a nucleus composed of protons and neutrons. Each proton and neutron is composed of what we call "quarks": subatomic specks that bear a minuscule electrical charge. There are three quarks inside of every proton and neutron. Two of the quarks always spin in the same direction, up or down, and the other spins in the opposite direction. This creates a positively or negatively charged particle, depending on the direction the majority of quarks in the particle spin. Two spinning up and one down is positive, and two down with one up is negative. All of these particles, however, have one thing in common: they make up everything that is in the universe. Different particles come together to make up all that is in our world.

Why is one thing a solid and another a liquid, a gas—or even light? The answer does not lie necessarily in its atomic makeup; rather, it is more about how its atomic makeup interacts within what is called the Higgs field.

The Higgs field is a field of energy that is thought to exist in every region of the universe. The field is accompanied by a fundamental particle known as the Higgs boson, which is used by the field to continuously interact with other particles, such as the electron.

For example, we know that the desk that holds the computer I am typing on right now is a solid. If I were to push on it, it wouldn't break. And I cannot walk through my desk either. On the other hand, if I were to take a flashlight and turn it on, I could walk right through the particles of light that would emit from it. And those light particles would travel through space for what would seem like forever, or until they hit something that stopped them from traveling any farther. The same could probably be said for water and gas as well. However, my desk does not act that way. It stays stationary and seems to remain quite solid.

Essentially, this is due to the field in which the particles interact, rather than the particles themselves. Particles interact with the Higgs field, and the Higgs field determines whether those particles will vibrate very slowly (as in a solid) or very quickly (as in a liquid, a gas, or light). The point that I'm making is that it is the Higgs field which determines how the mass particles behave. Why is this important? Because we know that everything, every particle, contains energy, and the Higgs field determines how that energy, and the properties of the particles, will travel through, and behave within that field. This explains how matter interacts in the entire universe. Especially as it pertains to its vibration and frequency.

We know from Albert Einstein's theory of relativity that all matter can become energy, and all energy can become matter. What scientific theory ties all this together? The answer is: string theory. String theory proposes that the fundamental constituents of the universe are one-dimensional "strings" rather than point-like particles. What we perceive as particles are actually vibrations in loops of string, each with its own characteristics and frequency.

I have quoted him many times in this book; Nikola Tesla once said, "If you want to know the secrets of the universe, think in terms of energy, frequency, and vibration."

Our thoughts are also a form of energy, and each thought vibrates on a different frequency. If you recall, I wrote earlier that thoughts are things. Thoughts contain energy. And all energy travels through the field. We know this to be true. Nikola Tesla showed us that electricity can travel through the electromagnetic field that surrounds the earth. The earth's own electromagnetic field travels through the Higgs field as well any other Quantum fields. (You probably see where I'm going.)

As we think them, our thoughts are released into these fields that pervade the universe. Scientists have begun to find ways to measure the activity of thoughts and now realize that thoughts have mass. From EEGs to Delta or Theta brain waves, we are now able to measure some form of thought waves. As a thought travels through the field, similar to how light, water, or gas behaves, it will continue until it meets with resistance. This includes, but is not limited to, colliding with someone or something. In fact, thoughts are so light, they probably travel faster than anything, including light.

Since different particles behave differently in the Higgs field, not everything functions the same. My desk will just sit here—it probably won't attract much to it, except for the notes that go into my books and several empty cups of coffee, which are actually items that were manifested by me and not the desk. But energy can travel through Quantum fields indefinitely, and interact with other energetic particles. For example, when you turn on a radio, the signal it receives may emanate from the other side of the world. Radio waves transmit sound waves from a satellite in outer space to your cell phone, radio, or other electronic device. This serves as an example of how energy can travel to other parts of the universe. The other very important thing to remember is that similar vibrations, or similar energetic particles, attract one another. So my thoughts and their vibrations, often triggered by my emotions, have a specific frequency that goes out into the universe and attracts other, like vibrations. I can also send out those vibrations from my thoughts repeatedly and wait for other, like vibrations to be attracted to me.

This is how the laws of vibration and attraction work. "I think, therefore I am," wrote René Descartes. I am able to attract things to me simply by using my thoughts. (Voila!) I can create, and make things happen in the universe as well. Using the scientific discoveries of Tesla, Einstein, and Higgs, we can prove this is so.

"What you think, you become. What you feel, you attract. What you imagine, you create." — The Buddha.

He said this about 2,400 years before Tesla's famous quote. How do you suppose he learned that?

Journal Entry, October 10, 2020—"Hold Your Head Up"

The first time it happened it was awesome and freaky at the same time. I began my meditation like any other, the only difference being that I changed my intention a few minutes into it. My typical morning meditation lasts a mere five minutes; it is before bed that I usually do a much longer, deeper meditation. My intention is always to express gratitude, but in the evenings, before sleep, I like to go deeply into a manifestation mode. On this day it was too late for my habitual brief morning meditation and too early for my bedtime session.

I began, as usual, with chanting, then decided to switch over to a deeper state, focusing on my breath and allowing it to take me to another realm where I might meet an available energy being. I don't know whether it was the sudden switch in programs or what, but I began to feel as though someone or something was pulling on my head, drawing it up into the sky. I was sitting upright with my head level, and it felt as if someone were pulling up on my ears and the crown of my head, like the pull of a magnet or something above, tugging on it lightly. It wasn't painful or uncomfortable.

I wanted to see what would happen if I moved my head, so I inched it forward ever so slightly, looking down a bit. Sure enough, the spot at the back of my head, which was now the highest point, was the part being pulled up by the "magnet." I changed the position again and went back to level-headed (if that were possible for me). The pulling sensation returned to the ears and the top of the head. When I tilted my head back, the pull was primarily on my forehead. It was as if the UCC was pulling me into its realm. I continued to move my head a little up and down or side to side, and each time, in each position, there was the same result: the highest part of my head would be pulled up. It was as if my head were floating above the rest of my body.

I had been experiencing some neck pain that day, but it went away: I could no longer feel my body, only my head being pulled on. I have since been able to repeat this process, and each time I have come out of it feeling better and better. It is a very deep state of trance, fully connected with the universal consciousness. I would describe it as a physical confirmation or sensation of that connection. Certain matching energies and frequencies attach to each other like magnets, and others that differ from one another often repel.

Journal Entry, October 27, 2020—"A Helping Hand"

Everything Jessica and I had been manifesting was coming to fruition very rapidly. We had formed several entities for business purposes and set many things in motion for our future. I had recently proposed marriage, and we had decided to live together. We were merging our lives and businesses. Life was great.

So much was happening so quickly that I began to get somewhat stressed. When that happens, it often shows up as a painful muscle cramp or knot in my neck or back, which has sustained several injuries. Stress will often manifest itself in the form of physical pain in a weak spot in your body. This time the gripping pain in my neck was worsening by the day. I could meditate to the point of not feeling my body, and that would provide relief, but the pain would return upon my emerging from meditation. I felt I needed to meditate much more so it would go away completely. I was hoping that meditating more often daily would relieve the stress or the cause of the pain.

On one particular day the pain was quite severe, so I entered a meditative state that was very deep. I crossed over to another realm where I encountered Jessica's dad. Being in severe pain I just took a chance and asked him, "Can you do anything about this?" I was referring, of course, to the severe pain in my neck. He turned his head and, with a smile, began to move his rather large left hand and forearm toward me, as if from the left side of a movie screen. The hand and arm were completely silver, like the color I sometime see in my guides. The hand moved toward me very slowly, before resting itself very lightly on the back of my neck. I could barely feel it. Within seconds, my pain was gone and so was the hand.

I felt no pain for the entire day. It did return late on the following day, though it wasn't as severe. Whatever transpired in those moments, I was grateful for it.

CHAPTER 15

FROM SELF-DESTRUCTION TO RECONSTRUCTION

If you read my first book you know that the first half of my life was rather unpleasant. It was filled with trauma, followed on my part by self-destructive behavior. I had repeatedly placed myself in bad, sometimes even life-threatening, situations. And yet, somehow or some way, I always seemed to get myself out of those situations and to a place of safety. Someone or something always showed me the way. When these messages first were given to me, I didn't believe that they emanated from a higher source. In fact, I believed in nothing after life on earth. I thought that when we died, everything would just go black. Just like Tony Soprano said in that infamous final episode on HBO, that everyone except me, hated. I completely understood what he was saying and would have agreed at that time. Even though I had seen the afterlife, through experiencing an NDE, before that show aired. I chose to live in denial. I liked the simplicity in the fact that nothing was coming next. I would blame others for my shortcomings and mistakes and continue down that path until everything went black. That was my mentality until so many crazy things happened around me that I simply couldn't deny any longer that there was something bigger than myself here that I didn't understand.

It wasn't until I met Jessica that I began to search for my own answers. It began with a simple question from her, "What are your spiritual beliefs?"

She asked me this when she and I began to get serious with our relationship. I suppose this can be a deal-breaker in a relationship if the two parties disagree or if either or both of them are not willing to go along with their partner's way of thinking. In any event, my answer was simple. I said, "I don't know," because at that time, I didn't. I went on to explain that it was something I had been meaning to explore. It really was on my list of things to do. It was also one of those things I could easily push off to the side while working on what I thought was more important. Wow, was I ever wrong. If I knew then what I know now, my life would have been so different. For the better, of course.

I had no one to teach me these things early on, so I had to put it together very slowly over time, like a puzzle. Eventually, Jessica helped me find my current mentors who have helped in so many ways and have shown me the way to use these abilities to help myself and others.

When we help others first, we are repaid in kind. On the other hand, if we are selfish, then we open ourselves up to shit coming our way. You get what you give, every time.

Understanding life is easier when you break it down and really think about it. Karma is forever circulating. So the people who fucked you over, you really don't have to dwell on them, or allow your anger toward them to consume you. Bad shit is on its way to them. The universe will fuck them so hard and all you have to do is move forward with your life and be happy and do good stuff for others. Simple, right?

What happens to our minds when we are victimized is that our subconscious changes, altering how we view ourselves. Remember that the brain and the mind are not the same thing. The brain houses the mind, but the mind controls the brain. If we view ourselves a certain way in our minds, we will inevitably *be* that way. If you think you are a victim, you will continue to *be* a victim. The way you picture your life and yourself as a whole is exactly how they will be. What happened yesterday does not have to materialize tomorrow, but you have to make a conscious effort to adjust your subconscious mind in order to change that.

We are all the sum of our experiences up until the present moment. Those experiences gather in our subconscious, creating an image of ourselves in our minds which we carry around with us wherever we go. If you define yourself in a certain way, you are likely to remain that way in the future as well. If you say something like, "Oh, every time I try to do that it never goes as planned," you have already decided what will happen next time. You have defined yourself as a person who cannot do something. Thoughts are things. If you thought it, you bought it. Now own it. Change your thought and speech patterns and you'll change your life.

This shift can begin by changing the way you speak to yourself and the way you think of yourself. You must retrain your brain. If you catch yourself saying or thinking something in the negative form, consciously stop yourself and reframe it in your mind in positive terms. Do this over and again thousands of times and you will rewire your subconscious self. You will bring yourself to a new starting point of "Yes, I can," rather than "No, I cannot."

I will share with you my own story of how I did this. I came from people and an environment in which the attitude was only the wealthy and powerful could do or have certain things. Then I began to wonder what was so different about them? I couldn't find anything. They were human also. Like me, they put their pants on one leg at a time. So I adopted a mantra which I applied to everything (and I really mean every single thing I did, or was planning to do). Here it is.

"If they can do it, then *I* can do it too."

That's it. So simple, yet so profound. I absolutely refused to accept that anyone could do something I couldn't. (Unless it was something like dunking a basketball—where one is hindered by a lack of gene-driven ability). Anything that took brainpower to accomplish, I knew I could do. I would think of a person who had accomplished what I wanted, and learn how they did it. From there I could choose whether to recreate the process it took them to achieve it. I set no limitations for myself or my mind. I never again uttered the forbidden words, "I can't do that."

Of course, I could perform brain surgery. Why not? There are some human beings who perform brain surgery, after all, and I am human. Therefore, *I* could perform brain surgery too. Now that I've established that fact, I consider what the other persons had to do to become brain surgeons—and of course the answer is: many years of schooling and residency. Am I willing to do that also? If I am not willing to do the work to become a brain surgeon, I won't become one, but that does not mean I *couldn't* become one.

Gone forever was the notion that I could not do something, replaced instead with the question, "What would I have to do to accomplish it?" I literally changed my mind. I reprogrammed myself to adopt a better perception of myself and my world. This entailed repeating to myself thousands of times that if *they* could do it, then *I* could do it too.

I wanted to write a book for as long as I can remember, but each time I tried I would barely begin before telling myself, "I'm not an author. I can't do this." I would then abandon the project.

Then I began examining the books of those who were not professional authors but who had a message to share with the world—and a light bulb went off. What made them so different? Absolutely nothing. I humanized them—I found errors in their writing: misspellings and grammatical gaffes. One of the authors even prefaced his book apologizing for the fact that English was his second language; he went on to ask the reader to please pardon his mistakes. These writers were no better than I was. I was misled by those in my environment. What you are reading now is my second book. It is written to help people realize that I am not special, and if *I* can do anything, *you* can as well. (And for the record, I *can* dunk a basketball—but only if I use a ladder!)

The mind is fully adaptable and programmable, but that process must begin with a conscious choice on your part to change your subconscious. It is a simple process, but repetition is the key. The neurons in your brain that fire together will inevitably wire together over time. Change your perception of yourself and it will change your entire existence. That, my friend, is the power of the mind.

(Currently, the National Basketball Association does not allow ladders on the basketball court. Oh well, I'll just have to become a fucking brain surgeon. MJ, your GOAT status is safe, at least for now.)

Journal Entry, July 25, 2020—"Thank You, John"

I was immersed in a full day webinar with Medium Joe and some of his other students. Although only about twelve people typically attended these classes, Medium Joe had invited alumni to this particular session, so we had more than double the usual number of people.

As we got to the end of the class, Medium Joe asked if any of the mediums on the webinar would like to connect to someone in the afterlife and share their session with the entire group. Fear took over. Absolutely no one spoke up. Medium Joe laughed and then asked again if anyone would like to step up to the challenge. There was silence for a while, but then a woman named Jackie said, "Sure, I'll give a try."

I was impressed. The webinar included not only our class but many others who had been trained by Medium Joe, one of the greatest mediums of our time.

She took over the webinar and with all eyes on her, began.

"I have a man in his fifties. He had heart failure or a heart attack very unexpectedly. He always had his family with or around him, and they shared a very strong bond. He worked with his hands, perhaps mechanical or some type of construction when he was alive. He died too soon and has unfinished business here regarding his family."

She paused and asked if anyone on the webinar knew this person. A few hands went up and she continued to find more identifiers. What she was describing sounded like someone I knew, but I was petrified.

"He had very dark brown hair. He would be described as jovial. He was the type that was loved by all. He was quite successful in business and generous with people. He joked about almost everything. He loved the holidays, and sharing them with friends and family."

She paused again to see if anyone could identify the person. Only two people still had their hands up, although mine should have been up as well. So far, she was describing Jessica's dad. *He speaks to me directly*, I thought, *so why come through in this roundabout way?* Plus, I was at that point too scared, or perhaps intimidated, to get involved.

Just then Jessica sent me a text message. It was an image of her and her dad, and under the picture she had written, "Hi!" Such a strange caption to go under that picture. I remember looking at it and thinking, *Which of them is extending this greeting?* This picture was the screensaver on Jessica's computer, and usually after two minutes had passed the computer would go into sleep mode, but her next text message was something along the lines of: "How strange is it that my dad's picture is still on my computer screen, well beyond two minutes?" Jessica was unaware of my situation.

I texted her back: "It might be because your dad is speaking to me right now through another medium in my class."

The medium went on: "The person this message is for is quite close to his living family and has helped his family tremendously, especially his wife, and this man is very grateful for all you have done for them."

My heart was pounding out of my chest: I knew now that this message was indeed meant for me. I was trying not to get emotional. My hand remained down at my side. I was texting this state of affairs to Jessica, though my hands were shaking uncontrollably.

"He values your friendship and is sorry he has not been around much lately, but he wants you to know he thanks you for helping him with his kids and staying in contact, bringing messages to his family. He will try to be around more."

(Notice how her dad said, "Thank you for helping me help my kids"? That was just like him; he was not going to give me all the credit.)

All hands on the webinar were down now. That last statement could only have been for me. Euphoria was passing through my entire body. I was laughing inside and trying not to get emotional at the same time. I placed my hand over my mouth and continued through the session as we all said our goodbyes to each other, and that was the end of our class for the day.

I called Jessica. She had been staring at her computer, waiting for me to call and give her more information. As soon as she picked up the phone her computer finally went into sleep mode, the picture of her and her dad slowly dimming away.

(Holy shit, John. You really know how to make an entrance—and an exit.)

Journal Entry, August 11, 2020—"The Workaround"

For a couple of weeks, I had been absorbed in my day-to-day life and not addressing those who wanted to make contact through me—precisely what my mentor had told me not to do.

Unfortunately, while it is happening, I don't notice that I'm doing it. It can become habitual to just say something like, "Not now," or "Leave me alone. I'm tired." Sometimes I need to work, or be present in the moment; and I can't always just stop and say, "Okay, dead person, what's up? What can I do for you?" If I did that all day, I would rarely have time for anything else. It seems like once they realize I can hear or see them, they never want to stop talking.

I guess on a few occasions Jessica's dad had wanted to talk and I must have blown him off. I can never say ahead of time who is contacting me—medium caller-ID has not been invented yet, or at least not for me anyway.

(Wow! I'm sorry, John! As I typed that something just rattled my insides. No one can do that like John. So now I know I was right.)

Jessica's dad, John, like I told you before, was a powerhouse in life and death. He did not take no for an answer when he was here, and he doesn't take it any better now post-death.

On this particular day Jessica was hanging out with one of her friends who we knew had some psychic abilities. She had been asking to chat with me ever since she saw my picture; she could tell I was a fellow medium. We have not been able to get together yet, but I'm sure it will be interesting when we do, and I'll write about it for sure.

Jessica and she were chatting privately when a large presence took hold of our psychic friend. She went on to tell Jessica in the middle of their chat that there was a man who really wanted to talk to her. Jessica grabbed her mobile phone and recorded the event as it happened. It was her dad. I guess he'd been wanting to give her some guidance, and I had been too busy (or thought I was), so he found a workaround. Once again John managed to not let a silly thing like death get between him and his daughter. This was the second time he had done this to me!

CHAPTER 16

THE WAR OF MULTIPLE MINDS

We all have what I call multiple minds. Or rather, to be more precise, we all possess multiple *parts* to our minds. Let us begin with the conscious mind and the subconscious. The subconscious sees all, hears all, and reads all. It also remembers all. Absolutely nothing can get past your subconscious mind. If you take something in through any of your physical senses, it will be stored in the subconscious. According to the Encyclopedia Britannica, your subconscious mind can take in, decode, and remember eleven million bits of information in one second. Your conscious mind can handle only about forty to fifty bits per second. Your subconscious basically makes your conscious mind look dumb as fuck, right? Not so fast. The conscious mind is what separates us from the animal world. Our conscious minds are far more developed, and as such, able to solve problems, invent things, build things, and so on.

Think of your subconscious as your hard drive in your personal computer, and your conscious mind as the RAM. RAM stands for "Random Access Memory," and it refers to how much of your computer's hard drive memory and information can be utilized at any one time. Most personal computers made today have on average a one-terabyte hard drive and about sixteen gigabytes of RAM. To put this in perspective, one terabyte is the equivalent of one thousand gigabytes. The RAM or Random Access Memory of your computer is much smaller than the hard drive, but this is where information gets brought up only while you are using or working with it. The second you close a program, the information is deleted from the RAM and returned to the hard drive. Do you think, perhaps, when they invented the personal computer, they modeled it after the human mind?

If a computer has more RAM, it can hold onto more information from the hard drive at any given time—but remember all the information is still coming from that hard drive. All your human information comes from your subconscious and unconscious minds respectively (more on the difference in a bit). Those two parts of the mind makes up over 80 percent of your mind and are the smartest and the dumbest parts at the same time.

Some people theorize that your subconscious mind can never be completely filled—that there is always room for more information somewhere inside it. However, Einstein did not believe that. He was convinced that the subconscious could be filled up, at which point it would have to delete something in order to retain more. Regardless of who may be right, let us return to the hard drive and the way it performs. A hard drive can overwrite itself. Meaning although the past information stored on it isn't completely gone, we can place new and improved information on top of the old stuff. This can be done over and again, until the old stuff is so far down that it has no effect on our computer anymore. Once again, the subconscious can act in the same way as that hard drive. You may not be able to delete your traumas, but you can overwrite them with new positive experiences. Does this take time and effort? Of course, it does, but it is worth every moment spent on it.

The foundation of your subconscious mind is programmed by and large during the first seven years of your life. During that time, from birth to about seven years old, your mind picks up everything around it. It learns everything, stores everything, and then begins to use that programmed information to make decisions based upon those first seven years of experience. During this learning stage, your brain typically remains and operates on a brain frequency or state known as "theta." Theta is great for imagination and learning. In theta your mind will absorb most everything. If you have ever been hypnotized to change something about yourself, (perhaps rid yourself of some bad habit like smoking.), the hypnotist will want to get you into a very relaxed theta state, to be able to speak directly to your subconscious mind.

The Jesuits have a saying: "Give me a child for the first seven years, and I will show you the man he will one day be." Before the age of seven, the child is just repeating the things he or she has heard. They have not yet formed an opinion on much of anything. That capacity is still emerging. Much of what they say is just being repeated like a recording. So, if you get mad at your seven-year-old for saying a bad word, chances are their subconscious mind recorded it from you in the first place.

Let us say a dad said to his six-year-old over and again, "You don't deserve this or that. You will never amount to anything." The child will take that in and record it as fact. As an adult, later in life, they will begin to act in a way that ensures they are living by the program they were given. This is done completely subconsciously. As adults, such children will most likely sabotage themselves to keep the program running correctly. This can be averted or corrected, but it must be done *consciously*. You must consciously reprogram your subconscious to change the outcome, to create a new program and discard Dad's, Mom's or any other authoritative figure who helped program the old one.

How does this information that we may not want, or that may not serve our highest and best selves, manage to sneak its way from the subconscious to control the conscious mind? Well, there is a weak link that connects them. It is called the egoic mind, or "ego" for short. I call it the "weak link" because it seems to cause significantly more harm than good. Of course, there are times when the information from our subconscious is healthy, good, and positive. But there seems to be no shortage of negativity that comes through time and again. The ego, according to Joseph Campbell, sits as a small spec in the conscious mind, but it can be activated and influenced primarily by the subconscious part of the mind. Think of the ego as the CPU in your computer. The CPU is the part of the computer that distributes the information it gets from all parts of the computer's memory, and ultimately tells the computer what to do with that information and when to do it.

We can delve a little bit deeper into the subconscious and break it up into two parts: the unconscious and the subconscious. The subconscious is made up of memories and experiences while your unconscious is composed of your feelings and emotions. When an experience occurs that is brought on by, or met with, a strong emotion, it becomes solidified as factual in your perception. A part of what you believe to be truth. Everyone's personal perception is their own truth. You've probably heard the saying: "There are two sides to every story, and then there is the truth." Two people can have the same experience and each walk away from it with a different perception and recollection.

Don't believe everything you think!

To the young boy who walks over to a hot stove and puts his hand on it for the first time, his experience is the feeling of pain. The intensity of that feeling creates an association and solidifies his perception about this thing called "stove": *stoves cause pain.*

Another boy comes along and touches the stove, but it isn't turned on, so no pain is caused. Boy number two says to boy number one, "Stoves don't cause pain. You're just stupid." Here we see the same scenario with two completely different perceptions of reality.

Boy number one then says, "No, you're the one who is stupid. Your mom doesn't cook; she makes reservations."

The boy who got burned (who may have a career in comedy) will remain afraid of stoves until he learns consciously that a stove can be used safely without pain and suffering. Please note that this must be done consciously, to override his subconscious perception of reality. That perception will never be deleted. The subconscious does not delete. You can write a new program over the old one, but you can never completely get rid of what was there before.

Since the subconscious is like a hard drive in a computer, it remembers everything you have seen or heard from your earliest memory on. In this sense it is quite brilliant. However, your subconscious does not know the difference between reality and imagination. Therefore, if you visualize or imagine something enough times using your conscious mind, and subsequently attach a feeling or emotion to it, your subconscious can make it real for you.

You have doubts?

Why do you go to scary movies and get frightened? You know that the serial killer in the film can't come through the screen and kill you, yet most of us become afraid and some of us even scream while watching scary movies. Why?

It is because your subconscious doesn't know what is real and what isn't. It reacts before your conscious mind can jump in and remind you that something isn't real. Then you can begin to relax as your conscious mind kicks in. The subconscious makes up the majority of your mind and reacts much more quickly, with all of its knowledge and programming stored in there from childhood (*stranger danger!*). The conscious mind is much smaller and works more slowly, so it comes to your rescue later and reminds you, "Hey. This isn't real, dummy. We're in a movie theater. Pull yourself together."

And this is when your ego chimes in with, "You looked like such a fucking idiot when you jumped out of your seat. Ha-ha-ha. Everyone is laughing at you now." Oh yeah, that is the ego.

Since we know that the subconscious reacts more quickly than the conscious, we have a problem. A big problem. Remember how we reacted during the scary movie?—first we got scared and yelled, and then we were reminded that it wasn't real.

Sigmund Freud described the "ego" as a small part of the mind that plays a very big part. In the English language we often use the term "ego" incorrectly. We might say something like, "You have a big ego," meaning you are arrogant or full of yourself. I do not use the term in that sense. I define the ego simply as the voice in our heads that advises us what to do, what not to do, and how to go about doing whatever we should do next. It also judges us and our behavior and appearance. That's quite a lot of control held by this ego; wouldn't you say? So then, why do we allow it?

Eckhart Tolle says that this part of your mind known as the "ego" is created and derived from one's memories, experiences, and past moments which affect future actions. The ego lies in between one's conscious and subconscious minds and acts as a bridge between the two. It transfers information back and forth, just like in the movie theater. Since we know which side of the mind reacts first, we know which way more traffic is headed over our mental bridge.

Your ego might say things like, "Why did you say that? Why did you do that? You are going to look foolish. You better not try to do that; you know you're just going to fail. You can't do that. I wonder what so-and-so thinks about that? Why haven't they called back? I'll bet they are angry with you about blah, blah, blah." *(Holy shit, I sound like my mother. Make it stop!)*

These types of negative thoughts are the result of past memories and experiences. The subconscious mind can be a great friend or your worst enemy. This subconscious mind wants to control you by influencing your conscious mind through its weak link—the ego. Your conscious mind, however, can take control, and decide what you will do, and say next. It has command of your actions. In order for the subconscious mind to gain access and control of you, it must infiltrate your conscious mind through the ego. The best way for it to accomplish this is to create fear or self-doubt by utilizing old information from your past. It will manipulate your conscious mind in an attempt to dictate what you can and cannot do. It is the subconscious mind, infiltrating the ego, that creates anxiety and fear.

It will repeatedly say things like, "You look fat in that outfit. Don't say that out loud, you will sound stupid. Don't you wonder what your boss thinks of you now? Why isn't he/she calling you back? Was it something you said or something you did? You will never be wealthy; no one in your family is. You will never own a house, a car, get married, be loved, . . ." These may have been many of the things others have said to you, or perhaps that you've seen played out in front of you, that you believed. After all, why wouldn't you believe them? You were only five years old.

You were four years old the first-time daddy called mommy a bitch. *Mommy must be a bitch. Why would daddy lie to me?* You were five when you saw your mom looking in the mirror complaining about how fat she was, over and again, in each outfit she changed into. *Women are afraid of being fat. Why would mommy lie?* Hell, you didn't even know what a lie was yet.

You get the idea. Now, the ego could say nice things as well, but often it prefers to tear us down and belittle us, as a much more effective means of gaining our attention. Why, you ask? Because it is an ego. Its purpose is to remind us of who we are, or what we are, from its perspective—the things we can and cannot do, and the things we should and should not do. It takes over our conscious mind and makes itself the primary factor in our decision-making process. If you try not to listen, it will repeat itself again and again. This stupid ego (manipulated by our past experiences) that no one else can hear, is the one we rely on the most for practically everything! Think about that for a second. You aren't making your own choices on just about everything. The ego pulls from the past. So you are making decisions for your future, based on past events, some of which aren't even yours! Many were implanted at a young age when you didn't understand anything about anything. Wow! Its no wonder we are all fucked up!

There is a constant civil war going on in your mind for ultimate control of your being, and subsequently, control of your existence!

The ego isn't always bad or wrong. When the ego tells you not to talk to strangers, or not to get into a car with strangers, don't take candy from strangers, that is most likely good advice brought forth from your subconscious mind. It will also prevent you from thinking you can fly, or jump off a hundred-foot cliff and live. But do you see how even its good aspects are often the warnings it broadcasts, to which we give our undivided attention? It thrives on our fears.

We inherently tend to assume that this ego always has our best interests in mind and therefore we ought to trust it. We believe that our ego has always been there for us when no one else was. We think it is our guiding light. And most importantly, we think it is not only a part of us, but that it *is* us! We think we created it, but we did not. If we had created it, or had control over its beginnings, we could do so much more with it. Instead, we typically have to spend a very long time fixing it because it has been programmed by others without our conscious consent.

"The first half of life is devoted to forming a healthy ego, the second half is going inward and letting go of it." -Carl Jung

Journal Entry, September 20, 2020—"Why?"

One Sunday Jessica and I had a lot to do, so it wasn't much of a day off for us. She had work and reports to write, and I was completing some additional schooling I had chosen to take on to become a certified practitioner of meditation and Reiki healing. Reiki and meditation came naturally for me, but I felt I needed the certification if I wanted to practice professionally.

Jessica was working in the downstairs office of the house, and I, upstairs. The children were playing and running back and forth between us. It was a beautiful Sunday, and we were both grateful for it. Jessica had received a phone call from a friend in the middle of the afternoon and called me down to her office to discuss it with me.

This particular friend was one of the very few people at this time who had full knowledge of my abilities. She was asking for help for one of her close friends who was struggling with the death of her husband. He had committed suicide and, as if that wasn't enough, he had done it in front of their little boy who was a toddler at the time. Jessica had told her to come over to our home and then asked if I would speak with her. I agreed and we waited for her arrival. Our friend arrived around 4 p.m. and went right into Jessica's office.

Jessica's office is actually the sunroom of the house converted to an office and art studio. She is an excellent painter—I know I am biased, but she is really good. She took one or two classes and now she is like Picasso. She loves when the sun enters the large windows with sliding doors to the backyard when she works; and she can also, due to the way this room is positioned, hear everything going on in the entire house, thereby keeping tabs on the little ones at all times. My office is at the highest point in the house, with windows that wrap around the corner, thus allowing me to see everything from a higher vantage point. Less natural light, but I don't mind that because I can see anyone coming onto or leaving our property. My hyper-vigilance and I like it that way.

Back to our story. Our friend arrived and was visibly shaken by the news she had just received from her friend. She had not heard from this person for the past year, which turned out to be because of this devastating event, so although it happened a year ago, she had just gotten the details. I suppose it took a while for the woman to discuss something as traumatic as this with anyone, especially given the fact that their son had witnessed the horrific event. The question our friend had for me was, Why? Why had her friend's husband killed himself and, more importantly, why had he done it in front of their small boy? For that reason above all, the widow was holding a lot of anger toward her deceased husband.

As our friend explained all of this to us, Jessica couldn't help but get slightly emotional herself. Why would any human being do such a thing in front of a kid? None of us could understand that part. I began to free my mind as I listened to Jessica and our friend talk about the situation, and I slipped into an altered state. The first thing I felt were such strong vibrations inside my body that my hands began to shake. Up until this point I had never shaken on the outside, only inwardly. I knew this was going to be bad. She showed me one picture of the man with his son, sitting by a swimming pool, both smiling and clearly enjoying the day and each other. There was no question that this man had loved his son, nor that he had loved his wife. *So, why then?* I thought to myself. I told our friend the man might not answer me even if I asked him, but I would try and see what I could get.

I looked at the picture of the two of them for perhaps a minute, then closed my eyes. I proceeded to see, in my mind's eye, a rather clear image and video of the suicide as it took place. I watched it replay a couple of times. I then opened my eyes to look at the photo once more, to make sure that in my mind's eye I was seeing the correct people. Then I returned to the vision with my eyes closed and spoke aloud what I saw.

On what looks like a movie screen in my mind, I see the man sitting to my left in the room. I also see a young boy. I think he is eight years old because he is wearing the same shirt I once had at that age. There is a gun concealed in the room. I see it between the cushions of the couch next to the dad. This may be accurate or just a metaphor that the dad had tried to hide the gun from the boy. A conversation takes place between the boy and the man. This conversation leads the dad to think the boy will leave the house. The boy does leave the room. He appears to enter a room, maybe a kitchen, with a door that leads outside the house. I believe that the dad expected the boy to go outside. The conversation the two of them had may have been something like the child asking if he could go outside and the dad saying yes. The dad watches his son walk out of the room. The man has assumed the child has left the house completely. He then picks up a gun with his left hand and proceeds to shoot himself where his neck meets his head. What the dad did not know is that the boy did not leave the house: he had actually turned around to come back to his dad just as his dad was pulling the trigger.

I shared these details with Jessica and her friend.

I was later told that the man was left-handed and that the boy was in fact exactly eight years old when this event took place. I told Jessica's friend to tell the wife that the man had not wanted his son to see this act and had thought the child was out of the house, and perhaps she could find some solace in that fact. The other thing I was able to infer was that the man was not thinking clearly at the time he did this.

While having visions such as this one, I can often "see" another person's thoughts. They appear as white lines that shoot through the air above someone's head. In my experience, most people have a couple of these at any given time; and sometimes if a person is dwelling on one of these thoughts in particular, I can pick up on what they are. With this man, however, literally hundreds of these lines were sporadically shooting around above his head. What this told me was that he was far from thinking clearly. No one can consciously process that many thoughts at once. He was unable to think this event through completely to be certain that the child would not see him or find him afterward.

When I see that many thoughts or lines shooting around a person's head, it usually means there is some serious mental instability or illness in operation. They can also be the result of significant drug and alcohol abuse, or a combination of both. In any event, as horrific as this was, one thing I could say for sure was that the kid was not meant to see this. I could not grab a hold of any of the man's thoughts because they were moving around too fast and too sporadically.

"I hope this helps your friend, at least a little," I said.

Our friend apologized for being the catalyst to my witnessing this horrific event. I told her, if it helps someone then it was worth it. I went on to relate a story of how just the other night, while Jessica and I were trying to fall asleep in bed, I received a vision of a bunch of children who were in a store during what I thought was an earthquake. The mother of one or more of the children was trying to reach or get to them, and they were holding on to the beams that support the building while the entire structure shook and began to come apart. "They are in so much trouble," I said to Jessica. "They are in Bermuda." I do not know how I knew that, because I have never been to Bermuda, and I have never seen pictures of Bermuda other than on a travel poster. But this was in more of a remote area, where those who live in that country year-round might go to shop— not any type of resort area. It was more of a poor neighborhood. Those poor kids were holding on for their lives. They desperately needed help, and quickly.

I sat up and grabbed my phone. I typed "Bermuda news" into the browser search field, which brought up a local news story reporting how a tremendous hurricane had just devastated Bermuda, and another was on its way tomorrow. It told of how Bermuda was in a state of emergency, and they were shutting down their local government until it was over. I passed the phone to Jessica, rolled into a fetal position, and tried my best to pray for them. Jessica said, "Are you alright?" I replied sarcastically, "It's just fucking great being a fucking psychic! I can do nothing to help those poor children. Why would the universe, or anyone, show me this?"

I see a lot of bad shit, which was the point of my telling our friend this story. "If I'm going to see horrible stuff anyway, I may as well try to help someone."

Update: "Why?"

About or week or so later, I hadn't heard anything in regard to the suicide. I asked Jessica to follow up. This is what the friend told Jessica:

I brought the information that Ray gave me back to the widow, and immediately she disputed it and said he had intended to do it in front of their son. "My son told me that and he also told the police that. My son told me that his dad told him to get the gun and then said something to him and shot himself." She was certain this is how it happened.

I wasn't as disappointed about being wrong, as much as I was disappointed that I couldn't help her, or offer her some sort of closure. I went back to the vision and watched it again and again. This was very confusing to me, and I'll explain why. I have always been taught that no one will ever be one hundred percent accurate, and I understand that, but this vision was amazingly vivid. Especially the parts the woman was disputing. I had been "off" a little bit, but I have never been outright wrong about the major portions of an event. I picked up my phone and brought this disparity to the attention of my teacher and mentor.

"You know how sometimes in a vision you are absolutely certain about some things, and then other things may be open for interpretation? This was one of those certain things. I was certain that the dad had tried to get the kid out of the room."

There was no question in my mind. I ran through the sequence of events with him, what I saw and how I saw it. There was a long pause on the line, but I could hear him breathing. I don't know where he went mentally at that point. Perhaps inside my head, her head, the universe, I didn't know; but then he came back to me.

"I think you're right."

"How can that be?"

"I am getting the feeling from the woman that she needs the story to be her way: where the man meant to hurt the boy by allowing him to see everything happen. You see, that way she can heal herself."

"I don't follow," I said.

"She needs to hold on to her version of events to maintain that anger toward her deceased husband. This is to help her move forward. She needs the story to be told her way. She didn't want to hear the truth from you; she wanted to heal and grieve by using her version of events and her rage toward him."

"Oh, now I see."

He went on to explain that something like this will happen from time to time—where a person you are trying to help is living in denial, and the denial makes it easier for them to handle their problem, whatever that problem may be. Her perception of the events represented *her* truth. She needed her version of the truth in order to grieve and heal herself. We all have our own perceptions of the things we see and hear, and to us they are the truth. Perception is personal truth.

CHAPTER 17

THE NEW YOU

Your ego is but a small part of your mind, and yet it performs in a very big and influential way. Perhaps it is the biggest of all determining factors in our lives, directing most of what we do, say, act, feel, and more. It will often present the negative side of things or make you question yourself. It was not originally created by your conscious mind, and therefore, it was not created by you. It was created by your subconscious mind. So, in order for us to make desired changes, we must look at what created your subconscious mind. Your subconscious is composed of memories from your past. Those memories and your past experiences were heavily influenced by the people around you each and every day since you were born, and quite possibly in your mother's womb (there is substantial evidence to suggest that unborn children are influenced by the things happening to and around their mothers).

The most influential folks, when it comes to your learned behaviors, are the people who have had an authoritative position in your world when you were very young. The first seven years of life are said to be the most important time in the creation of your ego. You had little if any control over that period of your life. You were just there, taking in everything and being influenced by it unwittingly. The ego continues to grow as you age, but its core foundation was laid out for you, very early on, by the thoughts and experiences of others. As you age, you will begin to make up your own mind more and more each day; but your mind isn't fully yours yet: it is filled with the images, thoughts and sayings of the others you interact with and those you observe. Their perspectives, their belief systems, and their egos, have become the founding components of your own.

This underscores the point I made earlier that your ego is not determined by your conscious mind. You have no choice in deciding what goes inside subconsciously. So, your reactions to your environment, or what you project outwardly, is being decided for you. That is, until you realize that it does not have remain this way. Remember, your subconscious mind remembers arguably everything from birth, especially the lessons you were taught, and others' treatments of you, up to the present moment. Your ego employs memories from your subconscious mind that in most cases you don't even consciously remember. I have written in many of my previous writings about my past traumas and I've had to admit that I have periods inaccessible to me; they are blacked out—certain parts of those episodes I simply cannot remember at all. In many cases, traumatized individuals do this unknowingly in order to protect themselves.

After I found myself in the middle of a shootout at one of my previous jobs many years ago, I began to take measures to protect myself at work. Up until about ten years ago, my ego would chime in while I was getting ready for work, "Hey, pack a weapon." Then I'd consciously tell my ego, "Thanks for reminder but we don't need that anymore. We haven't worked in that type of environment in over twenty-five years." Your subconscious is much faster at processing data that your conscious mind is, so it is of the utmost importance that we give our conscious mind a chance to catch up before taking any action or saying anything. It takes but a second for this to occur.

When we allow for the conscious mind to catch up to subconscious mind, we can then deploy our secret weapon. As humans we all this built in, but so many do not use it, and some don't know it is there to be used. It is your highest level of consciousness or your "Awareness." It has also been referred to as your "God-mind," your "Super-Conscious," and your "Higher-Self." We will get back to these superpowers momentarily.

In another example of the ego at work. Much less detrimental than the last, and perhaps a bit more relatable. When I was young, I often opened the door to the refrigerator in my parent's home with the intention of getting something to eat. Sometimes I would find myself drifting off into an altered state, or just stand there staring while looking inside the fridge. My mom, who was the almighty ruler of the kitchen, would say, "Close the refrigerator door before everything goes bad in there." She began to say it to me repeatedly, even when I opened the fridge for brief periods of time. It became an obsessive refrain. Before long, every time I so much as put my hand on the refrigerator door handle, she would say, "Close the refrigerator door before everything goes bad in there." Many years later, even to this present day, the second I touch the refrigerator door handle in my own home, in my own kitchen, I still hear my mom (through my ego) repeat those words as perfectly as though I were six years old again. "Close the refrigerator door before everything goes bad in there."

Now wait a minute. It is some forty plus years later. I own the food; I own the refrigerator; I own the house; I own the property the house sits on; and if I want all the food in my refrigerator, in my house, on my property to go bad, why the fuck can't I allow my food to go bad in my refrigerator? (And, for the record, it takes hours and sometimes days for food to actually go bad.) Completely senseless, and yet this is how the mind works.

The ego can take total control of you if you allow it, but this ego is not you! It is a construct of everyone else and their personal feelings that you have remembered and stored away for future use. Your ego brings them forth from your subconscious because it thinks they are real and relevant, but this ego is not you!

Your egoic mind is nothing more than a collection of everyone else's thoughts, views, and feelings, that you have seen, ingested, and subsequently adopted as your own. These are the thoughts and beliefs of others in your environment since your birth, that were forced upon you before you could make decisions for yourself, before you had time to pick and choose for yourself. They are made up mostly of the negative things that have been said about you or to you, by others, every negative thing done to you by others, and every negative feeling or emotion brought onto you by others. Past events you have experienced, or seen, or been told about, from an extremely young and impressionable age are all being held tightly in a little ball in your mind, just waiting for their moment to resurface and fuck you over. It is the old, outdated, outright poor, programming that has been done to you, by everything from advertisers to social media, news media outlets, and yes of course, your family, friends, and those who love you!

Take a pause before acting on old thoughts and beliefs and begin to allow your true self to come forth and shine through. Your beliefs likely differ from those of your ego.

Since all your ego knows is based upon what has happened in your life thus far. It only knows the past. If you let it run your life, it will dominate your future by using your past (including the things you have witnessed) and make you believe those same things are the current reality. As a result, the ego can inadvertently place limitations on you and what you can do. That is if you let it, and by doing nothing you are letting it.

It may even cause you to maintain a permanent negative or pessimistic attitude. I am here to happily tell you: it is not you! If you listen to your egoic mind, which was created by everyone else in your life and not by you, you are allowing them to decide who and what you are. They have shaped your whole fucking world before you ever had a chance to consider something else. Maybe they were right at the time, but maybe they were wrong, and now you are senselessly applying those beliefs and limitations throughout your existence—an existence only you (as co-creator of the universe) should get to decide.

You are a part of God and God is a part of you! Just about every religion in the world proclaims a version of this statement, and yet we allow the limitations of unconscious people to keep us ignorant of our divine nature and limitless capacity! (If you do not like the word "God," supplement another term here—it doesn't matter which: the Divine, the Source, the Light, the Universe, the Creator.)

You will always be a co-creator of your world. Do not allow someone else's views to dominate yours, thus ruling your perceptions, and along with them, your entire existence.

Once we know this is true, why don't we simply change our lives? The answer is that the ego will create a routine for you that is comfortable, that sits within the limits and boundaries preset for you by others, even if the process involved suffering. Let us say you wake up, eat something, head to work, do the same thing each day, and go to bed at night and repeat.

That habitual rhythm is comfortable for you, and your mind, by repeatedly steering you toward repeating it, is trying to keep you safe. That is its job, after all, to keep you safe. This mental mechanism stems from way back in the caveman days, when we learned to not venture out too far and risk getting eaten by lions and tigers and bears (Oh my!). Today, we do not require that exact mentality. Today we can be safe and try new things in a controlled environment; yet many of us choose not to, because to do so we must overpower our own subconscious mind, we must defy much that we hold to be true and sacred. Once you realize that most of that "sacred truth" is not comprised of your own thoughts and feelings, this inner "sea change" will become much easier to accomplish. Learn how the conscious mind works, then pick and choose *your* truths, and leave behind those of others you find not to be true at all.

Your conscious mind can overpower and override the egoic mind, but we typically do not follow this path. Instead, we allow the egoic mind to win over our superior consciousness or our awareness, which resides at the highest level and is connected to the universal collective consciousness. (We know this from Carl Jung, who was one of the founding fathers of psychiatry.) To override this natural occurrence, you must use your conscious mind to make the decision not to listen to, and abide by, your ego when it no longer serves your highest and best interests and allow your awareness to come through and make decisions from higher level of consciousness. I call this higher-level awareness because humans are one of the very few species that are "aware" that we are having a thought. Once you are aware of your thoughts, you have the ability to change them. By repeatedly practicing aligning your awareness with the universal collective consciousness, over time this process will begin to come naturally to you.

Accepting this concept may be difficult for skeptics, but once you realize there is more to you than your egoic mind, you will see the limitless possibilities to create, feel excited, positive, and relieved each day of your life. Let your higher consciousness guide you through life and leave behind the controlling, nagging, egoic mind in your head that wants to hold you back.

You can be limitless, but to do so you must rid yourself of the egoic mind's overprotective grip on your life.

Would you like to know how to ignore the egoic mind?

It's rather simple but it takes practice. Simply put, you must live in the present moment. You must always be present. This allows your higher self, in conjunction with your conscious mind, to guide your future, rather than abandoning the wheel to an ego obsessed with past events and instructions. Here is an example of what I mean:

Let us say that, although your current job is fine, you need to make more money, and there are no signs of it happening anytime soon. Your job has become the same monotonous thing, day in and day out: you can practically predict your entire day before you even arrive at work. Since you already know what will happen, you are comfortable being there; you feel secure at work because you have previously dealt with all the scenarios that can possibly occur and you know how to handle them.

Since you are so well-versed and experienced at your job, you know that you are fully capable of opening your own such business—the same type of business in the same industry that you already work in and know so well. You even have ideas to make it better and less expensive for the customer. You know everything you need to know, and you have some money saved up. However, you are scared to leave the comfort zone of the job. Even though you know you can deal with any situation that can arise, you are still apprehensive about opening your own place. Why is that?

You don't want to let go of what you have known and move into the unknown because your ego says that you could potentially fail. Your egoic mind reminds you of what your parents told you about work and money and what was expected of you. They told you things like, "No one in our family has ever owned their own business. We aren't wealthy people." They said things like, "We will never be able to afford that. Investing is too risky. This is who we are. What . . . you think we are the Rockefellers or something?"

Now when you think about opening your own business, this part of the mind reminds you of these "teachings" (or, more to the point, brain washings) from your parents and creates fear and anxiety in you. I am not trying to imply that your parents didn't love you, nor that they were trying to hurt you. You must remember that they were the product of their own upbringing as well.

You may recall that in the previous chapter I wrote that when a feeling or emotion (from the unconscious mind) meets an experience (held within the subconscious mind), it becomes solidified as a fact for you. It becomes *your perception* of the truth, and your perception becomes your truth. For instance: the thought of going out on your own petrifies you, but that fear isn't yours: it's theirs, arising from their feelings and beliefs echoing through you, giving you the perception that they are your own.

So you settle for where you are, and you continue to make money for the owner of your current company instead of having your own company and making money for yourself. Your decision to stay in that situation is based upon your past teachings. The subconscious mind does not have the ability to see forward, it only knows what has previously transpired; therefore, you continue to live in the past, repeating the same patterns over and over while hoping for a different outcome. Do you recall what Albert Einstein called this behavior? He called it insanity.

Your super-conscious mind, (higher-self, awareness, etc.) on the other hand, has different abilities. Learning to connect it with the universal collective consciousness can lead you down a new path. To get there, you must shut down your ego and follow it. New thoughts and new possibilities will open up when you shut down certain parts of your mind. This is because you won't be allowing the past to control the future. If your ego says, "You can't do that," tell it to shut the fuck up. Say, "I have been listening to you long enough. All you ever do is point out the negatives and remind me of the past. This is my life, and I will live it my way."

You are not your ego. You are your separate from it. Your awareness is your true self.

Living in the present moment literally means not allowing your past to come forth and convolute your current way of thinking or your future plans. Absolutely nothing that happened yesterday can or will be changed. We are here now, in the present, and from here we can move forward without the baggage, opinions, and emotions of others that we have picked up through existence so far. Tell yourself each time your egoic-mind tries to take back control, "That negative thought is nothing more than my fucked-up ego, trying to be a dictator, and take over my decisions."

Shut down your ego and begin to really live your life with the guidance of your awareness.

If you found parts of this chapter repetitive, that was no accident. I recommend going back and reading it again. We have many years of learned behaviors, from hurtful experiences, to overwrite on our hard drives. That takes much repetition. You are not your ego!

Shut down your ego and begin to really live your life.

Journal Entry, January 31, 2021—"The Mindful Gift Shift"

It was about 6 p.m. on a snowy Sunday night when I noticed something immensely transformative in myself. I was driving alone in my car, approaching a local high school. I remember this perfectly because I had missed my turn and was about to pull into the driveway of the school to turn my car around.

There is something that happens when I drive (and it is the reason why I choose, whenever possible, not to get behind the wheel): while driving or doing anything repetitive or mundane, I tend to go into an altered, receptive state of consciousness. Sometimes I get so caught up in messages or premonitions that come to me in that state, that I drive past my exit or turn. I wrote about this problem in my previous book, and it has yet to improve. Having discussed this issue with some of my medium friends, the consensus seems to be that mediums basically have no business being behind the wheel of anything motorized. We need a warning, like the label on a prescription: "Caution: Do not drive or operate heavy machinery while acting as a medium."

There was no one in sight as I drove along this quiet road. A blizzard was forecast for the next couple of days, so most people were staying at home or at least off the roads. Suddenly a deer jumped off the sidewalk directly in front of my car. By the time the deer and I realized we were going to collide, there was no preventing it. I slammed on my brakes as hard as I could, but with no luck.

Upon impact, I felt an adrenaline surge. This surge would normally have been accompanied by a great deal of anger—the type of anger with which I could destroy anything in front of me without a second thought and without regard for myself or my wellbeing. But that didn't happen. The adrenaline was there, but instead of anger or rage I felt a peaceful, calming sensation throughout my body. This was surreal because, normally I would have been so enraged at this animal who just fucked up my expensive automobile that I would have climbed out of my car and finished it off with great pleasure with a baseball bat. However, on this day that anger never surfaced, nor did the rage. I had no desire to hurt anyone or anything. Those feelings were replaced with an overall sense of calm, followed by concern for the animal. *Concern for the animal? What's wrong with me?* I thought. *Where is my anger? Where did it go?*

This wasn't me. This wasn't how I'd ever reacted to something of this nature in the past. *Who am I? What have I become?* At that moment I felt completely lost, in unknown territory, a stranger in a strange land. I didn't know who the hell I was anymore. Even though this was clearly an improvement in my behavior, at the same time I felt as if I were out of control, that I had no hold on my emotions. When most people say something like that, they usually refer to something bad. I, on the other hand, seemed to improve when losing control of mine. I was acting in a more positive, caring, compassionate manner, and yet I felt completely out of sorts. This was the part I found alarming.

I actually felt like a real, spiritual, caring being, without having to consciously make myself that way!

I remembered something I had learned from Eckhart Tolle. He is the greatest teacher of mindfulness I have come across, an absolutely brilliant, amazing person. In one of his classes, he explained that when something happens to you that triggers a very bad, unwanted emotional response that might be followed by actions you could regret later, just take a one-second pause in that moment. Then imagine yourself outside your body and look at the situation from a third-person point of view. Observe the "scene" and that which is about to take place. Then become the movie director of your own scene or movie, this movie that stars you, and as the director, tell your character how to act or behave.

For example, let's say I was driving by that accident of mine I have just described to you, observing someone else who had hit that deer, and I saw him get out of his car and start to go nuts: yelling, screaming, and acting foolish. I might say to myself, "Just look at that idiot over there, acting like a lunatic." Do I want to appear to be a raving lunatic in my movie? No, I don't. And so, as the great movie director I am, I will tell my character to act cool, calm, and collected. I want my character to be in control of himself. Just that single second of self-reflection and examination can make all the difference. That moment could prevent something from turning into something much worse that I might regret for years to come.

Back to the actual accident: I stepped out of my car to assess the situation. At first glance the deer appeared to be dead. I pulled the car off the road and fetched a flashlight from my trunk. I paused there, looked at the car, the deer, and myself, but in the third person. I automatically made myself a bystander in my mind, and in that moment, everything changed for me. Everything of late that I had been working toward came together.

The front of my car was badly damaged, but it was drivable. I was not seriously, physically injured, which was remarkable. I enjoyed a feeling of calm as I went to check on the deer's status, hoping it wasn't dead—or hurt for that matter. Gone were any inclinations toward revenge, replaced with an emotion so out of the norm, I have difficulty explaining it even now.

When the accident took place there was a split second when the adrenaline surged and my automatic thought was, *I hope that damn deer is dead; either that, or I am going to kill it myself.* But that was replaced with: *What's done is done. I can't go back in time. I can't change this event in any way, shape, or form. So I may as well accept this, move forward, and live now in the present moment.* In this calm and rational state, I noticed I was more concerned for the deer than for myself, as well as for the promise I had made to myself to seek to the best of my ability to obey the Buddha's five precepts, the first of which is to refrain from taking the life of any living thing.

I walked slowly with my flashlight to the place where the deer had fallen, but she wasn't there anymore. I immediately turned to my left, and there she was, standing by a large tree. She was upright! We were face to face, about eight inches apart, with our eyes locked. I have never been that close to a deer. I doubt most people have, because deer get frightened easily and they run away before you can get so much as a hundred feet from them. She just stood there and stared at me, and I back at her, for what seemed an eternity. I think she knew that I was sorry for what had happened. I felt that from her in return as well. (I know how crazy this sounds, believe me. I don't know if animals and humans can connect on another level the way two humans can, but it certainly felt real in the moment.) I slowly turned around and began to walk back to my car, periodically looking back at the deer, who continued to stay completely still, just staring at me.

My car turned out to be the big loser that day—it was in bad shape. As far as the deer and I were concerned, we both seemed to be relatively unharmed. How do such things happen?

I surveyed my car to make sure it was drivable, and it was. Then I began to dial Jessica's phone number. About halfway through I paused and realized something. Why should I call Jessica? Why would I call anyone? I was not stranded. I was not injured. Why call her and dump my bad moment onto her? Why should I give her my problem? Who would benefit from that? Would I feel better if I told her the story, and if so, wouldn't that be extremely selfish of me? It would upset her for no reason. I stopped the call and began to drive home slowly.

My calm, rational demeanor intrigued me. Had I achieved a higher level of consciousness and spirituality? Was I, perhaps, one step closer to enlightenment? I was so calm, and I remained in that mood for the rest of that evening, almost as if nothing had happened. I drove home, parked the car, meditated, and went to sleep.

I have read accounts of others who have felt this way after what they called a spiritual awakening or a raising of their consciousness. They claimed to feel somewhat lost—as though they didn't quite know themselves anymore. Even though this was for me a significant improvement, it still felt a bit strange.

Now I ask myself: Who am I, and what have I become? Have I lost control of my emotions, or have I gained it? I certainly feel better this way. I suffer from less stress and anxiety. Will this "new me," however, be effective if I need to be aggressive or confrontational to protect the people I love?

That was one of my concerns. Would I still have enough anger, enough steel within, if and when it is warranted?

This was a major ego fracture for me. I had others but this was most significant. I wasn't acting like my programming anymore, and it happened naturally. This can be wonderful but very confusing at the same time. *Who was I now?*

CHAPTER 18

Retrain Your Brain

Before we start tinkering around in your head, let us take a closer look at the immense power of consciousness. Consciousness is a form of energy which flows through every cell in our bodies and extend a few feet in radius outside of our bodies. The energy that radiates outside the body we often refer to as an aura. We know this to be true because of the people who have had near-death experiences and lived to recite everything that happened in the room even while they were clinically brain dead.

Scientists who study quantum mechanics describe a phenomenon they call "quantum entanglement"—when two quantum particles (such as photons or electrons) exist in a state that cannot be described independently of the state of the other, including when the particles are separated by a large distance. In other words, if one of the particles is in an "up" state, the other particle will be in the opposite or "down" state, or vice versa, no matter how far apart the particles are from one another—even on opposite sides of the universe.

In the simplest terms, this can be reduced to the fact that everything (and I really mean *everything*) can affect anything else. For something to affect something else, it must have, contain, or be derived from energy and that *is* everything. We have established that the conscious mind is made up entirely of energy. (By now you probably can see where I am going with this. Don't be alarmed; just come along for the ride.)

This brings us to the next important definition we will need, which is that of *decoherence*. Quantum decoherence describes how, since every quantum particle or system of particles is loosely coupled with the energetic state of its or their surroundings, entanglements are created between the system and its environment.

Simply put, any system cannot remain unaffected by its environment, and vice versa.

Your environment plays a huge role in who you are, even if you reject it. This means that if you are with the same people day after day and those people are a group of downers, always looking at the negative side of things, that negativity will mesh with you and mess with you. Get away from them because you cannot change them. If they ask you for help in changing themselves, that's different. It is more likely however, that they see their way of life as "just fine." In which case stay away from them. There are no exceptions to this precept. You must limit your exposure to such an environment. If you love them, do so from a distance. The people you spend time and interact with should be those who inspire you to be a better person. Now, you may say something like, "Well those 'downer' people are fun, even though they don't inspire me to be better." Here is the real deal: you were not put here to have fun. You are here to serve all life forms and evolve. You can and you should have fun while here, but that isn't your purpose or your right. Even the American Declaration of Independence only offers its people "the pursuit of happiness," not happiness itself.

The Buddha said, "There is no path to happiness; happiness is the path."

Revisit the story of the Buddha. He could have had everything he wanted so long as he remained living behind the huge protective walls of his parents' kingdom. He was a prince, after all. But he decided to leave all of it behind—food, shelter, riches beyond anyone's dreams. All of it was gone the second he walked out. He had nothing left. He could have snapped his fingers and had anything brought to him within minutes, but instead he threw it all away to be homeless and hungry. Why? Because he knew he wasn't whole, and he knew that in order to become whole he must experience the suffering that others had experienced. None of the peasants knew who he was and so he was able to walk around freely. He saw that the regular people who lived beyond the gates of his father's castle experienced much suffering. Why must they suffer while he did not? Why must anyone suffer? Why couldn't everyone have the same life he had? Could suffering be conquered? One thing he knew was if he didn't experience this other side of life, he would never become whole. He knew even then that a person who wasn't whole could never become enlightened. He realized that the only thing that made him different from those who lived outside the gates was his lineage.

The Buddha placed himself in the worst environment he could find so he could figure out how to get out of it and teach others to do the same. By getting out of it, he didn't mean just getting up and walking away from it. He meant making it so that you (your consciousness) could find fulfillment and happiness (contentment) whether within that environment or out of it. He was obviously successful, and, in that moment, he became the Buddha. I do not think you would have to go to the exact same lengths the Buddha had, nor would I recommend it. But I will say this: to become awakened or enlightened, you must first experience your own suffering. Watching other people suffer, and living vicariously through them, will not get you there. How can one be whole if one has only experienced only half of life?

Here is a quick and very simplified example of how environment can change one's decisions. Visualize yourself in an empty room. Another person enters the room. Even if they say nothing, they have already altered your energy, perception of the environment, and possibly your future actions. A third person enters. This one has an immediate effect on the second person, which then, as a result, changes your thoughts, your perceptions, and possibly your actions as well. One person leaves the room and five more enter. The room is getting crowded. Furthermore, one of the five makes you distinctly uncomfortable. You decide to leave the place even though you had previously planned on remaining there for the next hour. It may seem trivial, but your choice to leave could change the rest of your life, or the life of someone else in that room. What if one of those five people was going to start a conversation with you that would have resulted in you getting a big job promotion at work? This is a simplified example of a complicated topic. We will go more in depth. I promise you.

By no means is this phenomenon limited to people. Another simple example of how environment affects growth is the Mandevilla plant. If you place a tall lamp post in your yard next to a Mandevilla plant (which I actually did), the plant will begin to grow toward the lamp post and then up it, wrapping around the post. How does a plant know how to do this? How does it even know that the post is there? If I move the post away (which again, I actually did) the plant's growth is now limited. One's environment can produce a drastic effect in many ways.

On a quantum level, because of entanglement, one particle in the United States can affect another particle in Europe simultaneously. A particle on Mars may affect one on Earth simultaneously. There are no limitations at any distance. Einstein didn't like this theory because it seemed too magical (he famously called it "spooky action at a distance"), but he eventually had to concede that it was true, regardless of his efforts to disprove it.

What I am trying to show here is the power of the energy within the mind and how it has the ability to change or alter future events. If two pieces of matter (as mentioned above) can move or change one another, then imagine what one can do with the power of the mind.

When I was young my environment was quite unhappy and negative, and my thinking was shaped accordingly. To me, then, the glass was always half empty, so I needed to ration the water. If it were the opposite, if I always saw the glass as half full, I would have been in the habit of drinking some of that water before it overflowed. Do you see the drastic differences between those two statements and the mindsets of the persons doing the talking? It took me years to change my thought and speech patterns, and yet even now I sometimes find myself saying things in a negative way. Say something negative, believe the negative, and the negative will come to be. Flip the switch to positive, and the positive will manifest into reality.

"I had a car accident, and my car was damaged," versus "I had a car accident, but I came out of it unharmed."

"I never want to be in debt again," or "I want to always enjoy an abundance of money."

The way you speak to yourself affects your consciousness and the universe, determining what you will get, what you will have, what you will feel, and so on. You are creating your own quantum entanglement by putting your positive thoughts and statements into the universe to become entangled with other vibrating, energetic elements. Believe, that what your mind can conceive, you will achieve. Therefore, if your conception is negative, you will attract something negative, whereas if your conception is positive, the outcome will be positive. Quantum entanglement is the science behind the law of attraction.

The next obstacle I had to overcome was negative emotions. Something will trigger a negative emotion eventually, but how you acknowledge and react to that emotion is completely under your control. I assure you: if I can do it, anyone can. At one point in my life, my negative emotions were dictating my reality. Something as simple as a small disagreement with someone could trigger a chain of reactivity and angry exchanges with someone for the remainder of that day. If that isn't enough, I would continue to think about it for possibly multiple days thereafter. Keeping the angry energy circulating through me, attracting more of the same to me.

I will never forget an interview with Eckhart Tolle in which the reporter asked, "You mean to tell me that if a car cut you off while you were driving, you would not get angry at the other driver?"

"No, I wouldn't get angry," he said.

"How would you do that?"

Eckhart said, "I have simply learned to accept what is."

I am going to type that quote again, if not for you, then for myself: "I simply learned to accept what is." That is an enormously powerful statement.

What he meant was to accept what has already happened as fact, that which cannot be changed, and to maintain your presence and stay in the present moment. Obviously, the other driver didn't intentionally try to cut you off. He made a mistake. He didn't intend to crash his car into yours. If you stay in the present moment, you can see things as they really are, rather than based on your interpretations, emotions, or an ego flare. Accepting what is, as it is, allows us to respond appropriately, rather than potentially creating more of a problem.

Now if he had done it on purpose, with the intent of causing you harm, then you would have my approval to be angry; but I seriously doubt that is what happens in most cases (unless of course you happen to be driving in New York City—that changes things. —but let us move on).

Let's try something here. Think back and remember a time in your life when someone made a mistake that really pissed you off. Keep in mind that this was a mistake—perhaps something along the lines of a waiter dropping a glass of water on your lap. Think about it. Are you pissed off right now? If so, why? Who would be hurt or helped by your anger in this situation? Ultimately, *you* would get hurt because that anger can bring about a number of health issues; conversely, no one would be helped. Let us fast forward. The same thing happens again, same time next year. The only difference between then and now is you have finished reading this fabulous book by Ray Catania. The water drops the water and this time you remain in the present moment, which means you realize that nothing can be changed. It is over quickly; and it is only water. You don't get mad. The waiter, however, is in shock that you aren't swearing at him up and down. The owner of the establishment comes out to apologize to you directly, and even he is blown away by the fact you aren't mad at all. The owner and waiter are so incredibly appreciative, and they feel so badly, that they deduct 50 percent off your bill, and you get five-star service the remainder of the night. The waiter even offers to drive you home and walk your dog. A week later you return to the place on their busiest night ever, without a reservation (or a "rezzie" in Jessica's dialect), and now very quietly they are trying to shoo Liza Minnelli out the door just so you can have her table. You are the director. Tell yourself how to act until you do it enough times that it becomes second nature.

So you want to know how to control these negative reactions that could potentially flush your career, marriage, friendship, and so much else down the toilet? Don't worry. I've got your back. No one has flushed more treasures down the toilet than I once have. Here are the principles that will save you a lot of heartache.

Become "conscious of your own consciousness." This sounds more difficult than it is. Example: you get a phone call from your significant other, who says, "Tonight we are having dinner with the Smiths." You hate the Smiths. You've spent the whole day trying to please your unpleasant boss, and now you will have to endure the Smiths, who have a combined IQ of less than 100 and yet think they know everything. You are about to blow a gasket. STOP! Become the director of the movie you are in: the movie of your life. It stars YOU! You are the star of the show called "My Life"; but now, just like Clint Eastwood, you insist on both acting in and directing your own films. Look at yourself in the third person and give yourself some direction, "Clint." How do you want your character portrayed on the big screen? Do you prefer cool, calm, and collected or the emotional lunatic type? I am going to guess most people would prefer the former. Take another scenario. Let's say your two clumsy brothers are playing football in the driveway. One stupid brother throws the ball in your face, by accident of course. "Oh, my nose!" you scream, as the ball makes contact. Your big date that night with Doug is finished before it even gets started. Poor Marsha, Marsha, Marsha. You are pissed off. Get into your director's chair, stat! It was just a mistake. They didn't mean to hit you. Become conscious of your consciousness and remain present.

Practice "consciousness without thought." This is a technique that will help you from doing, saying, or feeling things that you do not want to manifest, and which may be harmful or may produce a negative consequence in your life. To practice this concept, look at an object. It can be any object, but let's make it a tree. Stare at the tree and see how long you can go without a thought from your ego invading your mind. Don't worry if you start out only being able to do this for a few seconds. That is pretty much where we all start out. Eventually you will graduate to several more seconds, and then longer. If you are worrying about what you will look like sitting in the yard staring at a tree, then you are actually allowing your egoic mind in from the start. If you need to work around this to be comfortable, then simply sit beside a window in a room with the door closed. Look at the tree. Look at it as if you have never seen a tree before. Really notice everything about it. Eventually, your ego will come through—that's okay. Just restart. The ego may say, "Who the fuck is telling you to stare at a tree?" Or, "Do you have any idea how much stuff we have to do today, and here you are, sitting around, 'being the tree'?" "I wonder who owns that tree?" "Who is their landscaper, anyway?" Okay, now you are in your egoic mind churning thoughts. Start over. It's fine to bring yourself back again and again. Just allow it to happen, don't get upset, and restart the exercise.

The more you practice the consciousness-without-thought exercise, the more you'll be able to pause when you really need to most, not allowing your egoic mind the opportunity to react to the situation at hand. This may sound like a silly exercise, but it just might be the one that saves you. You only need a second when a situation arises that would ordinarily piss you off to flip things around. There was a time when I felt silly doing this too, but trust me, this could really save your life. It can easily save your relationship, job, or friendships too. Consciousness without thought is something everyone thinks they have mastered, but truth be told, no one does. It can't be completely mastered (that I am aware of), only somewhat controlled. You only have a certain amount of time before a thought enters your mind.

Imagine yourself getting arrested for something about which you have no idea about. You are innocent, but instead of complying with the police, you yell and scream and reach into your pocket. Can you see how this story ends? It has happened many times, and entire cities have rioted after such a police shooting. This is real life, and it can really happen to you too. One extra pause for as little as one second to allow your conscious mind to take over and not allow your subconscious to react, can make a huge difference. Go find some trees and practice. (Not *that* one, though. That one's mine.)

Remember, your ego is not you!

Journal Entry, May 9, 2021—"Who Is This Guy?"

Mother's Day was approaching, and I really wanted to do something special for Jessica. She had been working her butt off lately on our list of projects and I wanted to express my sincere gratitude. I asked her what she would like to do or have for Mother's Day. "Anything you want, Babe."

She said, "I actually don't want anything." I thought she just didn't want to come out and ask for whatever it was. So, I asked her again. "No really, what would you like?"

She came back with, "I don't think you understand. I really want nothing at all. I would like a day to myself with no responsibilities, just staying home alone and relaxing. Go visit your mom."

At first, I thought this was one of her tricks. Jessica is notorious for saying "I want nothing," but actually she just feels awkward telling people what she wants. This time however, to my surprise, she actually meant "nothing."

Of course I had stuff delivered to her at the house, but I spent the day at my mom's without Jessica. This was still during the pandemic, so the only restaurants that were open would have very few tables available, if any at all. We decided that we would just order food, pick it up, and all meet at my mom's. We waited a little too long to order because apparently every single person in the area and at that hour had also ordered food for pick up and take out. We found one place that would take our order and they said it would be about an hour and a half before it would be ready. That worked out perfectly because my brother and his family were driving a long way to join us.

When my brother arrived, we decided we would go together to pick up the food as there was so much to carry. The restaurant was just a few short blocks from the house, so we waited until the full ninety minutes was up before heading to the restaurant. Everyone was hungry that late in the evening.

We arrived at the restaurant and saw several people ahead of us waiting for their takeout orders. They did not look happy. We got to the counter and were told that it would still be a little while. By the look of things, it seemed they might be running a little more behind than they were letting on. My brother and I found a table and sat down to wait.

I hadn't seen or spoken to my brother in quite some time since we were both busy with work and families. It was nice to take this time to catch up. But then I checked my watch and saw that the ninety minutes we had been quoted was approaching two hours. When I got up and asked if our food was ready, they said they were still working on it. I sat back down, and we talked some more. Time flew by, and then my brother's phone started beeping. Everyone at the house was concerned that we'd been gone so long. It had been two and a half hours with no sign of food. My brother got up this time to ask, and he received the confirmation that they hadn't forgotten about us, the food just wasn't ready yet.

My brother is habitually much less angry than I. When we were growing up, he could always hold back when I could not. My anger and rage would flare up easily, just like my father's did—at one point in my life I even had to attend court-ordered anger management. Now, here in the restaurant, we hit the three-hour mark and my brother fumed, "This is absolutely fucking ridiculous! I'm going back up there." I told him to wait a second and stay at the table. He asked me why I wasn't more upset by this delay.

"I just don't get it," he said. "Why aren't you angry? You must be, at least a little."

"Well, I don't think it's right that they are making us wait three plus hours for food, but why get angered by it? How will that help us? I don't feel like being angry today."

My brother stopped moving, speaking, or even blinking; he just stared at me with absolute amazement.

I explained it this way: "If we get angry, will the food come faster? We can't go back there and cook it ourselves; and if we left here, we would have no food at all because we would have to go to another restaurant and get back in line again for what may be another two hours. So, what's the point of getting mad?"

"Okay, I see," he said. Then he looked at me with strange stare. "Who the fuck are you, and what have you done with my brother?"

"Come sit down," I asked him. "I was enjoying our conversation.

"I have learned to stay in the present moment. There is nothing we can do except wait for the food. There are no better options for us. So we can sit here and be angry and miserable, or we can sit here and finish our conversation. This moment we are in right now is all we have, so love it and embrace it. Fuck it. The food will come when it comes."

"Is this the type of stuff that you have been writing about? Can you teach me this?"

"Yes, I have people who are my coaching clients that I work with one-on-one. My second book will focus more on this topic of being in the present moment, and many other perception and reality hacks that would make people happier."

"What about that phone call? What do I say to everyone at the house— and why aren't they texting you?"

"Well, first of all, they have been texting me. I answered once with, 'The food is not ready yet,' then switched my phone to silent mode because this is now their problem, not mine. They can't deal with the food being late, so they want us to be as angry and miserable as they are; but I will not give in to that. If there were something we could do to get food more quickly I would do it, but there isn't. Getting angry or upset about the things we can't control is actually rather silly, when you think about it. I won't allow someone else to determine my state of being."

"Neither will I," he said. "Thank you for that, Ray." He then turned his phone over and we went back to talking about life.

Upon our return to the house with the food, we were peppered with questions. "Did you get the food for free? Did you get a discount? Did you tell them we are never coming back to that restaurant again?" Everyone was hungry and upset.

I raised my voice just a little and said, "There are people who have *no food*, no money to buy food, and those who may wait days for their next opportunity to eat something—and I am supposed to be upset about a three-hour delay? Besides, I got to catch up with my brother in a way that wouldn't have happened otherwise. I choose to be thankful for the delay."

You could have heard a pin drop. Everyone's mood shifted for the better, and we enjoyed our food, which was quite good, by the way.

CHAPTER 19

THE LAWS OF ATTAINMENT

We discussed each of these laws individually in earlier chapters as they related to the practices I laid out, so they shouldn't be completely foreign to you. Now I would like you to see them as one collective list of some of the most important things anyone can learn. The laws listed here can be incorporated into a wide range of practices. In addition, these laws as listed here, when properly applied, can lead to the fulfillment of desires by peaceful means.

Law 1: Thoughts Are Things

I'd love to tell you I figured out these laws on my own, but of course I didn't. However, my own process of learning and applying these laws led to my bringing them together in a way that is easy to understand and implement.

This world we live in operates according to universal laws or principles. If A happens then B will happen, resulting in C. The laws aren't abstract; they are practical, and they play out the same way every time. Once you understand them, you must revise your way of thinking in order to live by them.

You will know the outcomes because you are part of their creation. Can you or I determine what will be given to us and make things happen the way we want them to? The answer is: you better believe you can!

I will explain these universal laws in simple terms, but it's up to you to retrain your brain and regularly apply them. Understanding them is the easier part. It is the implementation that some find challenging. This is because we are literally programmed from birth to see things a certain way. I am here to tell you that you must change that way of thinking completely to begin creating on your terms. If you do, you will likely get what you want. If you don't, you may very well get the opposite of what you want. There is not much middle ground.

Manifesting everything you want is just a thought away, but you must "think" correctly. That's right: *think correctly*.

The first law is: "*Thoughts* are *things*." They are not abstract or unreal just because others can't see or hear them. The universe must always listen to your thoughts. It cannot shun you or refuse to hear you. Remember, you are a conscious, living, breathing part of it.

You are a co-creator of the universe. You are a part of the universal collective consciousness. Therefore, what you think and how you think of it, will bring about changes in the universe. It may bring you what you want, or it may bring you what you don't want. That is why it is so important to master your thoughts, your thought processes, and your thought patterns. We accomplish manifestation primarily through thought, especially during meditation. There are some other important methods of communicating with the universe which also require a change in the way you think about things as well. There is a method for seeing your thoughts and visualizing them in a positive way. I will explain.

Thoughts contain energy, vibration, and frequency. Every thought you have is heard and felt by the universal collective consciousness that connects us all. Each thought matters, and each thought will have an effect. Each thought can become a reality. I'll give you an example.

You wake up in the morning of a day when you have an important meeting at work. The meeting starts at 9 a.m. and you must be present. So, you get up and say to yourself, "I can't be late; I can't be late." This thought is running through your mind as you get ready for work. "I can't be late; I can't be late!" What happens? More likely than not, when you arrive at work you will find that you are late. Why? Let's look at this more closely. By telling yourself over and over, "I can't be late," you created a picture in your mind of what it looked like for you to be late. Your focus inadvertently became about yourself and lateness. The universe does not speak English or any other invented language for that matter. It speaks "Universe." Therefore, you must learn to speak its language. Let's see how to correct your thinking to make things work better for you.

You wake up in the morning on a day when you have an important work meeting that starts at 9, and you must be present. This time you say to yourself, "I must be early; I must be early." This is the new thought going through your mind as you get ready for work. "I must be early; I must be early; I must be early for work!" So, what happens to you now? When you arrive at work you find that you *are* early. Why? You've created an image of yourself arriving early. You've reframed your thought into one that creates a positive mental picture of what you DO want to see happen. All the universe understands is the mental imagery projected from you which is converted to energy that vibrates at a specific frequency. The first image was of you being late; the second image was of you being early. Yes, it really is that simple. Never project the things you do not want. Lose those words from your vocabulary, your thoughts, and your written words.

I'll give you another example. Imagine if I were to say to you, "Don't think of a black cat." What would you immediately think of? A black cat. It would be impossible for you not to visualize a black cat. You must visualize what I am talking about in order to consider the notion that you are not supposed to think of it. Each and every thought we have is processed in part as a mental picture. This is how we are taught to speak as children. Mommy showed us a picture of a horse and said, "That is a horse." Once you fully understand this concept and how this thought process automatically occurs in your mind, you can begin to retrain your brain to think and visualize in a more constructive way.

Many of us are told from the day we are born what *not* to do. Then we proceed to do exactly what we were told not to do—repeatedly. It's not entirely our fault. It's the same pretense at work again. That is how thoughts function—they become images that direct our attention and energy in a certain way, which then creates our reality. Ideally, we would be taught what *to* do. Thoughts contain powerful energy.

If you change your thought patterns to always ask for what you *do* want (instead of what you *don't* want), you are more likely to get what you seek, because you changed the visualization that goes along with it. However, reprogramming your mind to do this every single time isn't always that easy. It depends on how you think or were taught to think. You must consciously repeat this exercise until your subconscious does it naturally, and that takes some time to accomplish. Start today and repeat each thing you say or think to yourself in an affirmative or positive way. If you wake up and say, "I don't want to be late," notice that error, and change it immediately to "I will be early." It's the visual aspect of your thinking that becomes the reality.

Here is another exercise. As you are going to bed at night, you say to yourself, "If I don't sleep well tonight, I will be tired tomorrow," guess what you will be like in the morning? Think for a moment how to reframe that sentence before you read on. You will be doing a lot of this reframing, every minute of every day, until it becomes completely natural to do so.

"I am going to sleep well tonight so I will be energized for tomorrow." Huge difference in your visualization! Get it? However, most of us do not naturally speak or think this way. That is the reason we must retrain our brains.

Knowing now that thoughts are things, how can we apply this principle on a larger scale to our benefit? Here are some more reframing ideas.

"I don't want to be in debt," . . . versus . . . "I always have an abundance of money."

Think for a moment. Run each of those sentences through your mind and then ask yourself what image was evoked in your mind. When you said the first one, you probably envisioned a stack of unpaid bills in your hands. When you said the second one, however, what did you see then? Perhaps a huge pile of money.

By the way, how many times have you thought about money in the positive or affirmative? We tend to say things like "I don't want to be in debt," or "I can't afford that." How many times have you employed the word "abundance" while thinking about money? Are you always telling the universe what you *don't* want, and thereby attracting the opposite of what you *do* want? How many times have you heard a friend say something negative and then they follow it up with something like, "Now watch, because I just said that it will happen." Why do you suppose they think that? Intuitively we know that is exactly how it works.

Tell the universe what you DO want. Automatically you will see that picture in your mind. The universe will then begin to rearrange itself to give you what you have visualized. Do this repeatedly and it will happen for you. It's universal law. Don't worry about how it happens; it just does. Do you understand how grass grows, or do you just accept and understand that it grows? It doesn't matter how it happens; it just does.

The Buddha said, "All that we are is the result of what we have thought."

Today you are the sum of the thoughts you have entertained up until this very moment. What you think of from this day forward can change your existence as you move into the days ahead. Start getting everything you want. Retrain your brain. It will change your life.

This is why making use of the principle of manifestation in your meditations is so powerful. In this type of meditation specifically, the only thoughts you should allow in your mind are your goals or your wants in picture form, said in an affirmative or assertive way. For meditation specific for manifestation, we suggest practicing in the morning and then again in the evening, preferably upon waking and just before going to sleep.

Here are a few more important pieces to this practice. You must repeat these positive visualizations multiple times. Just saying something once to yourself probably won't yield the desired result, but this also will depend to some extent on the complexity of what you seek. Continue to think of your positive visualization at various times throughout the day as well. It isn't possible to overdo this method. This is the same fundamental concept underlying affirmations. If you are familiar with affirmations, you know that you must repeat them many times in order for them to take effect. Also, just as with affirmations, you must believe in them. Believe that your positive thought can take tangible form, or at the very least, that it is possible. Believing will get easier for you as you begin to see the fruits of your early efforts.

Since believing is so important to the overall success of this law, try beginning with a few easier goals at first, and then work your way up to greater things.

Law 2: Maintain an Attitude of Gratitude

The next law is extremely important but often overlooked. You must maintain an attitude of gratitude. In other words, be grateful for the things you already have been given. This doesn't take very long to do, and it is extremely powerful because this changes your current mindset into one of positive thinking and receiving. It is great to think about all the things you want moving forward, but you'll get there much faster if you begin with thoughts of being thankful for what you have already received.

Attitude of gratitude shines brightly from within you, outward into the universe. Always begin meditations with those thankful thoughts. It can be done any time of day but especially each morning and evening. I find that if I do this just before my morning meditation, it instantly makes me feel more positive and connected to my higher self. It sets the tone to move forward.

If you are just beginning this practice, you may think you have nothing to be grateful for, but I assure you this isn't the case. We all have at some positive things in our lives. Maybe you don't drive the car you want, and you see a brand-new car across the street. Right away, your mind reverts to, "I don't have a nice car like that," or "I wish I had a nicer car." Fuck that! Start your day with, "I am grateful that I have this car to get me to work so

I can make an abundance of money to be able to get and drive one of those cars." Be thankful for what you do have and then put into the universe what you want to achieve next. Never say "I don't have." Change it to, "I want to have this." Or "I will have this." That is the proper positive thought form, and it is much easier to believe these things will happen when you start from a place of gratitude for what you already have. Obviously, there was a time when you did not have a car at all, then you made some money and bought one. So, if you did it once, you can do it again. You have accomplished this before. You have been given things, and shown the way to get them. Now we are just going to kick it up a notch, so to speak.

Whatever you think about, you will bring about. As soon as you start to think about the good things you have, you will begin to attract more of the good things you want; gratitude places your mind in a position to receive more. Gratitude is an important, significant law of the universe and must be treated as such. Having and putting forth an attitude of gratitude raises your frequency. Match frequencies with the things you want or need and watch them find their way to you. Like attracts like.

Have you ever come across a person who seems to have everything anyone could want, and they keep getting more? You see them living like that and you think to yourself, *What the heck did that person do to be so lucky?* It is not luck, my friend. They have learned, experienced, and believe that anything is possible, and they know what they must do to attract more. It is a cyclical thing: once you start receiving or achieving, you will find that you are able to do so more and more. However, once you start losing, you can continue that cycle also. We control this in our thoughts. You can place yourself into either category at any time.

Want a few more examples? You don't **have to** drive your kids to practice: you **get to** drive your beautiful kids to practice. You don't **have** *to* go to work: you *get to* go to work. You don't ***have to*** take care of your family: you *get to* take care of your family. Retrain your brain to maintain an attitude of gratitude. Check yourself. Some people have no job, no family, or perhaps can't have kids. Be grateful. Maybe you are in great physical health, but you lost your job. Thank the universe for your perfect health and ask for a better job. Maybe you went through a divorce, but you ended up with wonderful children from that marriage. Be grateful for them and tell the universe you want another person to love and with whom you can share those children. I don't care how fucked up you think your life is, you have many great things to be thankful for. In fact, when you put these things into practice, you come to a realization that it is often the bad shit we experience in life that yields the most important life lessons. Therefore, when you really think about it, there are no such things as negatives, because something positive is gained from all so-called negative things.

Law 3: Visualize to Materialize

The next law is: you must visualize in order to materialize. Since we already know that the universe can translate vibration generated through memorable imagery better than through words alone, we need to develop our capacity to visualize everything. Always visualize the end result of what it is that you want. Dwell on the end result. Let's say for example, your goal is to have a certain amount of money in your bank account. Picture that exact number on your bank account statement. Imagine logging into your bank account online and seeing that exact amount of money that you want in your account. Then sit and stare at it for a while. Then log off the computer in your mind. Meditate with that number in mind. Imagine yourself thanking the universe and being grateful for the achievement. Go ahead and actually thank the universe for what it is you don't have yet. It's okay. I know that it sounds insane, but just go with it.

This is one of the most powerful things you can do to speed up the manifestation process. Many motivational speakers suggest something very similar. They call this technique "acting as if" you already have what you want. I remember one of them saying that if you want to live in a ten-million-dollar house, go out and begin shopping for ten-million-dollar houses. Act "as if" you have the ten million already in the bank and are looking to pay cash for your new dream home. It helps maintain the belief and the continued motivation to continue on even if you get down on yourself from time to time.

The next important thing I will share with you is how to enhance your visualizations so as to make things happen quickly. I am not actually certain why we call them visualizations, given that to be successful we must use all of the five physical senses and not solely our eyes. We are going to dwell on those five senses and bring them into our mind, or our sixth sense, which is consciousness. (In my first book I explained that the earliest medical text proclaimed we had six senses, not five, with the sixth being consciousness.) Let us return to our ten-million-dollar house. Using our minds, we visualize ourselves entering the front door; . . . but I also want you to smell it. Then touch it. Then listen to the sounds around and inside it. Taste the food you will cook in the beautiful kitchen. You are now using all of your senses to experience it: all six of them. Bring the five physical senses up to your sixth sense. Always use every sense you possibly can in the midst of your so-called "visualization" techniques. The more senses you can experience and incorporate into the process, the faster it will unfold, enhancing the possibility of the thing you visualize becoming your reality sooner rather than later.

The universe can and will deliver, but you have to understand how to communicate with her in order to get started. Start small and build your way up to bigger and better things—and be patient. It may happen fast, or it may take a long while. In fact, the better things may take more time, but know in your heart of hearts that what you seek will come to you. Just be patient. Rarely do major changes come quickly. Don't give up early. In fact, do not give up at all.

Before we get to the fourth law, there is another very important aspect of this third one we should discuss. That is believability. What you want must be believable by you or it cannot happen regardless of how many times you attempt to manifest it. The truth of the matter is that if you don't believe that something can happen or come to you, it won't, and there is no way to override this concept. I have mentioned previously in my writings that I cannot try to manifest one billion dollars because I have no idea what it would be like to have such a superabundance of funds. I cannot relate to it or fathom it. I can't fully "visualize" it (using all six senses) because I have never experienced even being in the presence of a billionaire. But that is not my goal—greed has never been my thing. It is also my custom to ask to be shown the way to make an abundant acquisition through my own efforts, doing the type of work that will help others along the way.

If you can't "visualize" the item with all six senses, then use as many as you can. Also, I should mention that I often use money in these examples because everyone understands it. I'm sure hitting the lottery would be nice but, once again, I cannot visualize that, and I am certainly not going to waste my meditation time with it. I ask to be shown how to make, have, and hold onto an abundance of wealth *through my own efforts* of helping others. I have never gotten anything for free or without working for it, and therefore I cannot visualize that; and I am just fine with that.

Law 4: Take Action

Utilizing everything above without the final law will leave you quite frustrated and possibly thinking that reading this chapter has been a complete waste of time. It isn't as though we think of a new car and like magic it will appear out of thin air. Manifestation is not magic. I would also suggest that you refrain from merely "wishing" for material things. But if it is that car you want, ask to be shown what you have to do to make the money to get the car. Ask for those things on a higher level that give you the wherewithal to make such a purchase for yourself.

This law has more to do with your mindset, and less with your mind.

Let us examine the concept of materialism. Why do we want all these expensive things? Do you suppose it arises from a mindset of someone who thinks less of him- or herself, that they require these expensive items to make them feel that they are worth more? I can assure you from being both in poverty and well off financially, that one's happiness is derived from neither. Life is certainly easier with an abundance of money—this I can confirm. But fixating on money or the things we wear on our bodies or show off when we drive is not happiness at all. That is insecurity. That is showing a lack of respect for oneself. Money can make it easier to survive and thrive, but it won't give you what you need on the inside.

Many of us look for the instant gratification that comes in various forms from the outside world. I certainly was guilty of this much of my life, not realizing that even after I drew the jealousy of others, it didn't make me whole. It didn't fill the void. I looked to expensive items, intoxicants, comfort foods, and fancy labels, as if they would make me whole. They didn't. If you have chased after one of these categories you are not alone, but you are looking outside to cure an ailment that exists on the inside. The pursuits listed above are external forms of temporary pleasure, but none of them will bring permanent happiness. When we seek happiness outside of ourselves because we are trying to fill a void within ourselves, we only perpetuate the feeling that we are not enough. Stop looking outside and have a good long look at yourself on the inside. Changes made within you will last forever and can bring you peace and lasting pleasure.

Someone recently said to me, "I need a vacation." I thought about that. Why would someone actually "need" a vacation? They did not say, "I want a vacation." The difference is quite important. It was said as though the vacation were some sort of prescribed remedy to fix the person's woes. Furthermore, they seemed to be justifying this trip to themselves. This seems a poor reason to take a vacation. Wherever you go, there you are. You can never escape yourself. Even with intoxicants, you will not escape yourself. When the vacation ends or the intoxicants wear off it's you again, at home again, likely feeling worse than before because you now have less money and less brain cells.

The cure for internal pain always lies within you. It will never come from anything external.

Now don't get me wrong: there is nothing wrong with liking and buying nice things, so long as you are buying them for the right reasons. Jessica and I recently took a vacation, but we didn't "need" it. I can feel just as happy sitting at home on my couch as I can sitting next to the swimming pool of some hotel. One may be slightly nicer than the other, but neither serves as the source of my happiness.

The universe will give us things based on our beliefs about ourselves. You must feel that you are worthy inside in order to have more worth. If you feel less than whole, nothing external will bring you the happiness you seek. Nor will you acquire these things if you do not believe that you deserve them or that you should have them. I have struggled with this so often. I would see myself at the next level of success, or envision a pile of money, and then just before the action was about to become a reality, I would sabotage myself and lose what I sought. This habit was derived from growing up in an environment in which others did not believe in themselves, which rubbed off on me. I believed that way of thinking was my truth. To this day I often feel unworthy of receiving things. Even if it is a birthday gift, I have trouble accepting it. I had to overcome this feeling. I had to become whole.

This is what brings us to the next law: "Take Action." We must take the actions necessary to make ourselves feel and believe that we are worthy to receive anything, including happiness. Some very wealthy public figures have said things like "Hard work is what it takes to have more." That may be true in a way, I suppose. The speaker likely worked hard in his life, and because of that, he felt worthy of receiving such wealth. There is nothing better than hard work to get yourself to believe in your own self-worth. First, look inside yourself to find what is making you feel unworthy. Until we deal with that aspect of our life, we may have difficulty adopting a mindset of being ready to receive. Even if we acquire it, we won't find happiness there if we aren't ready for it.

It is time for you to reconnect with your higher consciousness. I say "reconnect" because you were born with this higher consciousness intact.

It gets lost as the years go by and other things we consider more important pull us away from it.

We were not born thinking less of ourselves. We were not born with any preconceived notions of what we could or could not be do or accomplish. Those limits were set into our subconscious minds by our overall environment during our early years of development.

It is time for your awakening. It is time for you to become whole. It is time for you to take action.

1.) The Buddha said, "There is no path to happiness; happiness is the path." What he is saying here is that happiness doesn't come when you buy a fancy car; happiness is the road to its acquisition. Each and every day your path will bring you closer to your goals. Live in each moment on the path and enjoy them as you follow through with your endeavors. Learn new things on the path. Welcome loved ones to join you on your path. Live and love the path, not only the outcome. The path may take a long time while the outcome may take only minutes. If you only enjoy the outcomes, you will do yourself a disservice. Love your path. It is where you will find true happiness.

2.) The Buddha also said, "All that we are is the result of what we have thought." Your subconscious mind does not know the difference between a real experience and a thought. If your subconscious doesn't know the difference, why not utilize this to your advantage? You can develop thoughts with your conscious mind. Make them real in your mind. Live them over and over in your mind, using the visualization process and all six senses. By doing this you are telling your subconscious that it is really happening. Your subconscious will eventually believe this as fact. This will put you in the mindset to receive.

3.) Eckhart Tolle said, "When you are not honoring the present moment by allowing it to be, you are creating drama." Living in the present moment means that the only moment that is real, the only moment that counts, is the one you are in right now. Anything that happened up until this very moment of your existence does not have to define you anymore. Let it go. We can't change it. We can't go back in time. Live in this very moment and allow what you do next to best represent you and what you are.

I had a conversation with someone a while ago; she was telling me about her father. She said that throughout his life he was almost always depressed and miserable. He would dwell on and obsess over things that simply didn't warrant the pain he was bringing onto himself and to others around him. Years later, as he aged, he was diagnosed with Alzheimer's disease, which strips a person of their memory. When she told me that I felt so bad and said, "I am so very sorry."

She said, "Oh, don't be. Once he developed Alzheimer's he was truly at peace and happy, right up until his death."

Obviously, none of us wish to be stricken with such a dreaded disease, but there is a lesson to be learned here. Once that man had let his go of his past, he was truly happy. He didn't do it voluntarily—his ailment forced him to live in the present moment; nonetheless, it was there that he finally found happiness.

Journal Entry, August 13, 2021—"Six-Figure Summer"

By August of 2021 Jessica and I were completely exhausted. We had poured our hearts and souls into building our platform to help others. At one point both of us were working fourteen-hour days. I wrote and published books, articles, and other forms of media. I was coaching people one-on-one at my office and trying to schedule as many speaking events as possible, including podcasts and online classes. I was also continuing my own education by working with my mentors, taking college classes, and completing various certifications as well. Jessica was working tirelessly on expanding the yoga and meditation studio, teaching yoga, hiring others to teach, and maintaining her medical practice.

We were so inspired (in spirit) collectively. She was receiving downloads from the universe faster than you can download a low-res JPEG of the Mona Lisa. We were spending money much faster than we were making it. The unfortunate reality of this world is that without money we cannot spread the word about the great spiritual shifts that are happening in the world today, and how to get out and be a part of them. We simply wanted everyone to know. We never started this to make money. The purpose of this work was always about something greater than profit. As Jessica and I would often jokingly say to one another, "We're just trying to change the world and shit." One person at a time. If we could just help one person's life become a little better each day, then we are accomplishing our mission. More and more however, we learned that to get the word out takes quite a lot of money.

Money for everything from expensive legal services to office supplies. We were fortunate to have so many people help us, and donate their time and efforts to assist us, but at the end of the day we were going to need money, a lot of it, to make a substantial change.

I know that I am co-creator of the universe. I know I am allowed to create my future reality as I want it to be. I know I am not controlled by something larger than me, because there isn't anything larger than my energy-based consciousness and its ability to attract what I need, when I need it.

Jessica was going out with the children to visit her mom. Before she left, I said, "One hundred thousand dollars. Every day and every night, one hundred thousand dollars." It's so wonderful to have a partner who understands the laws of the universe so that I can say something like that to her and she understands immediately. I was telling her that we were going to meditate collectively with the purpose of manifesting one hundred thousand dollars. She replied, "That's it?" Meaning, "Why not increase the number?" I said, "Let's start there, because that is what we really need right now."

"Okay, Baby," she said.

She left for her mom's place for a weeklong stay. I remained home to work. She was able to work remotely for a few days and write her reports from her mom's place and visit at the same time. I would text her periodically and remind her: "One hundred K, okay?"

She texted back, "I'm on it." And so we were. Each morning I did my "AH's," my attitude of gratitude, and my meditations. Then, after some more "AH's," I made my requests which were actually more like demands. "I need one hundred thousand dollars right now," I would say. Jessica would do this too from her mom's house. And so collectively, using our energy, beliefs, and knowledge of how the universe actually works, we were magnetizing one hundred thousand dollars so that we could continue to bring this information to the world—information such as how to get your own one hundred thousand dollars.

Some days I meditated repeatedly throughout the day. I spent a longer time with gratitude. I had a lot to be thankful for—make no mistake. Jessica and I were not starving. This was not the same as growing up without money. We weren't children. We had control of our lives.

The full seven days went by. We received nothing.

She and I were considering a small business loan to help us expand and grow. We put the application in and went back to the universe. Jessica received an alert on her credit report. It showed that we had applied twice for the loan. I was really upset because I knew we hadn't applied for two lines of credit. After all we didn't need two. If you have ever tried to reason with one of the credit reporting agencies, then you know what a waste of time and effort that can be. It also takes them months to fix an error.

A letter came in the mail, accompanied by an email to Jessica. She brought them to me happily. She said, "Remember when the credit borough thought we applied for two credit lines?"

"How could I forget," I replied.

"Well, it looks like we were approved for both."

"Both? We didn't ask for two. Holy shit!"

She said, "Will $250,000 do?"

"What?!?" I nearly fell off my chair.

"Should we call them?"

"Hell, yes!"

We called the bank and sure enough this was all legit. It was a business loan with decent repayment terms that would help us out quite a bit. We didn't take the entire sum offered, only what we needed. Within days it was in our account and once again the universe answered us with exactly what we needed. We were then able to use the money to expand our business. We are eternally grateful.

"Ask and you shall receive," Jesus said. He was right again. The catch is knowing how to ask, and asking for what you need without greed.

CHAPTER 20

Go Ahead and Lose Your Mind

When we hear the phrase "losing your mind," we often equate it with going insane. But losing your mind can also mean being mindful or practicing mindfulness. Mindfulness is the art of remaining in the present moment, not allowing oneself to use past events or memories to affect the present situation or the future. For example, if there is a certain "something" that really annoys you, but you have chosen to actively engage in being mindful, then you can let go of thoughts that would trigger negative feelings associated with it. You are no longer angry at the certain "something" because you have removed those thoughts that would have made you angry in the first place. When it comes to being mindful, less is more.

The only moment that actually is real is the present one. The past is gone, and the future isn't a reality yet. Where does that leave you? In between, and in the present. Why is it a good thing to practice mindfulness or living in the moment? We are the sum of our experiences, good and bad. All too often it is the bad experiences that determine what we may do next and in the foreseeable future. We allow what happened yesterday to dictate who we are in the present. Well, what if you could find a way to leave the past in the past and not allow it to affect your present and hence the future? Could this be advantageous to you? Let us look at it for a moment—the present moment.

Let us say that it takes you about thirty minutes to drive to work each day. Yesterday, however, it took you forty-five minutes because traffic was heavy and three other drivers cut you off, nearly causing an accident. That really pressed your buttons. Today as you get into your car and start the engine, you instantly feel anxious. You say something like, "If there is traffic, I'll be late again; and I hope there aren't any idiots on the road today." Well, remember that chapter on the laws of attainment? By thinking and speaking in those terms you may well find yourself in heavy traffic, and there may be a couple of idiot drivers too because you just visualized them in your mind. Let's see how practicing mindfulness can help in this case.

Mindfulness means we bring our attention to the here and now. Therefore, yesterday is not a thought that is allowed to enter your brain. You accept yesterday for what it was but have no preconceived notion of today. You've "lost your mind." Excellent! By letting yesterday's memory go away, all you see is this brand-new day. You are living in this new moment in time (the only one that is real) unaffected by yesterday's experiences. Now you get into your car and start the engine, but you don't experience any anxiety at all. Why would you feel anxious? What would it be based on? You aren't thinking about yesterday. You've let that shit go. It's gone because you lost it. You've lost that little part of your mind. By thinking less about yesterday, you are now practicing the art of mindfulness.

The more you accustom yourself to doing this the better you will feel every day. And it gets easier with practice. Forget about the bad shit of yesterday and focus only on right now! If you hit traffic again, just leave earlier tomorrow; but don't get worked up over it and carry it into the next day. The past is not reality, nor is the future. The only reality is the one you are in right now, this very second. Change the way you look at this moment as it happens. Don't define yourself by saying something like, "I am always late for work, and all the idiot drivers on the road seem to find me." You limit your own possibilities by anticipating something that isn't real and getting anxious over it. And if that isn't enough, you are making it happen again. Things do not happen to us; we make them happen to us by thinking them into being. You can determine whether you will be late for work. You will not decide how many cars are on the road, but you will decide whether you will be on time. Once you master this, your anxiety will diminish significantly, if not completely disappear.

When I began the process to become a student of Medium Joe, I completed and submitted his very in-depth and detailed application form. I waited weeks but heard nothing from him. I began to think: *I'm not good enough to be in his class. He must know this, and therefore he doesn't want me. I am not experienced enough. Hell, maybe I'm not even a real medium and this is all in my head. I guess I just suck at this. He will never take me.* I got myself all worked up.

I finally decided that I would just send an email asking if they received my application. His assistant replied that they did indeed receive it. "Medium Joe is reading the applications, he wrote. "Thank you."

I became even more upset because now that I knew he'd got it, I was sure I would be rejected. I doubted everything that had occurred during the past few years. I doubted the foundation of the entire first book I wrote before this one. I almost didn't publish it. *If Medium Joe says I don't have what it takes, it must be true.* This is what I said to myself, disregarding those who believed in me, including a certain woman who was my first mentor. *How could she not know I wasn't real?* I thought. How could this be? In my mind I had turned my life upside down, and nothing had even happened yet. I was completely distraught over something I didn't know was true.

Then one day I received a promising email. It was something along the lines of, "We thank you for your patience. Medium Joe has received hundreds of applications and must individually hand pick each student." At that point I thought, *Well maybe he hasn't read mine or evaluated me yet. Perhaps I still do have a chance.* But within the next twenty-four hours I was right back to, *I suck at this! He will never pick me. Why did I write a stupid book that no one will read? What an ass I am.*

I dismissed this situation from my mind and got on with my life. I had prepared myself mentally for a rejection, but deep down I was sure there was no way this wasn't real. My subconscious mantra that I wasn't good enough had energized my self-doubt. Then it came: the email that changed everything. It said, "Congratulations! You have been accepted to Medium Joe's two-year mentorship program." I nearly fell off my chair. It actually came with an apology for taking so long, but there had been hundreds of applicants and only twelve people made it into the program.

I had put myself through all that anxiety for months over nothing but speculation on my part. Everything I had thought about and stressed over hadn't been real at all. It turned out that Medium Joe loved my application and couldn't wait to begin teaching me. He told me right off the bat that he knew I was very talented, and he was looking forward to the next two years. What an idiot I had been for putting myself through something that was never real. I'd fabricated everything that caused my anxiety, and I almost made the potential failure real. Had I just lived in each moment from the time I sent in the application to the time I was accepted, I would have been much happier. On the plus side, I did visualize myself in the program many times during the weeks leading up to my acceptance. To that extent, at least, I was using my own techniques, yet I continued to harbor doubts that caused ongoing frustration.

I learned a few lessons that day. One was, "Don't be a complete idiot." And the other: "Always practice mindfulness."

Journal Entry, September 1, 2020—"Resting Bitch Face"

It was after work, about 6:30 p.m., and I was driving to Jessica's house. The entire day had been filled with an uncomfortable feeling of low and high vibrations running through my body from my knees to my head. I was rattled, and it became one of those strange days where for some unknown reason everything seemed to go wrong. I'm sure you've had them too—the type of day when big things don't work out and even the really small shit gets to you. I had texted Jessica earlier in the afternoon and told her what I was experiencing, and she said she was having that kind of day herself. I hadn't mentioned the vibrations yet because if I did, Jessica might wonder whether it may be her dad making contact with me, and she might get excited; but it isn't always he who is trying to get in touch with me (there are, of course, many millions of dead people), so I didn't mention it yet.

Driving to her house became increasingly more difficult and uncomfortable. While I was concentrating on the road I could feel multiple energies trying to connect with me. Once I had made it to Jessica's, she took one look at me and could tell immediately that something wasn't right. Jessica likes to joke with her friends that, even when completely relaxed, my everyday face appears to suggest that I am angry. She refers to it as my "resting bitch face." I wasn't angry, I was just shaken up. So, I asked her to meditate with me. She wasn't in the mood to meditate but joined me anyway to write down the things I saw once I entered the trance state. We set up my phone to record, and Jessica had pen and paper in hand. I began.

I saw the back of a woman's head. She was being pushed forward. I saw the hand pushing her: an angry hand. I thought it was a man's hand. Someone she loved was hurting her physically. I paused there because I fucking hated shit like this. The worst part of having these abilities is seeing this type of repulsive shit. Jessica asked me if the woman was alive or dead.

"Alive," I said. "She is here in our world and being hurt by a family member, a male, perhaps her husband. Either way it is disgusting. She has brown hair. It's a bit puffy." That was the only way I could explain it. I couldn't yet see her face. I couldn't see the man at all, only his hand, but I could feel the anger in the room. "The man isn't trying to kill the woman," I said, "but it is still a bad situation. It's an abusive situation." I gave Jessica the woman's name that came to me. She said she knew who it was and was aware of the situation—most likely the male person was one of her sons. They had gotten physical with their mom before. I felt disgusted, but I moved on.

The next thing I saw were the two people I had allowed to read a few chapters of my unreleased book. They were film producers who wanted to make a movie about our lives. I was hesitant to do this but something in the universe told me to consider it. I reminded myself that I had been in the presence of a divine being more than once. Who the fuck was I to question the universe and its plans for me? Anyway, in my vision I could see that they were both very happy with what they were reading and excited about moving forward. I told Jessica. A few hours later, that same night, we got emails from both of them. I'll paraphrase them here: "This is amazing! Can't wait to talk you guys again. This is going to be great."

I continued to move on and saw motion in the lower right-hand corner of the "movie screen." This is how I see things in my third eye. I have a primary go-to guide who will indicate things to me. He was emphatically pointing to a notebook with writing in it. I could see it, but I couldn't read it. My guide kept pointing. I asked, "Do I need to find that notebook?" I heard the sound in my right ear that he makes when he answers me in the affirmative. I can only ask this guide yes or no questions, for now anyway, and he answers with a sound. I have referred to it as Light Language in other writings. This is the term I was taught to use when referring to it.

I told Jessica about the notebook, emphasizing that we absolutely must find it. I didn't know why, only that it was imperative. Jessica then explained to me that she had searching for some lost paperwork that was quite important and she had a deadline to find them. Were the papers inside that notebook?

So there we were: me in meditation with Jessica, and my guide emphatically telling us to find the notebook. I ended the meditation, explaining to Jessica that the process sometimes becomes fragmented, so if there is more that I need to know it will come later. I wrote everything down and we went to have some dinner. By this time, we were both famished, but there was no way I could eat in that heightened state of consciousness—I would have thrown up. Hungry or not, I had to wait a bit before I could get any food down. I had just witnessed a horrendous scene of domestic violence. It can take as much as two hours for me to remove negative energy from a vision like that.

Later on, I had begun to think about finding the notebook. I didn't know whether my skills would serve for that sort of purpose, but I was up for the challenge. I agreed to do it and asked Jessica to give me some time to work on it. She let me know what the deadline was to find them and a name that would appear on the papers. That was pretty much all I had to go on. I had three days to find them.

The following day, we went for a walk in a park and sat down for a moment to meditate while we were there. The trees were beautiful. I don't know what it is about tall trees, but being under them just makes me feel like I am closer to higher realms. Trees have so much energy. Nature has so much energy. I guess the Buddha found that out. Anyway, that is when I saw it. I told Jessica then and there that I could see the notebook with the papers, and it was in our office. Back to the house we went.

We ripped through everything, but the notebook wasn't there. I was puzzled because I had seen it so clearly on the black desk in the office. Even though I felt it was on the desk, I had searched in the file cabinet, and I grabbed a file. "I got it! I got it. Look, the name of the person is on it." Well, that part was right. It had the person's name on it, but it wasn't the papers we needed and there was no notebook to be found. I said, "Sorry, Babe. I was close."

She thanked me for my efforts. I felt bad that I hadn't found the file she was looking for, but I was pleased that the process kind of worked.

The next day while at work I got a text message from Jessica. It was a picture of five notebooks that were in her office on a black desk. Inside the notebooks were the important papers. Above the picture of the five notebooks was the name of the person on an envelope with the papers she needed inside. The text read, "Please thank your guide. He is awesome." I texted back, "Yes, he is. I'll let him know. And so are you, my love. So are you!"

CHAPTER 21

THE ART OF SURRENDER

As a societal norm we tell ourselves and others we care for to fight and fight, and never surrender. "Win always. Win at all costs. You can do it. Just hang in there and make it so. Push with everything you have to make it to the top." This isn't bad advice, but what if there were a better way? What if I told you that manifestation through meditation will undoubtedly grant you all your wins and wants all the while, with far less worry and anxiety?

There is a saying I learned a long time ago. "Believe you deserve it, and the universe will serve it." We spoke earlier about using the manifestation meditation techniques to put your conscious, energy-based thoughts into the universe, and then letting the universe take it from there and deliver. You will receive what you need, or you will be shown the path to get it. I cannot stress enough how important it is to ask for the things you want *properly*. The universe does not speak English, Spanish, French, or any other language for that matter. The universe speaks by means of frequency and vibrations.

A quick recap of the practice itself:

After you wake up in the morning, meditate with an attitude of gratitude, followed by the "AH" chant. You will then tell the universe, "Give me _____ (fill in the blank)," expressing clearly your need. At night repeat this meditation, using the "OM" chant. This is 100 percent real. It works. Own this concept. You have a right to live happily and comfortably in this realm. Take it!

This brings us to the second concept of living only in the present moment. Let us assume that you have a serious issue that needs to be addressed in a timely manner. Most people would be consumed with thought that would likely lead to anxiousness and in severe cases, can even become debilitating.

If you truly wish to succeed in these practices, living in the present moment is paramount. Ask yourself this question: "Are you anxious about something right now?" Right this minute. "Are you concerned that you are taking up too much time reading this book instead of worrying about something?" Is there something pulling at you telling you to stop reading because you have something else to do? Now, ask yourself this: "In this immediate moment, do I have a problem?" I'm not talking about yesterday or what may come tomorrow. I mean, in this very second right now, do you have a real, threatening problem that requires my immediate attention? The answer is most likely no because you are still reading this book. I don't have to be psychic to know that you have no threatening problems right now, because if you did, you'd be forced to stop reading. The point of this is, you don't have to worry about, what you don't have to worry about, right now.

For example, if tomorrow, you have a flight out of JFK to Timbuktu, and flying makes you uneasy, you need not worry about that until tomorrow. Relax and read my book. You do not need to carry that anxiety around with you until you board the airplane. Everything else is just you, torturing yourself, for no reason. Don't worry about, what you don't have to worry about right now.

Once you have mastered these two concepts you can move on to the art of surrendering.

The practice of surrender is very effective. If you fear that surrender will cause you to become weak and ineffective, that would be a delusion. **In surrendering you say, "This is what something is, and I may as well say yes to it, and accept it for what it is. I may as well welcome it as though I have created it and own it."**

There is an effect from surrendering to "what is" that will bring you to victory. Surrendering can be difficult because it goes against all natural instincts, but I assure you there is much to be gained by it. And there are some things you will lose, including anxiety, depression, unhappiness, misery, worry, anger, despair, and much more. Simply surrendering to what is, will release all of those negative emotions the second you adopt and implement its practice.

Let's look at this more closely. Take a hypothetical: you have invested your retirement plan in the stock market and, if all goes well, you plan to retire in the next ten years. However, something triggers a recession, and your portfolio of investments takes a 40 percent loss. Is this tragic? Yes. What can you do about it? Little or nothing. It just is. The same would be true even if we made this scenario worse by adding that you recently moved around some investments you thought would do well, but they went in the wrong direction. Now you feel as though you caused this predicament to happen, which might make you feel even worse. But again, what can you do? It simply IS this way now. There is no traveling back in time to change it. So, surrender to what is because you will have to do so eventually anyway. Is it really necessary for you to dwell on the unfortunate occurrence until it begins to drive you crazy? Of course not. Yet how many people do you know who have done just that, obsessing about their unfortunate circumstances so much, they literally changed their mental health for the worse as a result?

The faster you accept "what is" and move forward with your life, the happier you and everyone around you will be. Will the money come back if you hurt yourself or become depressed over it? Not hardly. So then why do people do it? Why do folks torture themselves? Maybe there is a lesson here—a positive takeaway to be learned about money and investing. Be thankful for any learning experience. Find that learning experience, inherent in the situation, and dwell on only the positive derived from it. Surrender to "what is" and allow yourself to be happy again. Go back to gratitude and manifestation. Give thanks and be grateful for what you still have. You got to keep 60 percent, after all. Be thankful for the fact that you are still alive and able to take action to make the money back. You "get to" make it back, instead of "having to" make it back. Do you see the amazing difference in those two statements? You "get to" make it back. You have the opportunity to manifest it once again. Perhaps there is even a better way to do it that you learned along the way.

It may be a considerable challenge to retrain your brain to think in this manner, but once you do, you will be happier all the time. **Surrendering is a win-win (even though we often can't surrender until after we lose, lose).**

I was working on the first draft of this chapter during a weekend trip with Jessica. We were on a quick two-day getaway to a relaxing place we love. I spent the majority of the first day writing this chapter. When I was done, I read it back to myself. Jessica walked into the room at that moment and asked how it was going.

"I hate what I wrote," I told her. "This is such an important concept, and I don't feel that I got the point across." I was quite disappointed that I had spent a full day of my two-day vacation writing something I didn't like. I began to rant about how upset I was, and that I could have done something different that day. I had thrown away a full day of relaxation with the woman I love only to write something that would never see the light of day! We love our weekend getaways. We enjoy having the time to just relax, recharge, meditate, get naked, and have sex all day. And half of the weekend was gone with nothing to show for it!

She said, "What were you writing about?"

"The art of surrendering," I replied. "One of the most important concepts in the entire book."

"Is that so?" she said with a smirk. "You mean surrendering to what cannot be changed because it is already in the past? Accepting and not dwelling on what cannot be changed? Is that the form of surrender you're talking about?"

"Um, well . . . I guess, um . . ."

Jessica interrupted my stuttering with, "I am going to surrender myself to a hot bath. When you are done dwelling on your past you can come upstairs and join me in the pleasant and present moment I will be experiencing and enjoying the bath water, filled with bubbles. You will get to rewrite your chapter whenever you want."

I fucking love this woman!

Smart, sexy sarcasm—that day just got a whole lot better! *(Where's my snorkel? I'm going deep!)*

CHAPTER 22

QUANTUM CRAZINESS

The Higgs Particle (or the "God Particle" as it was nicknamed) may be the most substantial scientific discovery of my lifetime. As I mentioned before, Peter Higgs (who predicted its existence), helped prove to the world that there is at least one Quantum field in the universe. We discussed this in the chapter on the law of attraction, and it is worth discussing again. The Higgs field, if you recall, is a Quantum field that all particles must pass through. It exists between your body and this book right now. It lies, at this very moment, in between the Earth and Mars. It is everywhere. It controls how all mass will behave on earth or in space. As particles pass through this field they speed up or slow down, which is how different types of masses are formed. In other words it is the Quantum field which determines the particle's behavior and not the particle's make-up.

All particles begin their life with zero mass, but when they enter the Higgs field, their mass becomes a reality. The best way to visualize this was given to us by the famous theoretical physicist Brian Greene. I will borrow his explanation here. The Higgs field is like a sea of molasses that slows down certain particles to the point where they can hold steady. This explains how mass exists. If there were no Higgs field, all particles would float around aimlessly forever and behave more like light than anything solid.

Light (or photons) travels right through the Higgs field because photons seem to be unaffected by the field. Mass can be transformed into energy and energy can be manifested as mass. While some particles are almost completely unaffected by the field, other particles upon entering the field are directly affected and slow down to a halt (or what appears to be a halt), creating all the solids in our world.

This discovery may lead scientists to uncover the secrets of dark energy, which is said to account for 23 percent of the universe. As you recall from what I wrote in a previous chapter, it is my belief that dark energy is derived from the energy that remains (consciousness) after the body dies. Our consciousness (or what the Church would call a "soul" or "spirit") lives on after physical death in the form of dark energy, becoming part of the structure of the entire universe at its most fundamental core. Again, this is just my own theory, and has yet to be proven scientifically.

Knowing that the Higgs field is a reality may allow scientists to find solutions to many unanswered questions in theoretical physics. Everything that travels though the field seems to be affected by its existence in some way. It may be the "glue" that holds everything together in a perfect functional matrix.

We are now beginning to think that it is more likely, that we have, multiple Quantum fields in the universe. Evidence of this, was brought forth by David Tong, who is a professor of theoretical physics at Cambridge University, who specializing in quantum field theory. Each field may be responsible for different energies and particles.

That isn't what this chapter is about, but I'm using it as a lead in here to better explain our universe, how incredibly beautiful it is, and how you can become "one" with it, always.

There are three levels of existence in our world.

1.) The subatomic level: where particles appear to act similarly, to the way, water in a pond behaves after you drop a rock into it. The particles ripple outward like strings vibrating at their frequency.

2.) The macro level (or our material level): where these stringy vibrating waves appear to be solid matter, and we experience them with our five physical senses. (You will notice that I omitted the sixth sense.)

3.) Higher levels of consciousness: where no matter exists, only energy (including the energy of thought) vibrating at various strengths and frequencies through Quantum fields.

The core commonalities that are the foundation of all three levels are energy, frequency, and vibration—exactly what Nikola Tesla told us during his time. Suddenly, everyone wants to uncover all secrets of how energy and matter travel through a Quantum field. Some scientists have given up trying to figure out how it happens, preferring instead to focus on how this phenomenon can be turned to financial profit.

Quantum phenomena are already in use in our everyday lives. Many of our electronic devices perform as quickly and efficiently as they do because of the discovery of concepts like superposition and entanglement. Computer scientists are attempting at this moment to create the first quantum computer. If such a computer existed today, it would work one hundred million times faster than the computers we have in our homes.

Let me explain why this is such a big deal and how it relates to this book.

I want to return for a moment to quantum entanglement and what it means. The best analogy I've heard for quantum entanglement goes like this: imagine that you have a magical pair of dice which when rolled always add up to seven. If one die lands on six, you know for a fact the other will land on one. If the first die lands on four, you know undeniably that the other will land on three. Well, in the quantum world, this is how entangled particles behave.

Now, here is where it gets crazy. If you were to take one of these dice and roll it in New York while your friend took the other one and rolled it in California, the rule would remain the same. Depending on who rolled first, the outcome of that die will determine instantly the roll of the other die in order for both dice combined to make a seven. How can this be? One of the dice (it doesn't matter which one) is determining the other's outcome. How do you suppose they communicate? Currently, no one knows.

Related to quantum entanglement is another concept called "quantum superposition." If we have a pair of entangled particles in two different rooms, one red and one blue, and I walk into the first room and see that that particle is blue, I automatically know for certain that the other one is red. That being said, once I leave the room there is no guarantee that the particle in that first room will remain blue, nor that the other one will remain red. If I turn around and go back into the same room, that particle may now be red; if so, I will know that the particle in the other room is blue. Before either particle is "measured" or looked at, they are both said to be in a quantum state known as *superposition*. In a state of superposition, either particle can be red or blue; but once I look at one, the other one will be its opposite. This happens every time without fail, as proved by John Stewart Bell in 1964.

What this means is that one particle can communicate with another particle regardless of physical proximity. This happens instantly regardless of how far apart the two are located. Communication of any kind, as we already know, is transmitted by means of energy, therefore we must assume that information in the form of energy is being transmitted somehow from one to the other. In our examples they are informing each other what color to be or what side to fall on, but the type of information being passed from one particle to another is irrelevant to the fact that two particles at a distance can communicate at all! What's more, they do this silently, and possibly faster than the speed of light. It's completely mind-blowing!

You may wonder why I insert physics lessons into the texts of these books. It is because these scientific discoveries show that we are not as separate and limited as we ordinarily take ourselves to be, giving skeptics a way to understand how telepathic communication is possible. You cannot tell me, if two particles of matter can communicate with each other, when one is here in on Earth, and the other is situated on the former planet known as Pluto, that the human mind cannot communicate with someone else's mind, on the other side of the earth. Are particles of matter more advanced than human consciousness or the human mind? I think not.

By the way, as a side note; I am still a mite upset with the 2006 demotion of Pluto "the planet" by the International Astronomical Union (IAU), which officially downgraded its status. Poor Pluto: with no true identity, it is simply lost in space. To make matters worse, in 2016 they began saying that they may have discovered a new ninth planet in our solar system. This went unnoticed? Where are the conspiracy theorists when you need them? Please forward my letter below to the potentially new ninth planet as soon as possible.

Dear New Ninth Planet,

Before you commit to joining our solar system, just consider the way this whole Pluto thing was handled. Thank you.
Your pal,
Ray

Let's return to our topic.

Here are some of the more common technologies, involving principles of quantum mechanics, that have been in use in our everyday lives for quite some time:

1.) Computers

2.) Smartphones

3.) Lasers

4.) Telecommunications

5.) Atomic Clocks

6.) Global Positioning Systems (GPS devices)

7.) Magnetic Resonance Imaging (MRI machines)

Below are some of the more common examples of quantum mechanics at work in the lives of Jessica and Ray:

1.) Jessica thinks to herself . . . "The garbage has to go out." Ray takes out garbage.

2.) Jessica thinks . . . "It's been a while since we had a date night." Ray makes reservations.

3.) Jessica thinks . . . "He doesn't buy me flowers anymore." Ray calls a florist.

4.) Jessica thinks . . . "That pool boy is cute." Ray plots to kill the pool boy.

I realize things at my house may be different than at yours, but with a little work on your own sixth sense you, too, can plot a pool boy's demise.

By the way, if anyone is in possession of a quantum pair of dice, let me know and I will meet you at the nearest casino.

Journal Entry, February 13, 2021—Little Tibet in New York

One early morning I was sitting on a couch in a cabin, looking out windows that stretched nearly floor to ceiling. The cabin was situated in a valley between two mountains, one in front and one behind the property. At least two feet of snow covered the mountainsides. The majestic trees before me must have been fifty feet tall. I was facing east, and the sun was beginning to rise above the towering, tree-lined mountain. The weather forecast called for more snow later in the day and a temperature of about twenty degrees Fahrenheit. The view, the energy, and the peacefulness were breathtaking.

The cabin was a four-bedroom, three-bath cottage that Jessica and I had all to ourselves for four days. It was my birthday weekend, and each year at this time Jessica and I would take a trip somewhere special. (Anywhere is special when we are together—we could be sitting in a cardboard box with a candle for light and I would still consider it heaven if Jessica were near me). She was still sleeping in the master bedroom. I had placed a cup of coffee at her bedside and come upstairs to meditate in this beautiful, breathtaking environment and see the sunrise. You might be wondering why two people would pay for a cottage that sleeps eight? The answer is that the Dalai Lama once stayed in this cottage, which they have since nicknamed "Little Tibet."

I remember that upon entering the cottage I noticed a picture on the wall of the Dalai Lama standing on the front balcony, shaking hands in a crowd of what appeared to be hundreds of people. I went through each bedroom and stopped at the top floor corner room. "This is it," I told Jessica.

"Say what?"

"This was *his* room."

"How do you know?"

"It's kind of what I do."

"Oh, yeah," she said.

It wasn't the nicest bedroom by far, but I could tell it was the one. We did not sleep in it nor do anything else there for that matter. (Get your mind out of the gutter, people.)

There are many cottages of all sizes you can rent at this site, but if given the option, why not choose this one? As you can probably imagine by its nickname, there are no televisions or clocks, and no cellular service in "Little Tibet." In an emergency, or if you simply can't take being unplugged from the world, Wi-Fi is available, but we tried to limit our usage.

The idea of a retreat like this is to do nothing, to just allow yourself to be. If you are new to this type of thing, then it is about finding yourself. Jessica came upstairs to find me sitting on the couch, smiling and staring out the window.

"Good morning, Baby. What are you doing?"

"Good morning, my love," I said. "I am doing nothing. I am just being." With that she sat beside me, and we both looked out the window; just being present and in the moment, we forgot about life and all that goes with it for a while. A long while. Both of us passed in and out of meditative states and went deeper and deeper into ourselves. There was absolutely no unnatural outside stimulation. We had a beautiful view of nature and one persistent ladybug which had found Jessica and would not leave her. Even when Jessica switched places in the room, the ladybug followed. Ladybugs usually aren't around in the winter: a time when they go into some form of hibernation. We were not experts on this topic, but we knew that mid-February up in the mountains was no time or place for a ladybug to be out and about.

There is no greater feeling than getting to the point of not needing any external stimuli to make me happy. I often say to Jessica, "I don't need anything from the outside world to make me happy because I'm happy inside and I can visit myself inside my consciousness anytime, any day, anywhere." I know this sounds nuts, and at one time I would have been the first to say so, but now I'm of a different mind. I am still trying to figure out how it all happened so quickly. How the heck did I go from an angry, depressive materialist, to happily sitting like a monk in complete silence in the middle of nowhere. And not only happy but feeling extraordinary! I'll admit that Jessica and I visited the local spa for Tibetan massages once, and that experience was incredibly euphoric, but other than that we had barely left the cottage other than to go for walks in the luminous natural beauty. Is this what they mean by inner peace? Had I achieved that treasured state? *Another level up in my quest for enlightenment,* I thought.

I would like to share this with you. I wish I were able to reach through the pages of this book and give you this feeling that's inside me of true inner peace, where there is everything and nothing at the same time. I am having difficulty finding the words to describe it. Perhaps that is why we can't easily teach one another how to get here. It takes time and effort. There simply isn't a direct way to explain it. We each have a slightly different path that we must take, but we can all end up eventually in the same place. It's similar to how you set up GPS in your car, I suppose. You can choose the fastest route, or the shortest route, or the route without paying tolls, the way that uses less fuel, or even shut off the GPS and just drive. They will all eventually get you here—if here is where you really want to be.

Jessica and I had made this trip to celebrate my birthday, but it was also about something much more than that. It was once again soul-searching time for me, and some big decisions had to be made. *Was I going to leave my day job and devote the rest of my life to helping others? If so, what was the best way for me to do that? What about our children, who need us to supply them with just about everything, including their educations?* We were by no means in a place where we could stop making money. However, I also had to do what I was being called on to do.

This was a huge decision for me, and admittedly a scary one as well. Jessica wanted me to take the plunge, but she would support my decision either way.

These next few paragraphs are from my first book, *The Atheist and The Afterlife.* In that book I related how the first medium I had met had confirmed for me that the strange occurrences and things I was seeing and feeling were real. I had brought her my first journal, filled with descriptions of the so-called psychic phenomena I had been experiencing. She could personally identify with each episode, and went on to explain that she saw and felt things the same exact way. I have abbreviated this excerpt somewhat for our purposes here:

On January 25, 2020, I arranged a meeting with my teacher Medium Bonnie. She was extremely busy with other projects, so she hadn't come to our area in quite some time. I was very excited that she was going to be in my area, and I took the opportunity to have face-to-face time with her.

We then discussed the release of this book and my apprehensions about doing so. I didn't tell her I was apprehensive, mind you, she just knew. She asked me if it was because I was still doubting my abilities and I said, "Yes, absolutely." She said I had to stop doubting myself. She told me that I was advancing in months what it takes most mediums years to develop.

There was a brief silence in the room while she looked at me. I could tell she was receiving a message due to the pause in our conversation.

*She returned to me and then said, **"You must let yourself die, Ray."***

"WHAT? What do you mean?" I responded, shocked and very confused.

"You won't publish the book because you know that once you do your life as you know it will no longer exist and you will become someone else. Just like in death, we transform into someone or something else. You must let yourself die," she said again, quite emphatically. "Do it now, or you may lose your opportunity. Just let yourself die."

I understood exactly what she was saying to me, but this was still scary as hell. What would happen if I released this information to the world? What would my new life be like?

Up in the valley of the mountains, I sat and meditated in our cabin for hours, asking the universe for an answer I really needed. And then it began. The movie screen in my mind opened for a very short while; but in that moment, I saw something. I saw myself writing this book. Only this time I was writing in my own office. It wasn't the day-job office I had at that time. This was a brand-new office. And then eventually I saw people come into my office, one at a time, and I would sit with them individually and help guide them. Was this what some call an *"akashic* download"?—a visionary gift from my higher self, telling me it was time to move forward? I sat with this for as long as I could, but like I said, overall, this experience was brief.

Later on, in the evening more of the same vision came through, and more still the next morning. There was no mistaking the message now. I often must "see" things more than once to verify them. I told Jessica, "It's that time again. As nervous as I am, I have to let myself die."

I came home from the mountains, and that same week I had a meeting with the president of my firm and explained that I was giving three months' notice. I recall him saying, "I did not see that coming." I replied, "Neither did I; believe me, neither did I."

Oh, and as for which room the Dalai Lama had stayed in: around May 21, 2021, Jessica found a photo online of His Holiness in a meditative state sitting atop the bed in the exact room I had thought was his.

Journal Entry, April 14, 2021—Coaching Others for Success

After publishing my first book I decided to abandon my then-current job, which consisted of a well-paying executive position, to embark on a career dedicated to helping others through writing, publishing, teaching, and personal coaching. I created Limitless Publications, Media, and Coaching. Jessica and I opened a yoga, meditation, and wellness center together. In order to start my coaching practice, I had to go back to school once again; but I was starting to really enjoy school at that point, especially when it pertained to anything related to my new mission of helping others. I received my Life Coaching Certification and went on to receive my Master Certification. I went back to college at the University of Sedona where I completed their master's program in Metaphysical Parapsychology, and I am currently pursuing my PhD. I am also an ordained minister with International Metaphysical Ministry, a nondenominational organization founded by the late, great, Rev. Dr. Paul Leon Masters. Since it is a nondenominational church, it is founded on metaphysical principles and spirituality and not on traditional religions.

I also continue to attend classes and private sessions with my chosen mentors, and I read voraciously, including the works of Eckhart Tolle, Deepak Chopra, the Dalia Lama, Dr. Brian L. Weiss, Dr. Joe Dispensa, Dr. Dean Radin, Bruce Lipton, and many others. The combination of learning from those who are knowledgeable while experiencing my own phenomena has empowered me to explain this path to others. In addition to Limitless Coaching and Limitless Publications LLC and the studio, Jessica also continues to work in the medical profession as a pediatric neuropsychologist. We often say tongue-in-cheek to one another, "What have you done today, Babe?" "Oh, you know, just trying to change the world and shit."

Aside from the humor, we really are trying to change people's lives for the better, one person at a time. It is a business and a spiritual mission combined.

I was once full of nightmares and now I am living my dream.

Journal Entry, April 23, 2021—The Rebirth

This is my final day of work at my day job. As of today, I am a teacher of metaphysics, a spiritual coach/advisor, author, publisher, and business owner. In addition to metaphysical coaching, I coach people from all walks of life, who want to make significant changes in order to achieve more success and peace in their lives.

Jessica and I have found that the two of us working together can make a person's transformation much easier. Jessica says the key to my success is that I am relatable. I am still involved in the business world, raising children, saving money for retirement, putting kids through college, working sixty-plus hours per week and still a part of the rat race. I am a regular guy. I feel different, but that is on the inside. I rarely get angry, when once it was a regular occurrence. That old me seems to have faded away, though I am still quite far from perfect. Sometimes, Jessica will say something like, "That isn't very Eckhart of you, Honey" (referencing renowned author/ spiritual teacher Eckhart Tolle). My retort would be, "Well I guess I ain't that fucking spiritual, my Love."

I remain a work in progress, but I think that maintaining some of my less-evolved human side helps me to help others. I am no guru, and I am certainly no smarter than you are. I have taken ownership of myself and my life. I am whole. I wish to become better each day, love more, be loved, and above all remember, "I am That I am," and so are You!

CHAPTER 23

THE PRINCIPLES OF ASCENSION

A re you ready to reach a new level of conscious thought? Are you ready to change your perception of reality to one that benefits you, and to release the perception given you without your consent? Would you like to see the world differently? I believe there are certain principles you must take ownership of to ascend to your next level of consciousness. I am not referring to one's state after death. I mean the ascension that will take place right here while you are very much alive. It will require much acceptance, and certain realizations on your part, with which you will need to come to terms. It won't be all sunshine and rainbows, but I suppose that would depend on how you choose to view the things I am about to share. Your acceptance of these principles will include facing some facts that will be challenging but necessary to face head on. These reckonings may not come easily, and this is in part, why many people choose not to do this work.

Shall we continue? What the hell, you made this far?

Principle One: You will die.

The fact of the matter is that we are all going to die someday. I imagine that thought may make you feel somewhat nervous, anxious, and maybe even angry. Believe it or not, it shouldn't. To become whole, you must accept that there will be an end to this lifetime. In fact, the acceptance of such can be one of the healthiest things you may do for yourself. It will bring you peace and calm. For death is not the end: it's a new beginning. Accepting that it will come one day should be something of a relief, giving you the freedom to live more in the present moment. Treating each day like it may be your last can help you truly appreciate all that you have. Tell everyone how much you love them. Live and love each day.

According to the current posting on the website of the United States Deaths Clock (and yes, there is such a thing), a person in this country dies every 11.4 seconds. On planet earth 0.8 percent of all humans die each day—that is approximately 64 million people. This information is not intended to make you feel morbid but rather to give you freedom. Granted, with about eight billion people populating this earth the odds are considerably in your favor that you will not be one of those people today, but there is still tomorrow, and the next day . . . So, my question to you is: What will you do today?

Suppressing the awareness that you will die will only make the feeling of unrest that much stronger. Many studies have been done with folks in hospice care or who have incurable terminal illnesses, showing that acceptance allows them to gain a new perception of life, death, and their future. Yes, their *future*. What they found is nothing short of amazing. Those who were told that they would die and were given an approximate date of their own death (whether it was one month or five years) lived with a feeling of comfort and relief once they accepted it as a fact that couldn't be avoided. They experienced a sense of peace. They took nothing in life too seriously. They made the most of their time. All of their anxiety was gone. It gave them the freedom to do the things they wanted. Isn't that the way we all should live each day?

Studies like these have been done numerous times by psychologists who wished to know what comes with the realization of one's own death.

The findings have all been quite similar. There can be nothing more powerful, and dare I say more positive, than changing your relationship with death.

Hospice patients who were analyzed by psychologists repeatedly displayed or expressed the following:

1.) A rearrangement of life's priorities.

2.) A sense of liberation.

3.) Deeper communications with loved ones.

4.) Fewer fears.

5.) Fewer concerns about rejection.

6.) A greater willingness to take risks.

Not long ago I was quite uncertain about writing a book because I feared what others would think of me or say. Of course, that was my ego speaking. I try not to take the advice of my ego anymore since I know it is flawed, like a computer program with a virus. And since I am going to die one day, what the fuck do I care what people think?

Principle Two: Set yourself free.

Your past is just your past. It does not have to define your tomorrows.

Unfortunately, it is the negative things that have transpired in our lives that rest comfortably on top of our subconscious minds. Those are the things that feed the ego. I recall an interview with Tiger Woods in which he was asked about the times he played his best professional golf, and when he played his worst. Well, he instantly began to talk about the worst he had played. That part was easy. Such memories came to him in a millisecond, but then, he struggled significantly, to answer the other part of the question. He said something like, "Wow, that is difficult to answer."

How can that be? How or why is it so easy for us recall the worst shit in our lives, but when it comes to the best of times, we struggle to remember?

To be able to write this book I first had to change myself. I had to become whole. To become whole, I had to accept all of myself, including my dark side and such things I have done, and the evil dark things that were done to me.

We all boast about our accomplishments. Well, guess what? Doing that will never make you whole. This is because your good side is only one part of you. Hopefully, it is the larger part of you, but for some that may not be the case. It doesn't matter. When trying to become whole what matters is that you take ownership of your past and then choose consciously to live in the present moment while not allowing the past (subconscious/ego) to own you or dictate to you what is possible. For many, it is admitting the dark shit you have seen, been part of, or exposed to, that will set you free. It is going to be painful. It's supposed to be painful. It is easy to tell everyone something kind you did for someone else but try owning your dark shit and telling someone about that. Own your shit and set yourself free.

You will never have an awakening or become enlightened until you become whole. Until you stand up and say, "This is me. This is all of me!" The point of this exercise is to come to terms with who and what you are—the good, the bad, and the ugly. Give yourself the freedom to "be." You can then change, but you first must know and acknowledge who you are or who you were, in order to come to terms with what has to be changed about yourself. I am not saying necessarily that you must write a book and put it out there for the world to see, but find someone you can express this with and let it come out of you. I do **not** suggest doing this with a friend or family member. Get a professional licensed psychologist or certified life coach. You cannot be awakened while burying your past.

You cannot be awakened through denial. There can be no enlightenment without suffering. There is no light without darkness.

This isn't meant to be a penance either. The purpose of this is to look back at what no longer serves you. It is to help you live in the present. Acknowledge your programmed ego, and then release it. That way when you are about to make a decision predicated on your ego's programming, you can consciously kick it aside and do what is right for you, and not what was right for those who programmed you. You are not your ego. Separate yourself and set yourself free from what is not you any longer.

Principle Three: Good and bad is a choice.

Remember this quote (one of my favorites):

"Nothing is either good or bad but thinking makes it so." ~William Shakespeare, *Hamlet*

Who decides whether something is good or bad? You do. That's it. No one should ever have that power over you, to decide that for you. What I mean by that is your preprogrammed subconscious mind, made up of others' viewpoints, should not determine this for you. No one other than you and your conscious self should decide what is good. I think the following parable will help you see what I mean.

One sunny afternoon a man takes his dog for a walk. While going past a wooded area the dog sees a rabbit and immediately takes off running. The man's hand isn't holding the leash properly and the dog gets away from him. The man tries to keep pace, but the rabbit and the dog are just too fast for him, and both get away. The rabbit finds a safe place to hide, but the dog runs off and gets lost. The man looks for his dog all day and finally gives up when it gets too dark. He is distraught and angry with himself that he wasn't holding the leash correctly at that exact moment in time when the rabbit came out of nowhere. *What bad luck*, the man thinks.

The following week the man hangs up signs asking folks to please help him find his lost dog. Another week goes by, and he thinks his dog is gone forever. Almost two weeks after the dog went missing, a woman rings his doorbell. The man answers the door to see the most beautiful woman he has ever seen, and she has his dog. The man and woman exchange phone numbers and decide to keep in touch. The dog is safe at home, and a romance ensues between the man and the woman. They fall in love and eventually get married. They still have the dog.

One day the man is driving to pick up his wife from her place of work. While in route he thinks about how lucky he is that this exact woman found his dog at the exact moment in time when they both were looking for a soul mate.

The man pulls up to an intersection with a green light and proceeds to move forward when a truck runs the red light, crashing right into the side of the man's car. The man is rushed to the hospital where he undergoes a series of tests for head injuries. The doctor says they won't know the severity of his injuries until they get the scans back. The man thinks how unlucky he was to have been in his car in that exact spot at that exact time when that truck crashed into him.

The doctor comes in to see him with the results of the tests. He says, "I have good news and bad news. Well, they are technically the same news."

The man looks very confused. "I don't understand."

The doctor says, "Well, the bad news is we found something in the scan—a brain tumor."

"Is there good news?"

"Yes, we found a tumor in your brain scan. You see," the doctor goes on to explain, "the tumor was not caused by your accident. In fact, you have no damage from the accident at all—but this brain tumor we found must be removed quickly. Usually, we don't see these types of tumors until it is too late because there aren't any symptoms until the tumor is too far along to operate on. Currently, it is small enough to remove it completely without any permanent injury to your brain. So, technically speaking, this accident saved your life."

The man's thoughts are all over the place between the bump on his head and the good news and the bad news, which are the same news. He decides to let all these thoughts go and get some sleep.

The man undergoes a successful surgery to remove the tumor. He is released from the hospital within days. He then returns home to his loving wife and dog, with just a scar on his head to remind him that nothing is either good or bad but thinking makes it so.

Principle Four: You are God

What I am about to tell you should change your life forever. You are God. Your consciousness and that of all other conscious beings make up what we often refer to as God. He isn't a separate entity. You and "He/She" are one and the same. The energy within you and everyone connected collectively is what Carl Jung called the "universal collective consciousness." Here is where I believe you'll find God, by whatever name you may call Him/Her. Jesus told us this, and the Buddha as well; but here we are thousands of years later, and we still prefer to believe that God is a separate entity that judges us, and who must "accept" us into His world or kingdom. I am here to tell you that you already are there. You always were part of God. You never had a choice, because God is the energy that lies within you. "I am That I am," as Yahweh (Jehovah) proclaimed in the Old Testament. That "I am" is you. Moses brought us that truth. The list of the greatest minds in the world, including Tesla and Einstein, described to us their versions of the universal collective as well.

Why do you suppose most folks ignore this truth? I think it is a combination of things, the biggest being the world is fucked up and some people dislike certain things about themselves, and they need to hold someone else responsible for their actions. If you come to realize you are God, then you are simply out of excuses. You must then take ownership of your shit, and who would do that unless they had to? It is far easier to remain a pawn in life's game and blame others for everything. It is easier to hide under a blanket of lies than expose yourself to the truth. But once you accept this as your truth you can begin to become whole. Then you can help change your world for the better. As a god can do. Make things better for yourself, your family, your loved ones, and perhaps society as a whole.

If you take one message from this book, please make it this one: **you are the co-creator.** You are responsible for all things, especially your own life's things. You can ask for change, but you must be a part of that change. Accept responsibility for all the good and bad in your life and your world. Then begin to fix the mistakes. Create the miracle of life. Create the miracle of love. Create the miracle of happiness, forgiveness, abundance, kindness, compassion, giving, caring, and so on.

This entire book was written to share with you this simple fact. To make you realize that you are in charge. To share with you that you are the co-creator and, as such, you have a responsibility to go out and **create**

goodness and kindness. Make this a better world, even if the change comes one person at a time. Live with this feeling of power that lies within you. You may not be happy with all of your previous choices, but that's okay. Many people aren't. It's what you do from here that matters. **Live only in the present moment.** Free yourself from the negativity in your subconscious mind, or at least stop allowing your ego to flow through your energy being. Wake each morning with the feeling of power and the emotion of love within you and go out and **design your life** as you want it to be. **Help others** who have yet to realize this fact. Lift them up, to show them the power they have, and together we can change this world.

Use this newfound power you possess to **end suffering**. Start in your own back yard and work your way outward. Go and put this to the test. I have shared with you how to create using the power that lies within you. Your consciousness is part of the one and only consciousness. This is why so many say, "I can't find God": they haven't looked within themselves. The answer was hidden in plain sight; it was right in front of you the whole time.

The power of creation comes from within you.

Now that you know this truth, what will you do with it? Will you hold it within and use it for yourself, or will you share it with others as I have found is so important to do? Will you make your world a better place, or will you toss this book aside and suppress this powerful, perhaps inconvenient truth?

If you begin your words with "I am," and you understand and believe that the "I" means "God," what you say afterward will harden into fact.

Believe it, and you will achieve it. So it is said, and so it shall be.

Thank you for taking the time to read my book. Among millions of options, you chose mine and for that I am eternally grateful. I hope parts of it will prove to be of value in your future endeavors. Perhaps there is a reason you chose this book. Remember, there really are no coincidences.

The light within me honors the light within you.

The End.

Printed in Great Britain
by Amazon

39472282R00178